CONTENTS

Dedication	
Acknowledgments	7
Introduction	8
Opening Statements	10
Penn State Football Countdown	14
"The Greatest Show"	15
Marching Band Moments :: by Blue Band director Dr. O. Richard Bundy	18
A Penn State Education :: by Lee Stout	21
Greatest Athlete in Each Sport	27
Penn State National Champions!	31
Momentous Football Decisions	36
Top Reasons Why Joining the Big Ten Has Been Good for Penn State	41
Top Reasons Why Penn State Should Not Have Joined the Big Ten	43
Top Five Reasons Why Penn State and the New York Yankees Have the Greatest Uniforms in Sports :: by Sweeny Murti	46
Why the Grand Experiment Works at Penn State :: by Dave Joyner	47
A Top Place to Tailgate :: by Joe Cahn—the Commissioner of Tailgating	49
Tailgate Treats	50
Top Tailgate Foods :: by Marc Fetters	52
Whatever Happened to . . .	53
I Am So Done With . . .	55
Historic Teams	57
On the World Stage	59
JoePa Has Outlasted . . .	61
Lessons from Joe Paterno :: by Matt Millen	63
Top Coaches Not Named Joe Paterno	64
Most Inspirational Athletes	67
Top Comebacks from Injuries :: by Dr. Wayne Sebastianelli	69
Greatest Freshman Seasons	72
Top Rec Hall Moments	74
What Made Rec Hall Special :: by Dan Earl	78
Atlantic 10 Memories	79
Top Ten Penn State Wrestlers :: by Jeff Byers	82
Top Penn State Wrestling Moments :: by Jeff Byers	83
Greatest All-Time Penn State Basketball Players	85

Favorite Lady Lions :: by Lisa Salters	88
PSU Memories :: by Lisa Salters	90
Top Movies that Reference Penn State	91
Which Film/TV Fictional Coach Would Be a Great Replacement for JoePa?	92
Characters of the State	94
Memorable Personalities :: by Steve Jones	96
Thrilling Endings	98
Heartbreaking Losses	102
Memorable Weather Games :: by Joe Bastardi	107
Greatest Penn State Football Players from Pennsylvania	110
Greatest Penn State Football Players from Maryland	111
Greatest Penn State Football Players from New York	112
Greatest Penn State Football Players from New Jersey	113
Greatest Penn State Football Players from Ohio	114
Greatest Penn State Football Players from Delaware and West Virginia	115
Why Joe Paterno Is a Great Coach :: by Lou Holtz	116
Top Football Nicknames	117
Salt and Pepper :: by Bruce Clark	119
The Biggest Shoes to Fill	121
Top Assistants Under Joe Paterno	124
Top Reasons That Explain Penn State's Football Success :: by Jim Caldwell	126
Penn Staters Who Coached Elsewhere	128
Our Favorite College Football Announcers	131
. . . And Those Announcers We Don't Like	134
An All-American Education	137
Traditions No More :: by Lee Stout	139
Top Pittsburgh vs. Philadelphia Moments :: by Jeff Byers	144
Top Philadelphia vs. Pittsburgh Moments :: by Scott Henry	146
Top Ten Penn State-Pitt Games	148
Pitt-Penn State Memories :: by Chet Parlavecchio	154
Penn Staters by the Numbers	156
Saturday Night Live Alumni and Penn State	167
Top 25 Bryce Jordan Center Events (non-PSU athletic) :: by Bernie Punt	169
Top Off-Court Memories :: by Kelly Mazzante	172
We All Scream for Ice Cream :: by Jennifer Pencek	174

THE GREAT BOOK OF PENN STATE SPORTS LISTS

MATTHEW AND DAVID PENCEK

RUNNING PRESS
PHILADELPHIA · LONDON

© 2011 by Matthew Pencek and David Pencek

Published by Running Press,
A Member of the Perseus Books Group

All rights reserved under the Pan-American and International Copyright Conventions
Printed in the United States

This book may not be reproduced in whole or in part, in any form or by any means, electronic or mechanical, including photocopying, recording, or by any information storage and retrieval system now known or hereafter invented, without written permission from the publisher.

Books published by Running Press are available at special discounts for bulk purchases in the United States by corporations, institutions, and other organizations. For more information, please contact the Special Markets Department at the Perseus Books Group, 2300 Chestnut Street, Suite 200, Philadelphia, PA 19103, or call (800) 810–4145, ext. 5000, or e-mail special.markets@perseusbooks.com

ISBN 978-0-7624-4107-5
Library of Congress Control Number: 2010937312

E-book ISBN 978-0-7624-4235-5

9   8   7   6   5   4   3   2   1
Digit on the right indicates the number of this printing

Cover and Interior Designed by Joshua McDonnell
Edited by Greg Jones

Front cover photography:
  Top: © Derek Demeter
  Bottom left: © 2011 The Patriot-News. All rights reserved. Reprinted with permission.
  Bottom right: AP Photo/Gene J. Puskar

Running Press Book Publishers
2300 Chestnut Street
Philadelphia, PA 19103–4371

Visit us on the web!
www.runningpress.com

We Are . . . Penn State—From an Outsider's Perspective :: by Shannon Pencek	176
Top Ten Famous Nonsports Figures Who Attended Penn State	178
Why the 1982 Polls Got It Right by Voting Penn State Over SMU	180
Why the Voters Got It Wrong in 1994	182
1959—The Season That Almost Was :: by Richie Lucas	184
Could'a . . . Should'a . . . Won the Heisman	186
Greatest Quarterback Controversies	191
Linebacker U	196
The Start of Something Special :: by Jack Ham	198
Dynamic Duo :: by Lydell Mitchell	200
Top Penn State Non-BCS Bowl Games	203
Top Major Bowl Victories	205
Most Memorable Calls :: by Steve Jones	208
The Greatest Games Against the Big Ten	210
Road Trip Eats :: by Frank Bodani	213
Best Pizza in the Keystone State :: by Mike Munchak	215
All-Time Bars in State College :: by Jeff Byers	217
What's in a Name?	219
JoePa Commercials	221
Joe Paterno Fashion Statements	223
Favorite JoePa Press Conference Moments :: by Neil Rudel	225
Greatest Penn Staters for Each NFL Team	227
Pro Championship Game Performances by Penn Staters	231
Lion Killers	234
Surprising Football Heroes	238
Top Walk-ons Under Joe Paterno	240
Missed Basketball Opportunities	242
Family Ties	245
Why I Love Happy Valley :: by Mike McQueary	249
All-Time Top Athletes from Centre County :: by Ron Bracken	251
A Happy Valley Bucket List	253
Top Ten Things We'd Love to See at Penn State	255
All-Time Football Team	257

DEDICATION

Matt: I formed the initial concept of this book in December of 2008 while preparing to fly out to California for Penn State's Rose Bowl game with USC. In a time of economic uncertainty, why was I spending money on a trip across the country to watch college football instead of staying home in Delaware and watching it all on TV? Because I am a Penn Stater, and I have my dear family to thank for that. This book is for my parents, Jack and Diane, and for Uncle Rich and Aunt Carolyn. In my childhood, all were part of memorable fall Saturdays at Beaver Stadium. It also is for Jeff "Ironhead" Byers and Scott "Scooter" Henry, who both contributed chapters and are the two greatest friends I have. I also would like to dedicate this book to a man I have never met, ESPN.com's Bill Simmons. In more than one of his columns, Simmons has offered inspiration and advice to would-be writers. After years of reading his work, I finally decided to attempt to join the world of sports literature with this project.

To my brother and fellow collaborator, David, who has been with me on so many of my life's greatest experiences. Finally, to my wife, Shannon, whose love and encouragement were a great asset during this project, and sons, Jack and Connor, who understood my need to spend hours away from them while researching and writing this book.

David: First, to my brother, Matt, who conceived the idea for this book and really pushed it to make it become a reality.

This also is dedicated to some of the same people Matt mentions—our parents, who have always been there for us, Uncle Rich and Aunt Carolyn, and Scooter and Ironhead, who are not only the greatest friends anyone can ask for but also have become like family to the Penceks.

Also, I would like to dedicate this book to all the reporters who worked the Penn State football beat during my ten years of covering the team, especially to former *Times Leader* writer Jerry Kellar, who passed away in 2007. Besides helping my career, he provided a tremendous amount of heart and humor to the beat, and those who worked in the press box with him won't forget him.

Finally, to my loving and understanding wife, Jen, who, thanks to me, now enjoys the blue and white of the Nittany Lions more than the blue and white of her alma mater UConn Huskies; and to my son, Ryan, who I took to his first Penn State football game in 2010 when he was 13 months old, and I look forward to watching many, many more games with him.

ACKNOWLEDGMENTS

A sincere thank you to all of the guest contributors and everyone who helped us publish this book. Special thanks to Dwight Spradlin of the Tennessee Titans, Jackie Cook of the Indianapolis Colts, and Ron Rossi.

David also would like to thank his coworkers at *Town&Gown.* They have been supportive of this endeavor while continuing to put out the best magazine in the region and the best Penn State football and winter sports preview magazines that anyone publishes.

INTRODUCTION

Here it is! The book that will settle all those debates about Penn State sports that you have with coworkers, at tailgates, or in a bar. Or is it the book that will spark new debates? Either way, we discuss the great moments, the great players, and, yes, even some events that led to heartbreak in the land of Nittany.

What does former Notre Dame head coach Lou Holtz really think about Joe Paterno? For that matter, what is one-time Penn State problem child Matt Millen's opinion of the Nittany Lions' head football coach? What are former All-American running back Lydell Mitchell's recollections of forming a powerful one-two punch with teammate Franco Harris?

How and why did the 1994 football team get robbed out of a national title? Who was the greatest Penn State athlete to ever wear the number 22—the only Heisman Trophy winner or the most dominant basketball player in school history? What are the pros and cons of the Lions' membership in the Big Ten conference?

We look to provide the answers to all these questions and more.

Though sports themed, we also want this book to cover the entire Penn State experience that generations of students and fans—from tailgating to nightlife—have cherished, and there's even some space dedicated to taking classes. And did we say sports themed? When Penn State sports is referenced, it normally means football, football, and—wait for it—football. Go to the book section of any of the Penn State stores on College Avenue in State College, you will find dozens of titles on the subject of football and very few on the other Nittany Lion sports. Even a quick look at the table of contents of this book offers a football-heavy list of topics. But we also recognize the great moments and great athletes of the nearly 30 other athletic programs carrying the Penn State banner.

In addition to the three names mentioned previously—Holtz, Millen, and Mitchell—we asked, among others, former athletes, former Paterno assistant coaches, and current media personalities to be a part of this project. You will find chapters written by NFL Hall of Famers Jack Ham and Mike Munchak, Indianapolis Colts head coach Jim Caldwell, one of the greatest Lady Lion basketball players of all time Kelly Mazzante, and one of the nation's top meteorologists Joe Bastardi.

One objective of this book is to be a final say on many topics. When ranking the greatest players, we put an emphasis on those who won multiple All-American awards balanced with the dominance of their play. Then there are those topics that are just ripe with some good-old biased opinion, as some ESPN announcers and Big Ten officials will find out.

Our favorite college sports program is one of the greatest in the history of the NCAA, with legendary coaches and set in an awe-inspiring natural backdrop. When talking about Penn State, we are reminded of that line from the Mac Davis song that says it's hard being humble when you're perfect in every way. And although PSU isn't always perfect, it is *Dear Old State* to the hundreds of thousands across the Nittany Nation.

—Matt and David

OPENING STATEMENTS

Sure, Penn State has had memorable bowl wins. Season-ending games with Pitt have had a major impact on national championships. Since joining the Big Ten, the Nittany Lions also have had some big moments against Michigan State, including clinching two conference titles. But what about season openers? Stop that snickering. Yes, of late and probably for the foreseeable future, the Lions' first games have been against the likes of Youngstown State and Coastal Carolina. There were those openers in the past that seemed to, for good or bad, set the tone for the rest of the season. In the court of Penn State public opinion, here are our opening statements on season openers.

10. September 23, 1961: Penn State 20, Navy 10. The return of running back Roger Kochman from a knee injury the previous season highlighted the game. Don Jonas scored a touchdown and kicked two second-half field goals in the victory.

> **How did they finish:** The Nittany Lions would complete an 8–3 season with a 30–15 win over Georgia Tech in the Gator Bowl and tie for 18th place with Arizona in the final AP poll of the season. Navy would finish 7–3.

9. September 3, 1994: Penn State 56, Minnesota 3. This is ranked not because the Golden Gophers were a solid team that Penn State could measure itself against—the Gophers finished 3–8 this season; rather, it's here because fans, and the rest of the nation, got their first looks of the incredible offense the Nittany Lions unleashed in 1994.

> **How did they finish:** A perfect 12–0 season, their first Big Ten championship, and another missing national championship.

8. September 1, 2001: Penn State 7, Miami 33. Following a losing season in 2000, the Lions were looking to rebound in 2001. The south end zone upper deck in Beaver Stadium and Mount Nittany Club were complete, as were the suites atop the east stands. The expansion added more than 12,000 seats, increasing Beaver Stadium's capacity to 107,282. Emotions ran high as Adam Taliaferro jogged onto the field less than a year after his serious injury at Ohio State, when some questioned whether he would ever walk again. The stadium was electric—and then the game started. The eventual national champion Hurricanes raced out to a 23–0 lead four minutes into the second quarter, and the rout was on.

How did they finish: After starting the season 0–4, Penn State made a nice run and nearly ran the table, but ended up with a 5–6 record.

7. September 4, 1993: Penn State 38, Minnesota 20. Again, this was not because the Gophers provided a good measuring stick for the season—Minnesota finished 4–7. The reason for including this contest is that it was the first-ever Big Ten game the Nittany Lions played. Bobby Engram hauled in four touchdown passes from John Sacca, including three in the first quarter.

How did they finish: A third-place finish in their first season in the conference. The Lions finished 10–2, including a rout over Tennessee in the Florida Citrus Bowl, and ranked eighth in the final AP rankings.

6. September 19, 1959: Penn State 19, Missouri 8. The game at Columbia, Missouri, showed both Penn State fans and the nation that the 1959 team had the makings of something special. Richie Lucas began his Heisman campaign completing 10 of 11 passes, including a 52-yard touchdown to Jim Kerr in the victory over a Tiger team that would play in the Orange Bowl.

How did they finish: The Nittany Lions were in position to be a contender for the national championship, but two losses in their final three regular-season games (Syracuse and Pitt) ended that dream. The Lions did defeat Alabama in the Liberty Bowl. The 1959 team is probably one of the most underrated teams in school history, and it was much closer to winning the championship than its 9–2 record would indicate.

5. August 27, 2000: Penn State 5, USC 29. The good old Kickoff Classic did not provide a good experience for the Nittany Lions and foreshadowed what was to come that season. Sultan McCullough rushed for 128 yards against the Lions, and future Steeler Troy Polamalu had a 43-yard pick-six touchdown off of Rashard Casey.

How did they finish: How did they finish you ask? *How did they finish?* Terrible—that is how they finished. The next week, the Lions were embarrassed at home, losing to Toledo, 24–6. Two weeks later, in a dreadful game at Three Rivers Stadium, they lost 12–0 to Pitt en route to a 5–7 season.

4. August 28, 1991: Penn State 34, Georgia Tech 22. This proved to be a more positive experience in the Kickoff Classic. Senior quarterback Tony Sacca threw for five touchdowns against the defending conational champion Yellow Jackets as the Lions built a 34–3 fourth-quarter lead.

How did they finish: The Nittany Lions finished 11–2, including a 35–13 victory over Notre Dame and a 42–17 rout over Tennessee in the Fiesta Bowl. They finished No. 3 in the AP poll.

3. August 29, 1983: Penn State 6, Nebraska 44. A rude experience for the defending national champion Lions in the inaugural Kickoff Classic, as the Cornhuskers avenged their "Miracle of Mount Nittany" loss from 1982. The game was so bad that many reporters in the press box paid more attention to MTV's Video Music Awards telecast instead of what was occurring on the Giants Stadium turf.

How did they finish: It was one of the worst starts to a season for a defending national champion. After the loss to the Cornhuskers, Penn State was shocked by Cincinnati, losing 14–3 in Beaver Stadium. The following week, Penn State lost a 42–34 shootout to Iowa and fell to 0–3. They did rebound to go 8–4–1, including a win over Washington in the Aloha Bowl.

2. September 1, 1978: Penn State 10, Temple 7. During the mid to late 1970s Wayne Hardin's Temple Owls played Penn State as tough as anybody on the schedule. On this Friday night in Veterans Stadium, Matt Bahr's 23-yard field goal with ten seconds remaining pulled out the win.

How did they finish: Penn State had to rally to defeat a cross-state rival in the opener, and then it had to rally to defeat cross-state rival Pitt in the season finale. In between, Penn State defeated everyone else as well and attained the school's first-ever No. 1 ranking. The Lions played Alabama in the Sugar Bowl for the national championship, losing 14–7.

1. September 7, 1985: Penn State 20, Maryland 18. For some reason this game does not rise to "great game" status among Penn State fans. The two-time defending ACC champion Terrapins were *Sport Magazine*'s chic pick to win the national championship and were ranked No. 7 in the AP poll. Penn State was coming off of a 6–5 season in 1984 and was ranked No. 19. It had to travel to a sweltering Byrd Stadium. One of the lasting images was the differing approaches the two teams had to battling the heat. Maryland had multiple fans and ice blocks to keep its players cool. Meanwhile, each time the USA Network cameras panned to the Nittany Lions sideline, all that could be seen was a rickety fan that had a slow-moving propeller. Another image was State's Michael Zordich's 32-yard pick-six off of Stan Gelbaugh on the second play of the game. The Nittany Lions built a 17–0 lead but lost it all as Maryland scored 18 straight.

Massimo Manca's 46-yard field goal put the Lions up 20–18 with under seven minutes remaining. The Terps were poised to win the game and end a 20-game losing streak to Penn State when Alvin Blount fumbled the football after catching a Gelbaugh pass. The Nittany Lions recovered the ball with 38 seconds remaining and escaped with the win.

How did they finish: The Lions went 11–0 in the regular season, taking a No. 1 ranking into the Orange Bowl against Oklahoma. The Sooners defeated Penn State to win the national championship.

PENN STATE FOOTBALL COUNTDOWN

In the tradition of Casey Kasem, let's count down the top Nittany Lion hits.

12. Kansas Jayhawks on the field in the 1969 Orange Bowl that allowed the Lions a second (and successful) chance at a winning two-point conversion.

11. The number of consecutive games in which Kerry Collins threw at least one touchdown pass in 1994.

10. Interceptions in a season, a record held by Neal Smith (1969) and Pete Harris (1978).

9. 100-yard games by Ki-Jana Carter in 1994.

8. Seasons out of nine that Penn State was ranked in the AP top ten (1967 to 1975).

7. Perfect seasons (1887, 1912, 1968, 1969, 1973, 1986, 1994).

6. Rushing touchdowns in a single game—Harry Robb vs. Gettysburg in 1917.

5. Nittany Lions enshrined in the Pro Football Hall of Fame (Jack Ham, Franco Harris, August Michalske, Lenny Moore, Mike Munchak).

4. Victories in the Orange Bowl (1969, 1970, 1974, 2006).

3. Heisman Trophy second-place finishes (Richie Lucas 1959, Chuck Fusina 1978, Ki-Jana Carter 1994) and, heading into 2011, the number of Big Ten championships (1994, 2005, 2008).

2. AP and Coaches polls (1982, 1986) national champions, and the number of titles recognized by some historians (1911 and 1912) but not by the university.

1. Spot on the list of all-time Division I victories held by Joe Paterno.

"THE GREATEST SHOW"

It is one of the largest stadiums in the nation and home to what's been called "The Greatest Show in College Football." Watching a game in Beaver Stadium is undeniably one of the great experiences in sports—and this is not just because of the action on the field.

10. The roaming members of the Blue Band. Sometime in the third quarter, teams of four or five members of the Blue Band's horn section move about Beaver Stadium playing a rift from one of the Penn State fight songs. No part of the stadium is off limits: from the upper reaches of row 78 on the west stands to the lower portion of the north end zone, these band members give a little music interlude to action on the field. The crowd "claps along to the beat" and applauds these musicians for making a trek to their section.

9. The Nittany Lion growl. Greeting the players as they take to the field during warm-ups, or signifying a Penn State touchdown, the Nittany Lion growl played over the public address system lets all in attendance know they are in Penn State Country. Other schools with feline nicknames use a similar growl, but they are just pussycats compared to the stately Nittany Lion.

8. The blue school buses. Escorted by some of Pennsylvania's finest, a small convoy of school buses wind their way to the stadium entrance. Large crowds of Penn State fans line both sides of Curtin Road as this parade passes by, hoping to catch a glimpse of coach Joe Paterno and the members of the team. The seat next to Paterno on the bus is normally reserved for the starting quarterback, who is the first player who exits. For those players making their first game-day trek to the stadium, the blast of cheering that they receive from the fans while departing the bus lets them know quickly the amount of enthusiasm that surrounds Nittany Nation.

7. "We Are . . . Penn State." A simple phrase that has become a chant, a greeting, and even clever lettering on license plates across the United States, "We Are . . . Penn State" lets all Penn Staters announce their pride. It can start at anytime during a game, but you can count on at least one round of the chant prior to the team running out of the tunnel before the opening kickoff.

6. Pump-up videos. A fairly recent development in the Beaver Stadium experience, the slick MTV-style produced videos featuring great plays combined with dramatic music drive the excitement level of Penn State fans up a few levels when played on the stadium's giant viewing screens. These videos have become a big hit on Internet sites such as YouTube.

5. Paternoville. Nearly a week prior to the Nittany Lions' big game with Ohio State in 2005, a number of students began to camp out in front of the stadium's Gate A entrance with the hope of securing great seats for the contest that ultimately decided the Big Ten title. As the days passed, the crowd grew, and a name for this gathering was coined—Paternoville. Coach Paterno himself even stopped by the day before the game to deliver pizzas for the residents. It was such a great time that Paternoville now has become a regular gathering in the days leading up to home games.

4. Tailgating in the parking lot. You have not had a true Penn State football experience without tailgating in the many, many parking lots that surround Beaver Stadium. For some, the weekend starts on Thursday, as RVs make their way to Happy Valley. The RV parking lot is an impressive sight: There are elaborate spreads of food, large TVs hooked up to satellite receivers to allow viewing of other games, and contests such as beanbag tosses. The fun is not limited to the RVs. Fans making their way into town the day of the game can put on an equally fun-thrilled scene. Just strolling through a parking lot on game day, you most likely will take in a variety of aromas coming from food cooked on the numerous grills populating the area. Throw in beverages and tunes, and you can almost have as much fun outside the stadium as inside. Almost.

3. The student section. Sometime during the new millennium there was a drastic change in attitude coming from the student section compared to previous years. The current generation has become an intimidating presence and can rattle any opponent. The students also sing along to many of the tunes played during the course of a game, whether it's Bon Jovi's "Livin' on a Prayer" or Creedence Clearwater Revival's "Have You Ever Seen the Rain?"

2. The Blue Band intro. It starts with a simple beat of the band's drumline. The beat grows louder and faster as the rest of the band takes the field. When all is in place, the west and east sections receive a brief rift of "The Nittany Lion." The culmination of this grand entrance occurs when the drum major sprints from the south end zone to the front of the formation, leaps into the air, performs a summersault, and, if successful, lands in a split of his legs. For an encore, he sprints back toward the south end zone and repeats the routine. After that, if you are not pumped up for the game to start, well, you must not have a pulse.

1. The White Out. This started out as a unifying thing for the students, but the trend quickly carried over to the entire stadium. Now there is a designated "White Out" game each season, and everyone (except for fans of the visiting team) wears white, shakes white pompoms, and creates one spectacular scene.

Honorable mention: "Kernkraft 400" by Zombie Nation. Sure, Penn State was not the first, but it is one of the best to utilize the song to pump up the crowd, whether after a TD or a sack on defense.

MARCHING BAND MOMENTS
:: BY BLUE BAND DIRECTOR DR. O. RICHARD BUNDY

The year 1966 wasn't only Joe Paterno's first season as head coach, but it also was the first season for O. Richard Bundy as a member of the Blue Band. Bundy was a trombonist for the band from 1966 to 1970. He returned to Penn State in 1980 as graduate assistant for the band and has been the band's director since 1996. Here are Bundy's top Blue Band moments and memories.

11. Waking up the echoes. The Blue Band had its first performance at Notre Dame University on November 14, 1992. Although Penn State lost, 17–16, for everyone associated with the Blue Band, performing at this storied stadium and campus was a memorable experience. This performance was the Blue Band's only appearance at Notre Dame prior to the 1997 stadium expansion, which now obscures portions of the iconic "Touchdown Jesus" mosaic on the Hesburgh Library façade.

10. Start of a "great marching-band tradition." On November 20, 1965, at Forbes Field, Penn State lost to rival Pitt, 30–27, but the day is significant to the Blue Band as the performance in which our trademark drill, the Floating LIONS, was introduced. Dr. Ned C. Deihl designed the drill, and it has become the centerpiece of the Blue Band's traditional pregame show. Originally written for the 120-member band, the drill has undergone several rewrites through the ensuing years as the band has expanded to its current size of 315.

9. Patriotic halftime. It was the 1967 Gator Bowl, played on December 30. Under the direction of Dr. James W. Dunlop, the Blue Band's halftime performance titled "Salute to the Armed Forces" received high praise from TV commentators and marching band aficionados around the country at a time when marching band halftime shows were routinely included as part of college football television coverage. The Blue Band's Gator Bowl halftime show featured a USA formation similar to the trademark PSU formation used in the band's pregame show—the "P" was changed to a "U"; an aerial photo of this formation was used as the cover of the 1968 Jacksonville phone directory, providing the Blue Band with its first significant recognition on a national scale. Coach Joe Paterno's first bowl game as head coach ended in a 17–17 tie with Florida State.

8. A heart-y effort. The legendary "12 men on the field" 1969 Orange Bowl game when Penn State defeated the Kansas Jayhawks thanks to Kansas's having 12 men on the field during the Lions' two-point try. The winning touchdown and both two-point conversion attempts occurred in the end zone right in front of the band's field-level seats. The game also was memorable because the band's halftime show featured the first-ever heart transplant performed on a football field. In 1967 Christiaan Barnard had performed the world's first heart transplant, and Sonny and Cher were at the peak of their popularity, having recorded one of their most successful songs, "The Beat Goes On." For the 1968 regular season, director Dr. Ned C. Deihl combined these current events into a memorable animated drill that was repeated for the Orange Bowl. The drill featured a prone stick figure that sat up on the "operating table" after receiving a "prop" heart. The "patient" then stood upright with his right foot tapping to the sounds of "The Beat Goes On."

7. Impressing the Big House. The Blue Band's first visit to Michigan Stadium on October 15, 1994, was an opportunity to share the field in a performance with the Michigan Marching Band, one of the country's elite band programs. The game resulted in an exciting 31–24 win over the Wolverines, with the decisive touchdown being scored in front of the band's ground-level seating area. A Penn State alumnus with connections to the Michigan band reported that one Michigan band staffer indicated that they "didn't realize the Blue Band was *that* good."

6. *The* parade and bowl. The Rose Parade and Rose Bowl are something of a "Holy Grail" for marching band directors and performers. The opportunity to perform in the Rose Parade is an honor for any band program in the country, and the first opportunity to do so is particularly special. For its January 2, 1995, performance, the Blue Band learned a military-styled "column turn at the oblique" to use, as the band negotiated the 105-degree right turn onto Colorado Boulevard. The live television coverage and celebrity commentators at this location were extremely complimentary of the Blue Band's execution of this movement. Recently, during its second Rose Bowl appearance on January 1, 2009, the Blue Band was credited with having "invented" this turn—untrue, but it was nonetheless flattering to hear it described as the "Penn State turn."

5. National Anthem before a national title. Penn State's 14–10 victory over the Miami Hurricanes in the 1987 Fiesta Bowl resulted in a second national championship for the Nittany Lions. The Blue Band was selected to perform the National Anthem during pregame ceremonies that would involve the presentation of the colors featuring an American flag unfurled and held by hundreds of volunteers. The flag covered the entire football field except for the end zone, where the Blue Band formed for the performance. The super-sized American flag continues to be an impressive Fiesta Bowl tradition.

4. Some 007—and a first national title. The Sugar Bowl following the 1982 season matched No. 2 Penn State against No. 1 Georgia in a national championship showdown. I was a graduate assistant with the Blue Band at the time and had written the musical arrangements and drill for a "James Bond" show that director Dr. Ned C. Deihl and assistant director Dr. Darhyl Ramsey selected as the bowl show. The thrill of that performance, combined with Penn State's 27–23 victory over the Herschel Walker–led Bulldogs, are a fond memory for me.

3. Celebration of the century mark. Penn State's hosting of the 1999 Pigskin Classic, a preseason counterpart of the Kickoff Classic at the time, was the season opener for the Nittany Lions. It also was the first halftime show in a season-long Blue Band Centennial Celebration. The halftime show for this game began with six students wearing replicas of the uniforms that the original six members of the Cadet Drum and Bugle Corps, founded in 1899, wore. As the show progressed, more current students joined the "original six" as the band performed music and drills associated with the band's growth at important milestones during its 100-year history. As for the game, Penn State defeated the University of Arizona, 41–7.

2. Homecoming honor. Homecoming 2005 was a memorable day for anyone ever associated with the Blue Band. More than 400 alumni Blue Band members participated in the ceremony, as representatives from the Sousa Foundation presented the Blue Band program with the 2005 Sudler Trophy, an annual award "recognizing a university band program which has maintained an exceptionally high quality of marching innovation and musical performance over a period of many years." Family representatives of the student drum and bugle corps founder and of all deceased former directors were recognized during the ceremony. Past director Dr. Ned C. Deihl and the current director (yours truly) accepted this accolade on behalf of all band members past and present. Then, to top it off, Penn State defeated the Purdue Boilermakers, 33–15.

1. A "white out" of a different sort. Members most often identify performing the traditional pregame show as a favorite Blue Band memory, and Beaver Stadium is by far the Blue Band's favorite venue. It is difficult to pick any one pregame performance in Beaver Stadium as most memorable, but the pregame experienced at the final home game of the 2008 season is one that many recall. As the Blue Band began marching out of the tunnel, a snow squall suddenly engulfed the field and continued during the entire performance. Blue Band students who experienced this "white out" from Mother Nature still count it as one of their most memorable pregame performances. On that day, Penn State defeated Michigan State, 49–18, and celebrated a Big Ten championship.

A PENN STATE EDUCATION :: BY LEE STOUT

Penn State fans and alumni might be able to tell you who was the Lions' leading rusher in 1975 (Woody Petchel), but what do you *really* know about Dear Old State? Penn State's retired historian and Librarian Emeritus, Special Collections, Lee Stout, gives us his top ten things you might not know about Penn State.

10. It's one of the oldest coed schools in Pennsylvania. The board of trustees made the decision in 1871 to admit women to the Agricultural College of Pennsylvania. Ohio's Oberlin College pioneered coeducation beginning in 1837, but there was little progress otherwise until after the Civil War. Then, coeducation took off, principally in western state universities where equality for women seemed to be more accepted. Back east, things were different. Despite being the eventual home of a number of well-known women's colleges, the East was more hostile to the need for higher education for women. By 1870 there were nearly 100 coeducational schools, but few were in the East. In looking for a new school president in 1871, the trustees settled on James Calder, who had headed Hillsdale College in Michigan, the second American college to grant a degree to a woman. He was a supporter of equal educational rights for women, and he could see no reason why it should not become the practice here, too. Overcoming prejudices that women's minds were of an "inferior quality" and couldn't do the same coursework as men, the faculty voted in favor of the change in June 1871. The trustees concurred in September, and the issue was settled. Calder brought two of his Hillsdale students with him to launch the "women's department" at the Ag College. They were Rebecca Ewing of Angola, Indiana, and Ellen Cross of Omro, Wisconsin, and four freshmen women admitted for the fall semester of 1871 joined them. Ewing became Penn State's first female graduate in 1873. In 1919 Ellen Cross was honored by the University of Wisconsin as one of the first women in America to receive a PhD. Although Penn State was not the first coeducational college in Pennsylvania, it was certainly one of the earliest.

9. It wasn't "Penn State" for the first 19 years. Most know that first it was the "Farmers' High School of Pennsylvania." But Penn State didn't maintain that name for very long. When President Abraham Lincoln signed the Morrill Land Grant Act into law in 1862, Evan Pugh and the trustees wanted to be sure that they received the designation as Pennsylvania's Land Grant College. They knew it would be a tough political battle, and it was. It was absolutely essential that there be no confusion about what this school was, so they took the precaution of changing the name to Agricultural College of Pennsylvania in 1862. Eleven years later the school was in trouble. Pugh had died suddenly in 1864, and his successors, William Allen, John Fraser, and Thomas Burrowes, had been largely unsuccessful in lifting the college from a miasma of financial problems and curricular disarray. Enrollments were bottoming out; rarely in the late 1860s were there more than a handful of graduates, and the number of students in the preparatory department outnumbered the four collegiate classes. With the arrival of President James Calder in 1871, the curriculum was redesigned to offer agricultural, scientific, and classical (liberal arts) courses. The trustees took the further radical step in 1871 of opening the college to women. By 1874 they reasoned that they were teaching everyone (men and women) almost everything with their broad curriculum, so, in hopes of persuading the legislature to begin regular appropriations to the college, they decided to rename the school the Pennsylvania State College. With another court decree, they accomplished the change. We've been Penn State ever since, and in 1953 the name changed again to the Pennsylvania State University.

8. Penn State was a hands-on college from the start. In today's jargon, the "vision" for the Farmers' High School of Pennsylvania was to build an institution where young men would learn to apply science to agriculture and enhance the productivity of Pennsylvania's farmers. It took Evan Pugh, a world-class scientist and first president of the college, to bring this dream to fruition. Pugh created courses in science that followed the model of the German research universities in which he had studied, with students working at the laboratory bench performing experiments. This would gradually translate into an institution where, as Fred Lewis Pattee said, a student "went in and heard a lecture on corn and then he went out and cultivated corn." As Penn State expanded its curricula into engineering and other fields beyond agriculture in the late nineteenth century, every student did a practicum of some type in their courses. Today, students participate in faculty research projects, and most seek out internships to both test their knowledge and learn new approaches in actual working situations.

7. Campus is the geographic center of the state—maybe. Many students believe that the geographical center of Pennsylvania is on campus, under the armillary sphere that is on the lawn in front of Old Main. Obviously, Centre County occupies the center of the state—hence the name—but the fact is that no one has ever established the exact geographic center of the state. Some believe it's near Aaronsburg, out in Penns Valley, although most believe it is closer to Fisherman's Paradise, near Bellefonte. Because Penn State's original location and main University Park campus is located in Centre County, many assume this central location was the key to the trustees' decision to begin here.

Back in 1855 there were seven counties that offered land to the board of trustees for a possible location of the Farmers' High School. A visitation committee examined most of them and selected Centre County. In those days and for many years to come, Penn State would be, in the words of President Edwin Erle Sparks, "equally inaccessible from all parts of Pennsylvania." Although many criticized the location, the trustees wanted their young men isolated from the evils of the city. But, also, Centre County made the best offer: 200 acres of free land and an adjacent 200 acres at below market price, backed up by a pledge of $10,000 from the citizens of the county (back when that was "real money"). Furthermore, Hugh N. McAllister, a trustee and past president of the Pennsylvania State Agricultural Society; Andrew Gregg Curtin, Secretary of the Commonwealth and governor-to-be; and James Irvin, ironmaster, former congressman and donor of the land, guaranteed the pledge. All three (as well as most of the trustees) were well connected with the Whig Party, which had pushed the charter for the school through the legislature.

6. We were never a high school. Many people know Penn State got its start as the Farmers' High School of Pennsylvania. So was this place really a high school in the beginning? The answer is no. It was a college from the start—the first graduates received bachelor of scientific agriculture degrees, the first college degrees in agriculture awarded anywhere. So why the disguise? In the 1850s "high school" didn't have the same meaning as today. There were virtually no public secondary schools, so the concept was more of a "higher education." Actually, they were trying to differentiate the school from the classical colleges that provided a traditional liberal arts education, reasoning that farmers would not send their sons to such a place if they wanted them to continue operating the family farm. This new school would provide a scientific education in agriculture. Thanks to the Morrill Land Grant Act, it would then later extend that education to include engineering, but it also would not exclude the liberal arts, thus becoming the forerunner of today's multidisciplinary universities. Students who planned to go to college in those days generally took advanced courses after eight years of grammar school at either a private academy or in a college's preparatory department. Penn State, like most colleges of the era, offered two years of prep work in addition to the four-year collegiate course. This lasted until 1910, by which time public high schools were well established across the state and college preparatory departments were no longer needed.

5. Old Main never burned down and the students didn't build the early buildings. Two of the most persistent myths are that the original Old Main burned down and that the students built the early buildings. In fact, the original Old Main lasted until 1929, when, due to structural problems—the top two floors were condemned and there were cracks in the walls—the original structure was demolished. The current Old Main was built on the same site, with nearly the same footprint, and re-using the limestone from the original structure, which was actually quarried from the southeast corner of Old Main lawn. Old Main did, however, have a fire in 1892, which destroyed part of the roof. The original roof and cupola were then replaced with a mansard-style roof and square clock tower in 1896. A related myth is that the students built the original Old Main, the College Barns, and the president's residence. Nope, actually contractors built these buildings, as they did all Penn State buildings. The confusion probably arises from the "labor rule." Early students were required to work three hours a day on the college farms or in other duties around the campus. The trustees considered it a practical part of their education as well as a money saver for the college, but students never liked it. Modern students apparently jumped to the conclusion that the labor requirement must have meant that the students built their own buildings.

4. Are we public or private? We've been "Dear old State" in the Alma Mater since Fred Lewis Pattee penned the words in 1901, and "The Pennsylvania State College" since 1874. But what's in a name: Are we the State University for Pennsylvania? Generally speaking, a state university is a public institution, founded and operated by a state entity and funded largely by state appropriations. Those are generalizations; reality is more complicated. A private organization, the Pennsylvania State Agricultural Society, founded Penn State. However, we were chartered by legislative act, as were all colleges in Pennsylvania in those days. We are operated by an independent board of trustees; there are state officials who are members by virtue of their offices and there are gubernatorial appointments to the board, but the majority of trustees are elected by alumni. We receive a higher state appropriation than any of the state-owned universities, but state funding composes only about 10 percent of our budget. The attorney general considers us an "Instrumentality of the Commonwealth," and our employees can be members of the State Employees Retirement System. We comply with the State's Right-to-know law to a greater degree than legally required, but fewer categories of Penn State information are "public" by statute than in the state-owned universities. Being the Land Grant University for Pennsylvania is indisputable, and at appropriations time, we are classed with the other three "State-Related" universities, but otherwise, public or private is not an "either-or" designation; it's a spectrum and we fall somewhere in the middle.

3. One university geographically dispersed—a PSU degree is a PSU degree.
Many have heard that Penn State's campus system is unlike any other, but how so? Many schools that have "branch campuses," such as Pitt or Indiana, are actually a system of semi-autonomous schools. Penn State has always said it is "One university, geographically dispersed." In other words, students have the freedom to move between campuses in pursuit of their degrees. Forty years ago, for example, most of the Commonwealth Campuses offered only one year of baccalaureate work; students then transferred to University Park to complete their degrees. Gradually this has changed; campuses began offering a second year of undergraduate work, and then Harrisburg and Behrend in Erie began to offer baccalaureate degrees, and now one can complete a four-year degree in a variety of majors at any of the undergraduate campuses. Sharing the same calendars, fee structure, credits, courses, and majors made this seamless ability to move around the system possible. Key to it all was a shared information technology system—student databases that unified everything from advising to transcripts. The Internet and the Web now make that even more transparent and efficient. In these times of bulging enrollments, campuses are relatively free to pursue their own initiatives, but the overall unity of vision and goals for the university remains stable. Regardless of which campus you call home, we are all Penn State.

2. What's "land grant" mean? There is a lot of confusion about our status as Pennsylvania's "Land Grant" university and what that means. One of the biggest myths is that it's the land on which the campus was built. Wrong. Penn State was the school the state designated to be the recipient of the funds provided through the federal Morrill Land Grant College Act of 1862. Senator Justin Morrill was the author of the law that designated a college in each state to specialize in agriculture and the mechanic arts (i.e., engineering). The "Land Grant" meant that each state received an amount of federal public land to sell; they then invested the proceeds of the sale to create an endowment for its Land Grant College. Pennsylvania received 780,000 acres, but the legislature dithered, so sales were not completed until 1867, by which time the net proceeds were only $440,000—less than half of what they had hoped to receive. Still, invested in state bonds, this could bring the college almost $25,000 a year, which was a valuable benefit at that time. Gradually, college budgets increased and the money became less significant. What remained vital to Penn State's future, however, was the fact that by accepting the Morrill Land Grant Act, the Commonwealth of Pennsylvania gave legal recognition to its special relationship with Penn State, unlike that of any other Pennsylvania institution of higher education.

1. Our unique campus system. Almost half of all Penn State undergraduates are currently at a campus other than University Park, so most Penn Staters are familiar with our unique campus system, but many may not know much about how it came about. PSU's campus system traces its roots back to the creation of Undergraduate Centers in the 1930s as a way for new students to live at home and take their freshman courses locally for reduced tuition. The initial centers were in economically hard-hit areas of the state, such as Uniontown and Hazleton. They were not really intended to be more than a temporary measure, and most closed when World War II began. Penn State already had a presence in other locations across Pennsylvania, however. Evening technical schools that began in the 1920s, teacher-training institutes, and County Extension Offices, beginning around 1914, put Penn State in virtually every county in the state. An exception was the Mont Alto campus, which traces its origins to the State Forestry Academy founded in 1902 as part of the State Department of Forests and Waters to train professional foresters. Eventually, the state closed the academy and gave Mont Alto to Penn State for forestry education and other programs. With the end of World War II and the flood of veterans wishing to use their GI Bill benefits for a college education, Penn State reopened the undergraduate centers and then added to them. By 1960 the campuses were separated from Central Extension (now Outreach and Continuing Education) and became Penn State's unique system of Commonwealth Campuses.

GREATEST ATHLETE IN EACH SPORT

Penn State has one of the largest athletic programs in the country, and it will become bigger in a few years when it adds Division I men's and women's ice hockey. Here are who we think were the best in the university's current varsity sports. The university's "official" list of athletic programs has indoor track and field and outdoor track and field as two sports; we considered track and field (indoor and outdoor) as just one sport, and we separated diving as a sport from the rest of swimming.

Baseball—Ed Drapcho. In 1957 he led Penn State to its best finish in the College World Series, finishing second. That year, he went 12–0 with a 1.52 ERA and 116 strikeouts. He is tied for the team record for most wins in a career with 29. He is one of four players in team history to earn first-time All-American honors.

Basketball (men)—Jesse Arnelle. He graduated as the team's career scoring leader with 2,138 points and career rebounding leader with 1,238, the program's only first-team All-American. He also led the Lions to their greatest seasons—three NCAA Tournament appearances in four years, including the 1954 run to the Final Four.

Basketball (women)—Suzie McConnell. She graduated in 1988 as the NCAA's career leader in assists. She also holds the Lady Lions' record for career steals and double-double games, and she is sixth in career scoring with 1,897 points. Her fast-pace style of play also brought new fans to women's basketball.

Cross country (men)—Curt Stone. Whereas his teammate, Horace Ashenfelter, is probably better known because he won the Gold Medal in the 1952 Olympics, Stone probably had the better cross-country career. He was a two-time All-American, including a runner-up finish in 1946. He also was a two-time IC4A cross-country and track champion.

Cross country (women)—Kathy Mills. She is the only national champion in team history. She won the championship in 1977, when she also won the Broderick Award as the top female in her sport. She was a four-time All-American.

Diving (men)—Chris Devine. He was two-time first-team All-Big Ten. He won the US Senior National Championship for 3-meter diving in 1994. That year he also placed third and fifth at the NCAA Championships on the 1-meter and 3-meter, respectively.

Diving (women)—Mary Ellen Clark. She is one of the more storied athletes in PSU history. A three-time first-team All-American, she also won bronze medals in the 10-meter diving competitions at the 1992 and 1996 Olympics.

Fencing (men)—Tom Strzalkowski. He won three consecutive national titles in saber—1992, 1993, and 1994. He also was a four-time All-American and left with a 109–10 career record.

Fencing (women)—Olga Kalinovskaya. She is the program's only four-time national champion. Kalinovskaya won the national title in foil in 1993, 1994, 1995, and 1996. She graduated with a 180–5 career record.

Field hockey—Char Morett. She is the program's only three-time first-team All-American and also is a member of seven national teams. She scored 50 career goals and was the first Lion to score five goals in a game. Of course, she has continued to help the program as the team's head coach since 1987 and recorded her 400th career win in 2010.

Football—John Cappelletti. There are so many great players, but, in order to be fair, we have to go with the one who has won Penn State's only Heisman Trophy.

Golf (men)—Dan O'Neill. He was a four-time All-American between 1970 and 1973. In 1972 he qualified for the US Open and made the 36-hole cut.

Golf (women)—Katie Futcher. She was All-American in 2002 and 2003. She graduated holding the team records for 18-hole, 36-hole, and 72-hole round.

Gymnastics (men)—Armando Vega. He was a six-time national champion. Vega won the all-around title in 1957 and 1959. He won three consecutive national titles—1956, 1957, and 1959—on the parallel bars. His other national title came on the still rings in 1959.

Gymnastics (women)—Ann Carr. She won back-to-back all-around national titles in 1977 and 1978 and ended her career with five national titles and 16 All-American honors. She won the Broderick Award for her sport in 1977 and 1978, and she helped the Lions win the national team titles in 1978 and 1980. She was inducted into the US Gymnastics Hall of Fame in 2001.

Lacrosse (men)—Gary Martin. He holds team record for points and assists in a career, and he ranks seventh in career goals. He was an honorable mention All-American in 1983. His 86 points in 1982 is still a team record.

Lacrosse (women)—Candy Finn. She was a three-time first-team All-American. She won the Broderick Award for women's lacrosse in 1981 and 1982. Second in team history in career goals and career points, she also led the Lions to national titles in 1979 and 1980. She is a member of the National Lacrosse Hall of Fame.

Soccer (men)—Dick Packer. He was a two-time first-team All-American. Packer led the Lions to two national titles (1954 and 1955). He holds the team record for goals and points in a season with 24 and 50, respectively. He also held the team career goal record with 53 until Stuart Reid scored 56 goals between 1992 and 1995.

Soccer (women)—Christie Welsh. She was the only player in program history to win the Hermann Trophy, which is the equivalent to the Heisman Trophy. She broke every Big Ten offensive career record and was a three-time first-team All-American.

Softball—Missy Beseres. She was a dominant pitcher from 2002 to 2006 and holds the team career record for wins with 53 and strikeouts with 745. She had ten games when she struck out at least 11 batters, including a 15-strikeout performance against Northwestern in 2005.

Swimming (men)—Eugene Botes. He was a three-time All-Big Ten first-team member. He graduated from Penn State holding three school records—100 freestyle, 100 butterfly, and 400 freestyle relay.

Swimming (women)—Fran McDermid. McDermid was Penn State's most dominant freestyle swimmer. She was a nine-time first-team All-American. She graduated in 1993 holding the team records in the 50, 100, and 200 freestyle.

Tennis (men)—Jan Bortner. He is the only player in team history to qualify for the NCAA Championships four times. He went on to be the Lions' head coach for 23 seasons before resigning in 2005.

Tennis (women)—Olga Novikova. She holds the team's career record for most singles wins (95) and most doubles wins (62). She was a three-time All-Big Ten member between 1995 and 1997. Her best season came in 1994–95 when she went 26–8.

Track and field (men)—Barney Ewell. Arguably, he was the greatest athlete in Penn State history. Ewell was a five-time national champion, winning three consecutive titles in the 100-yard run and two consecutive titles in the 200-yard run. His times in the 100 and 200 still rank seventh and fifth, respectively, in team history.

Track and field (women)—Kathy Mills. As dominant as she was in cross-country, she was equally impressive on the track. A three-time All-American and two-time national champion, both her titles came in 1978 when she won the 3,000- and 5,000-meter runs. She still holds the team record in the 5,000-meter run.

Volleyball (men)—Ivan Contreras. He was a four-time All-American. In 1997 he became the first non-California player to win the AVCA National Player of the Year award. He holds the team record with 2,089 career kills and, in 1994, helped the Lions become the first team outside of the state of California to win the national title.

Volleyball (women)—Megan Hodge. What didn't she win? Besides leading the team to three consecutive national titles, Hodge was a four-time first-team All-American, national player of the year in 2009, two-time Most Outstanding Player of the NCAA Championships, and she led the Lions to a winning streak of 102 matches. Yeah, she wasn't too bad.

Wrestling—Kerry McCoy. Although in another list, Jeff Byers, our wrestling expert, went with someone else as the team's top wrestler, we like McCoy in this spot. A two-time national champion (1994 and 1997), McCoy went a combined 131–1 in his last three seasons at Penn State. He is still the only Lion to win the Hodge Trophy, which is given each season to the nation's top collegiate wrestler.

PENN STATE NATIONAL CHAMPIONS!

Who could forget football play-by-play announcer Fran Fisher's signature call following the Sugar Bowl win over Georgia. By the end of 2010 the Nittany Lions and Lady Lions had combined for 68 recognized team national championships. Twelve are combined fencing titles (1990, 1991, 1995, 1996, 1997, 1998, 1999, 2000, 2002, 2007, 2009, 2010). As for the other 56, here is the list of Penn State teams to win a title.

1921 wrestling. The Nittany Lions clinch the intercollegiate title by defeating Iowa State, 28–18.

1924 boxing. C. Raymond Madera wins the featured bout against Navy.

1926 men's soccer. After a bit of controversy, Penn State and Haverford are named cochampions for their undefeated seasons.

1927 boxing. Another title, with Navy again finishing second.

1929 boxing. Allie Wolff's win at 160 pounds highlights the first-place finish.

1929 soccer. The Nittany Lions are awarded the title as the only undefeated team in the East.

1930 boxing. Marty McAndrews's win at 175 pounds led the way to a fourth crown.

1932 boxing. The Lions take the title at home in Rec Hall in an Olympic tune-up for many of the tournament's participants.

1933 men's soccer. Another controversial decision, as head coach Bill Jeffrey's (the guy who Penn State's home field is now named after) undefeated Penn State team is awarded the championship after battling undefeated Penn to a 3–3 tie in the season finale.

1936 men's soccer. Penn State is one of four teams declared cochampions.

1937 men's soccer. A fifth consecutive undefeated season and another shared title.

1938 men's soccer. A sixth consecutive undefeated season and, as the *Collegian* announced, this time "UNDISPUTED SOCCER CHAMPIONS!"

1939 men's soccer. The winning streak continues, standing at 53 games after the season. The Lions are named cochampions along with Princeton.

1940 men's soccer. Penn State and Princeton share the crown again.

1942 men's cross country. The Nittany Lions share the championship with Indiana.

1947 men's cross country. Running in three inches of snow, Penn State finishes ahead of Syracuse and Drake.

1948 men's gymnastics. Bill Bonsall's victory in the rings leads Penn State over Temple, 53.5–43.5.

1949 men's soccer. After years of committees determining the national champion, college soccer attempts to settle the title on the field and tries to encroach on football's hold on New Year's Day. Penn State meets San Francisco in the first "Soccer Bowl" held in St. Louis. Like many soccer matches before and since, this one ends in a tie (2–2), which means another shared championship for the Lions.

1950 men's cross country. Bill Ashenfelter is the top Penn State runner, as the Nittany Lions holds off host Michigan State.

1953 wrestling. With the championships at Rec Hall, the Nittany Lions become the first school east of the Mississippi to win the national title. Hud Samson wins an individual title and is one of five Penn State All-Americans.

1953 men's gymnastics. It's not even close, as the Nittany Lions' 91.5 points are 22.5 better than second-place Illinois.

1954 men's gymnastics. Jan Cronstedt wins four individual titles as Penn State sets a team record with 137 points.

1954 men's soccer. Back to committees determining the champion, and Penn State is awarded the title following an undefeated season.

1955 men's soccer. Lions share the championship with Brockport State Teacher's College.

1957 men's gymnastics. PSU is 8.5 points better than Illinois (88.5–80.0).

1959 men's gymnastics. Armando Vega helps lead the Nittany Lions to a record-setting 152 points.

1960 men's gymnastics. A wild March weekend at Rec Hall as Penn State successfully defends its title with 112.5 points to Southern Cal's 65.5. Jay Werner wins the individual all-around championship.

1961 men's gymnastics. Greg Weiss wins the individual all-around as Penn State wins its third in a row.

1965 men's gymnastics. The Nittany Lions are 17 points better than second-place Washington (68.5–51.5).

1976 men's gymnastics. Penn State's 432.075 (the scoring system was revised in 1966) helps out-distance Louisiana State and third-place finisher California.

1978 women's gymnastics. The first women's team to win a national title. The Lions are ranked No. 1 heading into the tournament and hold off Cal-State Fullerton, Southwest Missouri, Clarion, and Southern Cal to win the championship.

1978 women's lacrosse. Sharon Duffy scores 12 goals in the national tournament as Penn State defeats Maryland in the title game.

1979 women's lacrosse. Freshman Candy Finn scores two goals that are ten seconds apart with less than four minutes remaining to lead Penn State to an 8–5 win over Massachusetts.

1979 women's bowling. Valerie Bright is named tournament MVP, as the Lions defeat Hillsborough Community College, 193–180.

1980 women's fencing. The Lions' 83 victories at the national championships are two better than five-time defending champ San Jose.

1980 women's lacrosse. Maryland snaps the Lions' 38-game unbeaten streak in the regular season. The Lions get revenge in the championship game, winning 3–1.

1980 women's gymnastics. By the slimmest of margins, Penn State's score of 144.10 is just 1.40 points better than second-place Utah.

1980 field hockey. Candy Finn's second goal of the game comes with 1:30 remaining and breaks a 1–1 tie. It gives the Lions the win over California.

1981 women's fencing. Penn State defeats Temple, 9–1, in the final round in a successful defense of its national championship.

1981 field hockey. Penn State wins an appeal to gain an at-large bid into the tournament and then defeats Temple, 5–1, in the title game.

1982 football. Take your pick, Fran Fisher's aforementioned call or the *Sports Illustrated* cover exclaiming, "Number One at Last!" Either way, the 27–23 win over Georgia in the Sugar Bowl is surely sweet for all of Nittany Nation.

1983 women's fencing. The Lions win their third title in four years, defeating Wayne State, 9–6, in the final round.

1986 football. The 14–10 victory over Miami in "The Game of the Century" gives Joe Paterno a second national championship.

1987 women's lacrosse. Beth Stokes and Tami Worley each score three goals in the 7–6 win over Temple.

1989 women's lacrosse. Penn State defeats Harvard, 7–6, to win its second championship in three years.

1994 men's volleyball. The Nittany Lions become the first team not from the state of California to win the national championship. Penn State defeats defending champ UCLA, 3–2.

1999 women's volleyball. After failing in two previous trips to the finals, the third time is the charm for the Lions in a three-set sweep of Stanford.

2000 men's gymnastics. 0.125 was the difference between Penn State's (231.975) and Michigan's (231.850) point totals.

2004 men's gymnastics. A season-high 223.350 score was 1.050 better than second-place Oklahoma.

2007 men's gymnastics. To borrow from Motley Crüe, "Home Sweet Home!" Penn State wins the national championship in Rec Hall.

2007 women's volleyball. And a dynasty is born. The Lions win a dramatic five-game match over Stanford.

2008 women's volleyball. Megan Hodge wins the Most Outstanding Player Award, as the Lions sweep Stanford in the finals.

2008 men's volleyball. Playing in the final match of his Penn State career, Luke Murray has 63 assists, 12 digs, and 11 blocks in leading the Lions to a four-game win over Pepperdine.

2009 women's volleyball. Was there ever a doubt? Well, after dropping the first two games to Texas, there probably were some doubts. However, the Lions rally to win the next three in taking their third straight championship and, at the same time, pushing their consecutive win streak to 102 matches.

2010 women's volleyball. Although the Lions' unbeaten streak ends during the regular season, the finish is still perfect. Penn State sweeps California, 3–0, to win its fourth consecutive title and fifth in team history. Freshman Deja McClendon wins the Most Outstanding Player honor. The Lions lose just one game in its six tournament matches, including a 3–0 sweep of favored Texas in the national semifinal.

2011 wrestling. In just his second season as the program's head coach, Cael Sanderson leads the Lions to their second NCAA title in front of a record crowd in Philadelphia. Penn State has five All-Americans, including Quentin Wright, who wins an individual championship at 184 pounds.

OTHER CHAMPIONSHIPS THAT SHOULD BE RECOGNIZED.

2. Penn State Icers. Although Penn State will have Division I ice hockey again starting with the 2012–13 season—the school had varsity hockey from 1939–40 to 1945–46—the club team, the Icers, have had a great history, winning national championships in 1984, 1998, 2000, 2001, 2002, and 2003.

1. Football. Here is a push to add four more titles—1911, 1912, 1973, and 1994—to the football team's ledger. The National Championship Foundation crowned the 1911 and 1912 teams national champs (prior to the creation of the Associated Press Poll). The 1973 season saw the Lions go perfect for the third time in six years, yet pollsters, as they did in 1968 and 1969, denied them a national championship. Penn State's head coach announced that he had formed his own poll—"The Paterno Poll"—and the Lions were No. 1. He even awarded championship rings to the members of the team. The 1994 Lions also went perfect and were denied a national title from the major polls. But the *New York Times*, Sagarin Ratings, and basically all of the Nittany Nation ranked Penn State No. 1.

MOMENTOUS FOOTBALL DECISIONS

Penn State's uniforms may not be the flashiest—you know the cliché "no names on the back of the jersey." Its head coach is most likely the only coach currently not wearing a headset on game day. The school is situated in rural Pennsylvania. Yet for all the nonhip perceptions, Penn State, perhaps more so than most other schools, has had a huge impact on the college football landscape. At the root of these impacts were the decisions that the school and the coaches made. Here, in chronological order, are the top ten decisions.

10. Forming a football team—September 1887. There has to be a beginning to any great success story. For Penn State that occurred when school president George Atherton approved the organization of a football team. The first official game in Penn State history took place on November 5, 1887, as a squad led by George Linsz and Charles Hildebrand traveled to Lewisburg (now Bucknell University). Penn State was victorious that day, 54–0. Two weeks later Lewisburg returned the favor with a trip to State College. Again it was another Penn State shutout win, 24–0. For 1887, the Pennsylvania State College was undefeated, unscored upon, and (even though such things did not exist at that time) uncrowned as national champions. I wonder how many pollsters from Ohio voted Nebraska No. 1 that year.

9. Say goodbye to the power of pink—1890. There *was* a period of time when Penn State had very flashy uniforms. Pink and black were a popular color combination when the football program was born. Those were the colors of the uniforms for the first three Penn State seasons. A big thank you to the students in 1890: They changed the school colors to blue and white. Seriously, the image of Paul Posluszny or LaVar Arrington wearing pink uniforms is not a pretty sight.

8. Football scholarships reinstituted—May 1949. With multiple national championships and Big Ten titles, overlooking this incredibly important moment in the history of Penn State football can be easy. Starting in 1927, the school eliminated financial aid (scholarships) for football players. If it had continued that policy, Penn State most likely would have followed Ivy League schools such as Yale and Harvard who ceded their prestigious athletic past to having sports be an enjoyable diversion from the rigors of academic life. In short, not only football but also the entire university would not be the major player it is today. When the board of trustees rescinded the scholarship ban, it was the start of the pursuit of being a national football power.

7. Hiring Rip Engle—April 1950. Engle had some reluctance before agreeing to coach the Nittany Lions. When he was offered the Penn State position, the Somerset County native had a good thing going at Brown University. He had led the Bears to a combined 15–3 record the previous two seasons. In addition, PSU required that he keep all of the assistants from Joe Bedenk's 1949 staff, including Bedenk himself. Engle wanted to radically alter the offense and install the wing-T formation. He wanted somebody well versed in that system to help him with the change. So Penn State allowed Engle to bring one assistant from his Brown staff to State College. The trouble for Engle was that nobody on his old staff wanted to leave the Providence, Rhode Island, school. After those rejections, he asked the quarterback of his 1948–49 Brown teams to postpone his entry to law school, for just one year mind you, and assist Penn State with the new offense. What would Penn State look like today if one of Engle's assistants *did* agree to leave Brown and join the Lions' staff? Fortunately for Engle—and the future legions of Nittany Nation—the recently graduated Brown quarterback, Joe Paterno, agreed to "temporarily" take up residence in Central Pennsylvania.

6. Head east young men—November 1958. The word "visionary" best describes the board of trustees' decision to relocate Beaver Field, Penn State football's home facility, to the east side of campus. Doing so was part of an overall expansion project to meet the increasing size of student enrollment. The decision had mixed reactions. Those who opposed the move enjoyed the Fenway Park–like game-day atmosphere. Beaver Field was nestled near Rec Hall and the Nittany Lion Inn. It was a short walk for almost the entire student body living on a campus that basically encompassed dormitories and classrooms near Old Main to the West Hall dorms and Rec Hall. Returning alumni liked to enjoy a meal and a drink or two (or three or four) before and after the games at the Nittany Lion Inn or the pubs and restaurants two or three blocks away in downtown State College. Even Paterno thought it was a bad idea, stating he thought the move would *destroy* Penn State football. The bigger picture, however, was that both Penn State football and the university were growing. With the stadium at its west-campus location, the ability to increase the 32,000-seat facility was limited. Add to that the limited parking (or as some would say, "What parking?"), and the need to move was clear. Penn State is a school that takes pride in its engineering program. It was quite a feat of engineering that called for the dismantling of Beaver Field, moving the pieces to the cow pastures on the east side of campus, and creating a new 46,000-seat structure, Beaver Stadium. More than fifty years and an additional 60,000 seats later, it is home to one of the great venues in college football.

5. Promoting Paterno to head coach—February 1966. As the staff's top assistant, Paterno was the obvious choice to take over when Rip Engle announced his retirement. He had twice flirted with leaving PSU to take the head coach position at Yale. In 1963 the Ivy League school chose Johnny Pont over Paterno. When the position opened again in 1965, Yale offered Paterno the job. Although Paterno did have bigger football aspirations than to be an assistant, he also was eyeing the possibility of succeeding Engle, and his mentor had made it public he wanted Paterno to take over when he retired. To give Paterno some insurance, Engle promoted him to associate head coach in 1965, prompting one newspaper to run the headline "No to Yale . . . Yes to State." The Nittany Lions were only 5–5 in Paterno's first season, and after dropping the 1967 season opener at Navy, some thought that Penn State had made the wrong choice. Like he has most of his career, Paterno proved his doubters wrong—and then some.

4. Picking Orange over Cotton—November 1969. When they accepted the invitation to play in the 1970 New Year's Day Orange Bowl instead of the Cotton Bowl, the Lions made a move that prevented them the opportunity to play for the national championship. Many Penn State fans bemoan the fact that the undefeated teams of 1968 and 1969 were never crowned national champions. Longtime college football analyst Beano Cook, in his many forums (radio, Internet chats, television), has maintained the 1968 squad was indeed "robbed" and should have been voted the top spot in the polls. He disagrees with the 1969 team's claim and points to the fact that the Lions could have played eventual champ Texas in the Cotton Bowl and decided the matter on the field. For a little context to the decision, you have to remember that at that time bowl invitations were extended while there were one or two games remaining in the regular season. The bowls had become major sporting events, but there was still the "fun and reward for a great season" aspect to playing in the postseason. At the time the bowl bids went out, Penn State still had Pitt and North Carolina State to play. Ohio State was the No. 1 ranked team in the country and seemed destined to win the Big Ten, go to the Rose Bowl, and face the Pac 8 champion. All the Buckeyes had to do was defeat their arch rival, No. 12–ranked Michigan. Texas was ranked No. 2, and the Longhorns still had Texas A&M and Arkansas left on the schedule. The sentiment from the Nittany Lions indicated they figured Ohio State would win out and retain the No. 1 ranking. For the players who, in their minds, awarded OSU the national championship, spending the latter part of December on the beaches of Miami seemed a better option than in the middle of Texas. So the Orange Bowl it was. To borrow a line from the movie *This Is Spinal Tap*, "Can I raise a practical question at this point?" The OSU-Michigan game was played in Ann Arbor—why would the Penn State team and officials concede the contest to the Buckeyes? Even if Ohio State had won, it still would have to play in the Rose Bowl against USC, who was undefeated with a 9–0–1 record. It was a big assumption that the Buckeyes would automatically win both of those games. Assuming Ohio State would defeat Michigan, at the very least the winner of a Penn State–Texas or Arkansas Cotton Bowl would have put extra pressure on Ohio State playing later in the day in Pasadena. What did happen was that Ohio State lost to Michigan, and Michigan lost in the Rose Bowl to USC. Penn State beat Missouri in the Orange, and Texas ran the table, including a Cotton Bowl win over Notre Dame to claim the crown.

3. Playing and beating the best—mid-1970s. One of the knocks against Penn State had been that the eastern football opponents it traditionally played were inferior to the teams of the SEC, Big 8, Big Ten, and so forth (funny how those arguments did not apply to Syracuse in 1959 or Pitt in 1976). The 1973 Nittany Lions were 12–0, yet the voters slapped them in the face with a No. 5 final ranking in the AP Poll. It was time to take the fight to the rest of the nation. Ohio State appeared on the schedule for a three-game series starting in 1975. Starting in 1979, Nebraska was on the schedule for five consecutive seasons. It all came together in the 1980s. Including the series with the Cornhuskers, Notre Dame and Alabama also became regulars on the schedule. Add that to the improvement of eastern schools (Boston College in the Doug Flutie era, Syracuse in 1987, West Virginia's playing for the national championship in 1988, and Pitt's status as a national power during the first half of the decade), and all of a sudden the Lions had a monster schedule. How fitting that JoePa's two national titles occurred during this period of time.

2. Putting together the game of the century—November 1986. There were several decisions that led to the Penn State–Miami Fiesta Bowl for the national title. Penn State had the easy one. Undefeated and ranked No. 2 in the polls, Paterno and company said yes to a potential matchup with the No. 1 Hurricanes. The rest of the major decisions were out of Penn State's control. First, Miami had to agree to play in the game. The Hurricanes were strongly considering retaining their top ranking by staying at home and playing in the Orange Bowl. However, money talks, and to get the 'Canes on board, the Fiesta Bowl upped the funds for each participating school thanks to its corporate relationship with Sunkist. NBC (which had the broadcast rights) assisted in this area as well, but not without some reservation. The proposal called for moving the game from New Year's Day afternoon to primetime January 2, 1987. The problem for NBC was that doing this would mean that mega-TV-ratings monster and cash cow *Miami Vice* would not air in order to make room for the Fiesta Bowl. At the time this was a tough business decision, but NBC gambled that the power of Paterno and the "Good Guy" image of Penn State against the "Evil" Miami

Hurricanes would bring a good number of eyeballs to their television sets on this Friday night. Miami eventually agreed to play the game. NBC's gamble paid off, as that Fiesta Bowl is still the most watched game in the history of college football, earning a 25.1 rating with more than 52 million viewers. Most importantly, "Good" triumphed over "Evil."

1. Hello Big Ten—December 1989. After being snubbed by Pitt and Syracuse in his efforts to form an all-eastern sports conference, Joe Paterno and Penn State's officials felt the need to elevate the school's athletic standing. Football was trucking along fine in the 1980s as an independent; however, the rest of PSU's intercollegiate teams were confined playing in the barely mid-major conference of the Atlantic 10. After a series of conversations that were, impressively, kept secret, the presidents of the Big Ten schools officially invited Penn State to join the conference in December 1989. The reaction on both sides was not exactly positive. The athletic officials of the Big Ten schools felt that they were not consulted in this decision and, led by Michigan's Bo Schembechler, pushed to have the invitation rescinded. Once it became clear that this would not work, he advocated to delay the Nittany Lions' entry into the conference until the 1995 or 1996 football season. On the Penn State side, a large number of fans also were not pleased. After all, many perceived the Big Ten as a football conference in decline. It had not produced a national champion since 1968, and its teams seemed as if they were always getting pummeled in the Rose Bowl by the Pac-10—a 3–7 record from the 1981 Rose Bowl to 1990. The move also ended longtime rivalries with Pitt, Syracuse, and West Virginia. Furthermore, road trips to away games would become more difficult because of the conference's geography that stretched from the Keystone State to Iowa. Whether Penn State is now accepted by the other schools is debatable—the 1994 missing national championship is evidence against that theory. What this decision did prove, however, is that Penn State is a leader, innovator, and on the cutting edge of the college football world. Following the invitation, other dominos began to fall. The SEC expanded with the addition of South Carolina and Arkansas. The ACC expanded with the addition of Florida State. The Big East added football to its conference, ironically creating the all-eastern sports league that Paterno was pushing for a decade earlier. The Big 8 and four teams from the Southwest Conference (Texas, Texas A&M, Texas Tech, and Baylor) formed the new Big 12. Conference championship games began to take root—all because Penn State accepted an invitation to join the Big Ten.

TOP REASONS WHY JOINING THE BIG TEN HAS BEEN GOOD FOR PENN STATE

Penn State will likely always be considered an outsider to the rest of the Big Ten. And the fact that the Nittany Lions no longer have a team they can call their archrival or one that considers them their archrival makes it seem as if there's something missing each football season—face it: Michigan, Ohio State, and Michigan State will always hate each other more than they hate Penn State.

Still, overall, being a member of the Big Ten has been very good for Penn State, and here are the top reasons why.

5. Sticking it to former rivals. Some 30 years ago, a couple of Penn State's rivals joined the Big East in all sports but football, killing Joe Paterno's hope of an eastern conference encompassing all sports. How has Pitt football done since it stopped playing Penn State? How about Syracuse?

Why do you think Syracuse men's basketball coach Jim Boeheim made negative comments in 1990 about Penn State's joining the Big Ten, saying the football and men's basketball teams would never win in the Big Ten? Could it be he understood the ramifications for his university of not having Penn State on its football schedule? The simple fact is that Penn State is a member of the most powerful conference in the nation in terms of the influence it wields and the money it can generate.

4. Competition. Boeheim had one thing right: Penn State took a step up in competition in all sports, even football. There's no question fans have seen Penn State play better teams in nearly every sport since the school joined the Big Ten. And if you're wondering about football, the Lions have records of 22–2 against Rutgers, 48–9–2 against West Virginia, 35–1–1 against Maryland, and 42–23–5 against Syracuse. What kind of competition is that?

3. Exposure. This was never an issue for football. But now, thanks to the Big Ten Network, fans across the country can watch Penn State's other teams. And although this may not greatly help with recruiting, it can't hurt to tell the parents of a high school athlete who lives down South or on the West Coast that they'll be able to watch their son or daughter play on TV.

2. Necessity. Penn State's move to the Big Ten opened the floodgates to teams joining new conferences. If PSU hadn't done it, another school would have, and the Lions would have been forced to shop around for a conference to join—because being an independent in football and a member of the Atlantic 10 in other sports wasn't going to cut it. Even Notre Dame football is starting to realize that it may be necessary to play in a major conference—not just for the competition but also for the most important factor . . .

1. Money. This is always the bottom line isn't it? Thanks to the Big Ten's revenue sharing, Penn State can count on about $22 million a year from the conference, and that's before Nebraska joined and regardless of how football or any of the other athletic teams do. And although the Big Ten Network definitely helps with exposure, its biggest asset is that it could help the conference earn $2.8 billion over the course of its 25-year deal with News Corp.[1] Many schools in other conferences would love to get a piece of that pie.

---

1 "Big Ten Could Reap $2.8B from Network Deal," *SportsBusiness Journal*, March 3, 2008, http://www.sportsbusinessdaily.com/Journal/Issues/Archive/This-Weeks-News/2008/03/Big-Ten-Could-Reap-$28B-From-Network-Deal.aspx.

TOP REASONS WHY PENN STATE SHOULD NOT HAVE JOINED THE BIG TEN

The Penn State athletic world changed in December 1989 when it was announced that the university was joining the Big Ten conference. Ever since, some have felt that the other members of the conference don't think Penn State is really the caliber of a Big Ten school. Evidence cited includes referee Sam Lickliter's infamous call against the Nittany Lions in their initial men's basketball season as well as speculation that, in 2009, conference commissioner Jim Delaney lobbied extensively on Iowa's behalf, and at Penn State's expense, to the BCS bowls for the coveted at-large invitation. The relationship between the Nittany Lions and the Big Ten has not always been harmonious. Here are the top reasons why joining the Big Ten was the wrong choice for Penn State.

5. Arithmetic. Question: How many teams are in the conference of which Penn State is a member? Answer: 12.

Question: What is the name of the conference of which Penn State is a member? Answer: Big Ten.

For a conference that prides itself on the academic prestige of its schools, that they would flaunt their struggles with basic math seems odd. In this case, if Big Ten officials were on the show *Are You Smarter Than a 5th Grader?*, the 5th graders would win in a rout.

4. Geography. Continuing with the educational theme, road trips to other Big Ten campuses are quite the endeavor. The shortest trip is to Ohio State in Columbus, Ohio—a mere 276 miles. Compare that to the schools Penn State competed against on a regular basis prior to joining the conference:
- Pitt (Pittsburgh, Pennsylvania): 114 miles
- West Virginia (Morgantown, West Virginia): 136 miles
- Maryland (College Park, Maryland): 128 miles
- Rutgers (East Brunswick, New Jersey): 189 miles
- Syracuse (Syracuse, New York): 178 miles

Going on the road to watch the Nittany Lions when they played teams within their own part of the country was much easier and probably less expensive.

3. Loss of traditional rivals. Pitt and Syracuse helped kill the rivalries in all sports but football when they left Penn State on the outside and joined the Big East, so you can't blame Penn State's joining the Big Ten for that. Football, however, is a different story. Penn State has played Syracuse more than any other school. For most of their existence, Penn State and Pitt have been the top two programs in Pennsylvania. They share the same recruiting turf and they have been involved in a number of intense games that come with a big-time college football rivalry.

That rivalry ruled the college football world for a wonderful eleven-game stretch from 1976 to 1986. It started with Pitt's 1976 national championship. Two years later Penn State played for the national championship. In 1981 both teams held the No. 1 ranking at different points during the regular season, which ended with Penn State defeating the top-ranked Panthers, 48–14, in Pittsburgh, derailing Pitt's drive to a national title. Penn State won the national championship in 1982, played for it in 1985, and won a second one for Joe Paterno in 1986. No other rivalry in the country during that period impacted the national championship like Penn State-Pitt. There are many reasons why the schools no longer play against each other in football, but if it were not for Penn State's admission to the Big Ten, Penn State would likely not have allowed the series to end.

Proximity, a long history, and even a little hatred all added up to a good collection of rivals Penn State played before joining the Big Ten. Other than Ohio State and, perhaps, Michigan, no Big Ten school raises the ire of Penn State fans the way Pitt did—and, in some cases, still does. The Nittany Nation probably has more antipathy toward the commissioner and Big Ten referees than they do with the likes of Minnesota or Purdue.

2. They did not want us. The official invitation to join the Big Ten came from the presidents of the conference members in December 1989. Although they may have been welcoming, the athletic directors at the schools were not. They first tried to get the invitation rescinded. When that didn't work, they made it difficult for the Nittany Lions to begin conference play. After the invitation announcement on December 19, 1989, then-Michigan athletic director Bo Schembechler said, "It may be sound and for good reasons to have Penn State in the league, but I don't think it was very well thought out. . . . I don't see how we can play Penn State for 10 years." He even suggested that Northwestern, because it was the doormat of the league, would leave the Big Ten.[2] Other officials from Big Ten athletic departments expressed similar sentiments. A few months later commissioner Delaney told the Associated Press that the earliest Penn State could join the Big Ten for football and men's basketball was 1995.[3]

---

2 Mal Florence, "Inviting Penn State Ill-Conceived Idea, Says Schembechler," *Los Angeles Times*, December 27, 1989.

3 Associated Press, "Big Ten Conference Agrees to Make Penn State No. 11," *New York Times*, June 5, 1990.

The admission of Penn State literally changed the landscape of college sports. Soon after, the SEC added Arkansas and South Carolina. The ACC added Florida State. The Southwest Conference disbanded, with Texas, Texas A&M, Baylor, and Texas Tech joining the members of the Big 8 to form the new Big 12 conference. All these leagues immediately began to incorporate their new members into play. These actions exposed the fraud of Delaney's comments, and the timetable was moved up. The two basketball programs and wrestling began conference play in the 1992–93 seasons, while football played its first Big Ten season in 1993. And a not-so-beautiful friendship began.

1. 1994. In only its second year of conference play, the Nittany Lion football team went a perfect 12–0—the capper being a rout over Oregon in the Rose Bowl. The punch in the gut was that most Associated Press voters from Big Ten country voted Nebraska No. 1 over Penn State. This was a little surprising considering that many of these same voters thought Penn State would struggle in its new conference due to the false perception that the Nittany Lions had taken a major step up in competition. These same voters, who regularly touted the supremacy of the Big Ten, opted to vote for a member of the supposed inferior Big 8 as the national champion. One wonders if Ohio State or Michigan had a 12–0 season in 1994 instead of Penn State whether those Big Ten voters would have voted the same way. Well, it just so happens that three years later, in 1997, Nebraska and Michigan finished undefeated. That year, interestingly enough, the Wolverines and the Cornhuskers split the national title, with Michigan No. 1 in the AP and Nebraska topping the coaches' poll.

TOP FIVE REASONS WHY PENN STATE AND THE NEW YORK YANKEES HAVE THE GREATEST UNIFORMS IN SPORTS :: BY SWEENY MURTI

One wouldn't think that Penn State and the New York Yankees would have much in common beyond on-the-field success. Ah, but WFAN's Sweeny Murti, a 1992 PSU graduate who has covered the Yankees since 2001, sees that besides wins and losses, the teams have two of the best uniforms in all of sports.

5. Instantly recognizable—and intimidating. Just like seeing the pinstriped jerseys and pants, as soon you see one blue stripe down the middle of a white helmet, you know who's playing. No need to guess if it's Husker Red or Buckeye Red. No need to wonder if that's a Razorback or a Mustang on the helmet. You know right away it's Penn State.

And just as there are times when a team comes into Yankee Stadium, looks at the guys wearing the classic home jerseys, and recognizes that they are about to be beaten, it's the same way on crisp Saturday afternoons in the fall when teams walk into Beaver Stadium.

4. Simple is better. There's a reason the Nittany Lions and the Yankees don't have to change their uniform styles every couple of years: because classy never goes out of style.

3. No alternate jerseys. This is where Penn State has it over Notre Dame. Those "special occasion" green jerseys are over the top for me. Don't you sell enough of the regular ones? Same goes for the Yankees' jerseys and caps. The day I see either team wearing anything other than traditional home and road uniforms, I quit.

2. Producers of magic. Yes, there are legends that make the tradition. There's Mantle, DiMaggio, and Jeter just as there's Cappelletti, Ham, and Posluszny. But sometimes the magic in the jersey rubs off on the guy wearing it. How else do you explain Bucky Dent's home run over the Green Monster in 1978 or Craig Fayak's field goal at South Bend in 1990? Sometimes the tradition makes the legend.

1. No name on the back. The only stat that matters is getting the W. You put on the uniform and you expect perfection every time out. When you don't get it, you are disappointed. It's all about the team, and that's why we don't care whose name is on the back of that shirt. We know who you play for, and that's why we cheer for you. Like it reads on the scoreboard before games during the video montage: "I play for those who came before me."

WHY THE GRAND EXPERIMENT WORKS AT PENN STATE :: BY DAVE JOYNER

Joe Paterno called it "The Grand Experiment." It's the belief that a university can field a quality football program and have the team's players also be quality students who graduate. If anyone epitomized that philosophy it was Dave Joyner. An All-American offensive tackle in 1971 who Paterno said "may be the best tackle we've had at Penn State," Joyner also excelled in the classroom. He won a National Football Foundation and College Football Hall of Fame fellowship his senior season. In 1991 he was inducted into the GTE/CoSIDA Academic All-American Hall of Fame. These days Joyner is an orthopedic surgeon, specializing in sports medicine. He explains why the Grand Experiment does indeed work.

5. Help. They definitely have mechanisms in place with academic advisers. There's a structure in place, so kids don't waiver, don't drift. You can get great kids, but if you don't give kids a great structure and kids are left to their own devices, they will find a way to screw it up.

4. Results off the field equals results on the field. Joe made us believe that unless you were a complete person, you weren't going to be as good an athlete as you could be—in other words, to pay attention to all the details. What you do off the field has everything to do with your performance on the field. It's like the Japanese Samurai: They paid attention to everything. The Samurai paid attention to art and painting. If a Samurai neglected one part of his life, he wasn't as good on the battlefield. Discipline is a way of life: You can't turn it off or on.

3. Keeping up with your grades keeps you out of Joe's doghouse. There are two ways to get on Joe's bad side: You fumble a lot, and you screw up your responsibilities of going to school. Once you get into Joe's doghouse, getting out is hard.

2. It's a belief. You see some schools that have zero graduation rates, and the university president says, "We believe in academics." I believe they believe that, but coaches there don't give two hoots. Here, the belief has been going on long enough that this is the way we do things. When Penn State hires a new coach, they don't come here unless that's inbred with them. You don't attract people who don't want to be that way. People are attracted to the program because they want to be a part of that.

1. It's simply what Penn State does. There's an underlining aura and philosophy. The Penn State aura is that the athletic program is a reflection of the university as a whole—the faculty, the administration. The athletic teams are a reflection of the school in general. At a lot of places the exact opposite is true. But at Penn State, there's a sense that this is the way we do things. Athletes understand that; coaches accept it and embrace it. Athletes understand the expectation that they're here to be complete people. They're not just here to perform on game day.

A TOP PLACE TO TAILGATE
:: BY JOE CAHN—THE COMMISSIONER OF TAILGATING

For 15 years Joe Cahn has lived "the dream." With the start of each football season, he leaves his Fort Worth, Texas, home and travels to college and pro venues each week to tailgate with fans from across the country. By the start of the 2010 season he had traveled about 750,000 miles and hit around 650 games—although, he notes, he rarely goes into the stadiums to watch the games. He's there to tailgate, and he's become nationally known as the Commissioner of Tailgating. He has visited Penn State on several occasions and calls it "definitely one of the best places to tailgate." Here are his top reasons why.

5. Parking. Penn State's strength is the parking availability. There's an incredible amount of parking—and it's good parking. That allows people to get there early to the facility and tailgate. There's great RV parking. You have RVs coming in on Thursdays.

4. Fresh food. One of the unique things Penn State has is the butcher shop right by Beaver Stadium. (The Penn State Meats Laboratory holds sales most Fridays between 9:30 a.m. and 3 p.m. on Porter Road, across from the JoePa statue.) You can go Friday and get what you need. I love going over to the meat market. You also can go downtown on Fridays to the Farmers' Market. That's a giant bonus. You get your fresh goods from farmers around the area.

3. Diversity of food. With the diversity of alumni, there is a myriad of food one can expect there. During the early part of the season you'll have wonderful sweet corn and grilled corn. For breakfast, people make blue eggs. One of the all-time strangest dishes I've had at any time in any parking lot was at Penn State: scrapple with chocolate sauce.

2. Fans. The fans themselves are very hospitable. It doesn't matter what color jersey you're wearing. In the parking lot, everyone's a visitor. Inside you might be opponents. People coming to the game have made long trips, and they experience some incredible hospitality. And I love their loyalty to JoePa with Paternoville and how they are there to greet the players and coaches when they arrive at the stadium. . . . [On a side note], I don't know of a better chant anywhere than "We Are . . . Penn State." When the sides of the stadium go back and forth, that's an incredible feeling.

1. The Creamery. Now they have the new Creamery. Before the game you can get something or, afterward, head over and get your Peachy Paterno. The Creamery is something very special.

TAILGATE TREATS

In addition to watching great football in Beaver Stadium, part of the Penn State game experience is tailgating. Recreational vehicles roll into town as early as Thursday. Take a walk through the parking lot on a football Saturday morning and you'll see many people playing tailgate games, hear a variety of music, and catch some fans surrounding a television set rigged to a satellite, which is pulling in an early football game. And, of course, there's the aroma of hundreds of grills cooking up all types of food. What to enjoy with that food? Here are our top Keystone State–themed suggestions.

5. Iron City beer. A shout out to the Nittany Lion fans from the western part of the commonwealth. IC has long been associated with the Pittsburgh sports scene, and a can or two has been known to make its way east to a Beaver Stadium parking lot.

4. Nittany Blue and Nittany White cigars. Smoke 'em if you got 'em. We realize that lighting up a stogie may not be everyone's thing, but if you like cigars, take a trip to downtown State College and visit Your Cigar Den—the home of the Nittany Blue and Nittany White cigars. Although they are not made with any known Pennsylvania tobacco—they are produced and labeled elsewhere—a good cigar with a picture of Mount Nittany on the label is a nice complement to a tailgate full of Penn State paraphernalia.

3. Oak Spring Winery Game Day Blush. Oak Spring Winery is located near Altoona. Game Day Blush is similar to a rosé with a sweet taste. A good choice for those early season games when the weather is still warm.

2. Mount Nittany Winery Tailgate Red. When you have the words Nittany and Tailgate in your product's name, you are venturing close to John Shaffer's winning percentage. As its name implies, the winery is located on the southern slope of Mount Nittany. Tailgate Red is described as "a light, semi-dry blend of French hybrid grape varieties." The winery recommends that it be served chilled.

1. Yuengling Beer. America's oldest operating brewery is located in Pottsville. In 1987 Yuengling introduced its Lager, and it has since become the company's flagship beer. The beer is mostly sold in the mid-Atlantic states and some states in the South, keeping it a regional treat.

GONE BUT NOT FORGOTTEN

Rolling Rock. Yes, technically there is still a beer called Rolling Rock. What we are referring to is the beer that was brewed in Latrobe. The beer was a favorite of State College's, particularly the Rathskeller and the ever popular "case study," where many a case of Rolling Rock eight-ounce ponies were consumed. In 2006 Anheuser-Busch purchased Rolling Rock, and the beer is now brewed in Newark, New Jersey, ending a 67-year Pennsylvania tradition.

TOP TAILGATE FOODS :: BY MARC FETTERS

Although many fans prefer to bring their own grills and cook up their own tailgates, some don't mind letting the professionals handle things. That's where Marc Fetters, co-owner of Prospector's Allegheny Rib Company, can help. Fetters opened Prospector's in State College in 1996. For the past four football seasons he and his crew have set up a stand outside Beaver Stadium, and people can either come to the stand and buy food or preorder one of the restaurant's tailgate packs that can be delivered to their tailgate. ESPN's *College Gameday* called Prospector's "the best barbecue east of the Mississippi." Fetters gives us his top foods for any tailgate.

5. Prospector's Pig. This is a boneless pork cutlet smothered in barbecue sauce while on the grill. It's put on a Kaiser roll and topped with some creamy coleslaw.

4. Hot Sausage Sandwich. Fresh sausage comes in different styles—hot Italian, sweet, breakfast, and so forth. Put it on a sausage roll with roasted red peppers, onions, and one of several mustards that are offered.

3. Wings. Whether you have them with barbecue or wing sauce, you can never go wrong with some jumbo chicken wings at a tailgate.

2. Pulled Pork. Fetters says he does about 1,000 pounds of pulled pork for each game. The pork is slow cooked and smoked and then hand pulled. It has a mixture of two barbecue sauces that make it smokier and sweeter than the ribs. And speaking of ribs . . .

1. Ribs. Of course, this is what Prospector's is known for and fans love to eat. The baby back ribs are slow cooked and smoked "until they're ready to fall off the bone." They're slathered with the signature sauce, which has a little "kick to it" compared to other sauces.

On the side: Don't forget those side dishes. You have your choice of baked beans that have some of the pulled pork mixed in them, the creamy coleslaw, macaroni salad, potato salad, and more.

WHATEVER HAPPENED TO . . .

Other than Joe Paterno and many of the assistant coaches, there have been plenty of things that have come and gone at Penn State over the past 40 or 50 years. Looking back, we may not have all the answers, but one question comes to mind—whatever happened to. . . .

8. Ticket prices. When we went to our first game in 1978 the cost of one football ticket was $5. Yes, you read that correct—$5! Even as recently as 1998 the cost of a ticket was $28. Today there are NFL teams that offer cheaper tickets than Penn State.

7. 1 p.m. kickoffs. Though I feel like I am playing the "old man" card with this, there was a time when most of Penn State's games started at 1 p.m. Considering the distances many fans travel on game day, it was a perfect starting time—plenty of time for a good tailgate and, afterward, giving the fans the ability to arrive home at a reasonable hour. Now we have mostly noon kickoffs (better chug those Bloody Marys if you want to make it inside for the start), 3:30 p.m. (acceptable balance of tailgate time and arrival at home afterward), or 8 p.m. (a bit dangerous for the ride back home on Pennsylvania's deer-infested roads).

6. The Regatta. Not a football event, but for the most of the 1980s and early 1990s if you were a Penn State student, there was a good chance you partied at the Regatta held at Stone Valley and later Bald Eagle State Park. The Beta Sigma Beta fraternity sponsored the event, and it featured live music, canoe races, and tug-of-war contests. Acts such as Joan Jett and the Hooters performed during a time when they were not far removed from big hits. At its peak it was one of the largest fraternity philanthropies in the country. There has to be more than a few of you out there that owned a "You Gotta Regatta!" T-shirt. The Regatta is a nice transition to. . . .

5. The Phi Psi 500. Another large philanthropic event, the Phi Psi 500 had contestants race each other in downtown State College. The race included stops at many local bars to grab drinks (of the adult variety) as participants continued the event. MTV would give the Phi Psi extensive coverage. However, once the beer-drinking component was taken away, the event mysteriously lost is popularity.

4. Lionvision. This one never came to fruition, but in a way it was an idea ahead of its time. In 1989 Penn State began soliciting for subscribers to an all-Penn State, all-the-time TV network. The trouble was that in order to get Lionvision, you needed a special satellite dish that received only one station—Lionvision. That would cost a subscriber $995. In addition, there was the annual $300 fee to keep the dish and another $300 annual subscription fee. Even by today's finances, that was some big bucks Penn State was asking fans to fork over for the pleasure of watching Joe Paterno press conferences, tape-delayed football broadcasts, and other Penn State sporting events. I can't imagine why they did not get many takers.

3. Parody songs on pregame tailgate shows. As young Nittany Lion fans, riding into State College from Tunkhannock (most likely for a 1 p.m. game) one of the things that got us excited and let us know that we were getting close was exiting off of Interstate 80 and hearing the tailgate shows on the local radio stations. The hosts interacted with the fans in the parking lot, and part of the entertainment included a catalog of parody songs highlighting Penn State football. Our top three: 3. "Eye of the Lion" (Survivor's "Eye of the Tiger") 2. "Bowl Bound and Down" (Jerry Reed's "East Bound and Down") 1. JoePa ("Day-O: The Banana Boat Song"). One of the lines of "JoePa" says it all, "I work all week until weekend she comes. Football comes and I don't want to go home. JoePa top banana, make us number one. Football comes and I don't want to go home."

2. *TV Quarterbacks*. Perhaps the only time we were actually excited to watch PBS was the weekly show with Paterno, Fran Fisher, and Jim Tarman. *TV Quarterbacks* featured player interviews, Paterno's thoughts on the preceding and upcoming games, and highlights of the most recent game set to the soundtrack of 1970s-style NFL films music.

1. Numbers on the helmets. It was not just a passing fad; Penn State had a player's individual number on both sides of his helmet (University of Alabama style) for more than two decades. The numbers were on the helmets during the perfect 1968 and 1969 seasons and for John Cappelletti's Heisman-winning year. Starting in 1976 the numbers were gone—and have not returned since.

I AM SO DONE WITH . . .

There are many things to love about college football. However, if I were king for a day, there are several things I would eliminate. Borrowing from Sporting News Radio host Steve Czaban's (formerly of Fox Sports Radio) weekly segment, here are the top ten things that "I Am So Done With."

10. My butt hurting after games at Beaver Stadium. For those who have sat on the steel planks in Penn State's home field, you know of which I speak. Sure, I could bring in my own seat cushion (sometimes after a long afternoon of tailgating, I just plain forget that detail). I don't prefer the stadium's option of renting a seat cushion for the season, and you would think with the amount of money you pay for tickets, there would be more comfortable seating than a steel plank. I'm just saying.

9. Oregon's uniform of the day. Sorry, I don't think having 7,000 uniform combinations is cool. Who are they attempting to be, the Pittsburgh Pirates of the late 1970s? Thank goodness, Oregon didn't start its *Project Runway*-esque approach to attire until after the 1995 Rose Bowl against the Nittany Lions.

8. Audio delay of radio broadcasts. Yes, I am one of those headphone-wearing fans who enjoys listening to the Penn State Sports Network while watching the game live. Thanks to Janet Jackson's wardrobe malfunction at the Super Bowl, most broadcasts of sporting events are run on a delay. The problem is that the game action is out of sync with Steve Jones's and Jack Ham's call. I know they sell those devices to hear the game in real-time action, but why should I have to pony up for a radio that receives one station? Shades of Lionvision.

7. SEC speed. It seems as if every time Penn State plays a team from the SEC in a bowl game, the boys at ESPN pick the SEC team to win, citing speed as a primary reason; fast southern team against slow, plodding northern team. How many times do the Nittany Lions have to rout Tennessee in bowl games to put an end to the myth of SEC speed? Speaking of the SEC . . .

6. SEC programs that don't travel north of the Mason-Dixon Line. Joe Paterno stated during ESPN's broadcast of the 2010 Blue-White Game that they have tried to arrange home-and-home series with schools from the SEC. Alabama is the only school to ever agree to play in Beaver Stadium within the last 30 years. If the SEC is supposedly the greatest conference in the history of the world, why don't they man up and play a game in the northeastern or Midwestern part of the country once in a century?

5. The "*The*" in The Ohio State University. I am so glad Ohio State emphasizes *The* in its name. If not, people would probably confuse it with *A* Ohio State University.

4. Games on Tuesday nights, Thursday nights, Friday nights, or just about every night of the week except for Saturday nights. Elton John sang, "Saturday Night's Alright for Fighting." Add to that college football. Saturday is *the* day for the sport—from morning pregame shows to prime-time matchups. No need to dilute something that is near perfect by spreading it out over the weekdays.

3. Southbound traffic on Route 322 after a game. Just about every other part of Pennsylvania has four-lane highways in and out of State College—except for those traveling from the Harrisburg and Philadelphia areas. Only a few miles out of town, the four-lane highway becomes a two-lane country road. Traffic really bogs down in the area appropriately named "The Narrows."

2. Minor bowls laying claim to being January 1 bowls. I know the Nittany Lions have a few in this category, in particular the Capital One and Outback bowls, but January 1 bowls were and should still be the exclusive domain of the major events. The college football season should end on January 1 with the Rose, Orange, Sugar, and Fiesta bowls. Throw in the Cotton Bowl for old time's sake if you want. As for the others, there are plenty of dates in December at your disposal.

1. Having I-AA (Football Championship Subdivision) opponents on a schedule. There are plenty of I-A schools to choose from that there is no need to schedule Youngstown State, Coastal Carolina, or Indiana State. You don't see the Pittsburgh Steelers playing regular-season games against the Toronto Argonauts of the Canadian Football League. If you do feel the need to slum it at this level for a game, how about not charging full-price admission for what is basically a glorified scrimmage?

HISTORIC TEAMS

What's historic is not just that these teams won; it's what their success meant. Beyond the wins and losses during their respective seasons, their achievements had profound impacts that, in some cases, are still being felt.

5. 1994 men's volleyball. The Lions became the first non-California university to win the national title. Led by head coach Tom Peterson and All-Americans Ramon Hernandez and Ivan Contreras, the Lions defeated UCLA, 3–2, in the title match. The Bruins took two of the first three games and led 11–4 in the fourth, only to see Penn State go on an 11–1 run to win the fourth game. The Lions then went on to win the fifth game 15–12 to bring the national championship east. Besides being the first men's volleyball team outside the state of California to win a national title, no women's volleyball team east of the Mississippi River had ever won a national title. "We made history!" Peterson said after the match. "No one can take that away from any of us."

4. 1964 field hockey. In 1964 Penn State was preparing to field its first nine women's teams for intercollegiate competition. But when looking for opponents, the school had trouble finding other colleges in the region that had women's teams for most of the sports. Only field hockey was able to play a varsity season that year. On October 3, 1964, Penn State field hockey took the field against Susquehanna in the university's first female varsity intercollegiate athletic contest. The Lions, under head coach Pat Seni, won 2–0, and they would go 4–0 for the season. The next year Penn State added women's teams for basketball, fencing, golf, gymnastics, lacrosse, rifle, softball, and tennis.

3. 2007–10 women's volleyball. You have to put these four seasons together because they represent one of the greatest accomplishments by any college team in any sport. Head coach Russ Rose guided the Lions to four consecutive national titles with a streak of 109 consecutive wins included in these years. It's the second-longest streak in NCAA Division I team sports history, behind only the Miami men's tennis team's 137 consecutive wins from 1957 to 1964. During one stretch the Lions won 111 consecutive games! And a member of the Lions won the national player of the year honor in consecutive seasons, with Nicole Fawcett's winning it in 2008 and Megan Hodge in 2009.

2. 1967 football. On the surface, this was simply a good team—the Lions went 8–2–1, including a 17–17 tie to Florida State in the Gator Bowl. But what the future proved was that this team set the foundation for what Penn State football has become. In 1967 Joe Paterno was in his second season as head coach. After the Lions went a disappointing 5–5 in his first season, Penn State opened the 1967 campaign with a loss to Navy. Paterno wrote in his book *Football My Way* that after that game he, for the first time, felt concerned about his future as coach. The next week at Miami, he decided to start playing some of his talented sophomores. Among them were Steve Smear, Dennis Onkotz, Neal Smith, and Pete Johnson. Penn State upset Miami, 17–8. The Lions lost to third-ranked UCLA, 17–15, the next week, but it soon became obvious the future was looking bright for JoePa and the Lions—they would not lose again until nearly three years later. The legend had emerged.

1. 1947 football. Twenty years prior to what the 1967 team accomplished, the 1947 Nittany Lions had perhaps the best talent on the field the program has ever seen, and they made a statement off the field that should never be forgotten. The team included halfback and defensive back Wally Triplett and end Dennie Hoggard, the first two African Americans to play for Penn State. A year earlier coach Bob Higgins and the rest of the team voted to cancel a trip to play at Miami because Miami, like many teams in the South, refused to play against integrated schools unless they didn't bring their black players. In 1947 the Lions went 9–0 in the regular season. The defense gave up a total of 25 points and had six shutouts. However, a bowl trip appeared unlikely because the Orange and Sugar bowls didn't allow black players to play, and the Cotton Bowl had never invited a team with black players—and there was no reason to think it would start that year. But when SMU and head coach Matty Bell said they would play Penn State, the Lions were headed to Dallas, where they still endured some adversity; for example, they had to stay at the Dallas Naval Air Station because none of the hotels accepted blacks. The first integrated Cotton Bowl ended in a 13–13 tie; Triplett scored a touchdown, and he went on to become the first African American to be drafted by and play for an NFL team. The 1947 Lions' greatness on the field is surpassed only by their heroic stance and commitment to what was right off the field.

ON THE WORLD STAGE

Though competing for national championships and professional titles is nice, some Penn Staters have had opportunities to go against the *world's* best in various sports. Most of those have come in the Olympics, where the university has sent more than 100 individuals to participate in some capacity. Here are ten who showed their stuff not only representing the blue and white but also the red, white, and blue.

10. Christine Larson/Char Morett/Brenda Stauffer. America's boycott of the 1980 Summer Olympics seemingly took away Char Morett and Christine Larson's chance to compete for a gold medal in field hockey. But four years later Morett and Larson, who had kept practicing to be a part of the national team, joined another Penn Stater, Brenda Stauffer, on the 1984 field hockey team that won the bronze.

9. Allison Baver. The third time was the charm for Baver, who is one of the more decorated female short-track speedskaters. At the 2010 Winter Games in Vancouver, Baver finally earned a medal as she took home a bronze in the 3,000-meter relay. The team actually placed fourth, but Korea was disqualified for impeding a Chinese team. Baver had already won multiple medals in ISU Short Track World Cup competition. The 2010 medal also completed a remarkable comeback for her. A year earlier she collided with a teammate during a race in Bulgaria and fractured her leg in multiple places.

8. Kerry McCoy. The two-time national champion also enjoyed success in international competition. McCoy twice qualified for the Olympics—he finished fifth in 2000 and seventh in 2004. He also was a World Cup champion from 1999 to 2002; was a champion in the Pan AM Games in 1993, 2000, and 2003; and had a second-place showing in the world championships in 2003.

7. Suzie McConnell. One of the most dominant players in Lady Lion basketball history, McConnell twice showed the world her basketball skills. In 1988 she helped the US women's team go undefeated and take home the gold. She averaged 8.4 points and made a team-high five 3-pointers. Four years later she was back with the US team. McConnell averaged 6.8 points and had 18 assists as the US won the bronze medal.

6. Mike Shine. At the 1976 Olympics in Montreal, Shine nearly pulled off a huge upset in the 400-meter hurdles. He led the great Edwin Moses for most of the race, but Moses caught up to him at the seventh hurdle and eventually won in world-record time. Shine settled for the silver.

5. Mary Ellen Clark. A seven-time national champion, Clark won bronze medals at the 1992 and 1996 Olympics in 10-meter diving. The 1996 medal gave Clark the distinction of being the oldest women's diving medalist in Olympic history. That year, the US Olympic Committee nominated Clark as one of the top ten women athletes in the nation.

4. Gene Wettstone. Although Wettstone failed in his attempt to qualify for the 1936 Olympics as a gymnast, he wound up participating in five Olympics as a coach (1948 and 1956), judge (1952 and 1968), and team manager (1976). As Penn State's men's gymnastics coach, he also helped the school produce 15 Olympic gymnasts between 1948 and 1968.

3. Bill Jeffrey/Walter Bahr. Technically, Bahr had no affiliation yet with Penn State when he played for the US World Cup team in 1950—a team coached by then–Penn State soccer coach Bill Jeffrey. But Bahr would become Penn State's men's soccer coach nearly 25 years later, so he receives honorary mention here. The 1950 World Cup team pulled off what's considered one of the greatest upsets in sports when it defeated England, 1–0, in a round-robin game. Bahr had the assist on the lone goal. Some have called the match "The Miracle on Grass," obviously in reference to the "Miracle on Ice."

2. Horace Ashenfelter. A national-champion distance runner, Ashenfelter went to the 1952 Olympics and decided to compete in the steeplechase. The thinking was that his chances of winning gold were better in that event than to go against the great Emil Zatopék of Czechoslovakia in the 10,000-meter run. The steeplechase also was a challenge, however, because he had to defeat the world-record holder from the Soviet Union. The two were even for much of the race, but Ashenfelter ran the last 150 meters in 23 seconds to break the world record and win the gold.

1. Harold "Barney" Ewell. One of the top-ranked sprinters during and after World War II—he was a two-time national champion in the 100- and 200-meter races—Ewell pulled off an amazing feat when he won three medals at the age of 30 during the 1948 Olympics. After the Olympics were canceled in 1940 and 1944 because of the war, he qualified for the 1948 games when he tied the world record in the 100-meter dash. He also qualified in the 200-meter dash. He came close to winning gold in both the 100 and 200, but he had to settle for the silver in each. He earned a gold, though, while a member of the winning 4x400 relay team.

JOEPA HAS OUTLASTED . . .

Joe Paterno has been Penn State's head coach for more than 45 years. If you have been around at one place for any length of time, you are bound to see a number of changes. What about decades, even parts of two centuries? Paterno does have staying power. A good number of items had their beginnings in 1966 (Paterno's first year as head coach) *or* later, but they just could not match JoePa's endurance.

10. Elvis Presley's marriage to Priscilla. In Paterno's second season the King of rock and roll married Priscilla Wagner. They were divorced in 1973—the year John Cappelletti won the Heisman.

9. The WHA, WFL, USFL, and XFL. After the American Football League was successfully able to merge with the National Football League, other people attempted to start their leagues to compete with those that were established. None were able to last. The World Hockey League went from 1972 to 1979. The World Football League folded in its second season (1975). The United States Football League went only three seasons, 1983 through 1985. And, of course, the XFL, with players such as He Hate Me, lasted only one season in 2001.

8. Disco. Not sure if JoePa was doing the "YMCA" or the "Hustle," but disco music dominated almost every aspect of pop culture from 1968 to 1980.

7. CNN/SI television. There was a time when CNN was a serious sports competitor to ESPN. Its evening show, *Sports Tonight*, went up against *SportsCenter* and developed a strong following. It led to the formation of an all-sports-news network. However, ESPN beat its debut by one month when it started ESPNews in November 1996. CNN/SI lasted only until May 2002.

6. New Coke. Paterno's glasses have been referred to as "Coke-bottle glasses." We're not sure what the soft-drink giant was thinking when it unleashed New Coke on the public in April 1985. The beverage's name was changed to Coke II in 1992. It lasted until 2002. So did JoePa outlast one or two Coca-Cola products here?

5. "The U" as the Big East football standard-bearer. In reaction to Penn State's admission into the Big Ten, the Big East, mostly known as a basketball-powerhouse conference, thought it was an opportunity to exploit the Nittany Lions' leaving its eastern-independence heritage. The schools left behind (Pitt,

Syracuse, West Virginia, etc.) formed the Big East football conference. To help bring this new creation up to the level of the Big Ten and SEC, the league admitted Miami into the collection of schools in 1990, and the conference played its first season in 1991. The Hurricanes did win two national championships as a Big East member, but they also continued the conference's history of instability by bolting for the ACC in 2004.

4. Videos on MTV. Okay, not totally correct, but, seriously, unless you are watching MTV at 3 a.m., you are not going to see a music video. The "M" in MTV, which launched in 1981, is supposed to stand for *music*, and for the first 20 years, music videos were the primary source of programming. Now the network is almost exclusively reality and pop culture–related shows.

3. Veterans and Three Rivers stadiums. Philadelphia and Pittsburgh's multi-purpose stadiums opened in the early 1970s. They were unattractive, oversized concrete cereal bowls with some of the worst AstroTurf in sports. Thankfully, they no longer exist—with Three Rivers closing in 2000 and the Vet in 2003.

2. Super Bowls that end in daylight. The first Super Bowl was played after Paterno's first season. Up until and including Super Bowl XI, when the Raiders were crowned 1976 champs, the game ended in daylight. The following year the Super Bowl started in late afternoon, and it has started later every year since. Now the Super Bowl does not end until around 10:30 at night. All things considered, this is still a better deal than World Series games that conclude at 1 a.m. on the East Coast.

1. Big Ten coaches. Penn State's first Big Ten season was 1993. Since 2006 JoePa has been the dean, the longest-tenured coach in the conference. Every other program has made at least one coaching change, including Michigan State, which has made six.

LESSONS FROM JOE PATERNO :: BY MATT MILLEN

Matt Millen is one of the most unforgettable personalities who has played for the Nittany Lions. He's also one of the most dominant defensive linemen in the program's history, and he continued that dominant play into the NFL, where he won four Super Bowls. He and teammate Bruce Clark formed the best defensive-tackle tandem in the country during the late 1970s. Millen was an All-American in his junior season in 1978, when he had 54 tackles and nine sacks. He also blocked a punt and recovered two fumbles. But he also seemed as if he had a permanent residency in JoePa's doghouse due to his disagreements with his head coach. Today, Millen says the biggest problem was that he and Paterno are very much the same type of person and that's why they butted heads many times. The two get along great these days, but Millen still remembers some of the lessons his coach tried to teach him in college. Some he now agrees with, whereas others he thinks Paterno is still a little wrong on.

WHAT JOE'S STILL WRONG ABOUT:

3. White socks look good on any outfit.

2. Rolling your pant legs enhances your look.

1. You need to run a mile and a half to be a good football player. (Paterno took away Millen's captaincy in 1979 when Millen refused to complete two half-mile runs during the preseason.)

WHAT JOE'S RIGHT ABOUT:

Take care of the little things and the big things will take care of themselves.
He's 100 percent right about that and I still follow that one today.

TOP COACHES NOT NAMED JOE PATERNO

We all know Joe Paterno is the greatest coach of all time, whether you're talking college football or just coaches at Penn State. His amazing career, at times, overshadows the fact that the university has had many great coaches—some are even still coaching. I mean, the school has won nearly 70 national team championships, and football accounts for only two of those, so you know there have been some quality people leading these other programs. Here is our top ten sans JoePa.

10. Tom Peterson (men's volleyball, 1989–94)/Mark Pavlik (men's volleyball, 1995–present). It's tough to pick one or the other here because both Peterson and Pavlik have helped do away with the belief that only California schools can win national titles in volleyball. Peterson coached only six seasons at Penn State, ending his term with the 1994 national title, a win that shocked the volleyball world. Pavlik, who was an assistant under Peterson, has continued the program's success, leading the Lions to their second national championship in 2008.

9. Susan Delaney-Scheetz (women's lacrosse, 1986–89). It doesn't seem possible that someone who coached only four seasons could make this list—then you look at what Scheetz did in those four seasons as women's lacrosse head coach. The Lions went to the national title game every year, and they won two championships. Scheetz went 67–9 over those four years. The Lions haven't reached the title game since she left, but they have made it as far as the semifinals three times.

8. Rene Portland (women's basketball, 1980–2007). There is so much good and some not so good when it comes to Portland. The bad is obviously how the program slipped during her last few years, her controversial departure, and the lack of postseason success—one Final Four trip in 27 seasons. But you can't forget all the good. Portland made the Lady Lions a national power. In 1991 they became the first team from the Northeast to hold the No. 1 ranking in the AP Poll. When Penn State went into the Big Ten, the Lady Lions shared two conference titles in their first three seasons. They won three more conference crowns between 1999 and 2004. Portland not only improved Penn State's program, but she also helped improve and bring more attention to the women's game on a national level.

7. Charles "Rip" Engle (football, 1950–65). Just for bringing an assistant coach named Joe Paterno here should be good enough for Engle to make this list. But Rip did much more than that for Penn State. He brought Penn State football into national prominence, laying the foundation for what was to come after he retired following the 1965 season. The Lions went to four consecutive bowl games from 1959 to 1962, and they won three of them. Seven times they ended the season ranked in the top 20. Those feats might not sound like much now, but back then they were great accomplishments for the program. Engle finished with 104 wins, which ranks him second behind only his protégé on the team's all-time wins list.

6. Gillian Rattray (women's lacrosse, 1974–85; field hockey, 1975–1986). Rattray not only coached two sports, which is unthinkable these days, but also coached both teams to national championships. Combining records in both sports, she won 319 games and five national titles. In women's lacrosse she put together a 143–19–3 record and won three consecutive national titles from 1978 to 1980. She still holds the team record for wins by a coach. In field hockey she went 176–49–21 over 13 seasons and won national championships in 1980, when the Lions went 20–0–2, and 1981.

5. Russ Rose (women's volleyball, 1979–present). You have to say Rose definitely has a chance to move up this list, especially if he continues producing teams like he has over the past few seasons. Heading into the 2011 season, Rose has a 1,033–164 career record. He has led the Lions to five national titles, including four consecutive from 2007 to 2010, and guided them to the final match three other times. The 2007 to 2010 teams have become one of the greatest dynasties in college sports.

4. Bill Jeffrey (men's soccer, 1926–52). If you have a stadium named after you, you know you've done something great. Jeffrey Field is, of course, named after Penn State's legendary soccer coach. Jeffrey is the men's soccer program's all-time leader in winning percentage and for longest coaching tenure. During his 27 seasons as head coach—with never an athletic scholarship to grant—Jeffrey went 153–24–29 (.742 won-lost percentage), and the Lions won ten national championships. From 1932 to 1941 the Lions had an unbeaten streak of 65 games. Jeffrey's teams outscored the opposition 689–184. Beyond Penn State, he had a major impact on the sport, as he led the first US collegiate soccer contingent to travel abroad, and he coached the 1950 World Cup team that defeated England in what's considered one of the greatest upsets in the history of world soccer.

3. Charlie Speidel (wrestling, 1927–42 and 1947–64). Like Jeffrey, Speidel's impact on his sport went beyond his success at Penn State. He helped introduce and popularize the sport of wrestling in Pennsylvania and in other eastern states. He traveled extensively, holding clinics and helping wrestling become a major sport in high schools and colleges. During his 34 seasons at Penn State (he served in the military during the wartime seasons of 1942–45), he led the Lions to 14 top ten NCAA finishes and had six individual national champions. He also guided the program to its first NCAA team championship in 1953. From 1950 to 1954 the Lions won a school-record 34 consecutive dual meets. Speidel's 191 wins is still a team record. But as his biography on the Wrestling Hall of Fame website reads, his contributions "cannot be measured by victories and defeats. . . . He taught 'total wrestling'—not only the mechanics, but enthusiasm, self-reliance, and the importance of deep dedication, hard work, and the strength of the will to win."

2. Leo Houck (boxing, 1923–49). Besides helping Penn State win titles in boxing, Leo Houck was trying to change the perception of the sport. As a June 1985 article in *Town&Gown* reads, he was "advocating the science of boxing rather than the habit of brawling." Houck is considered the father of college boxing, and he sought to have high schools offer boxing as a sport. During his 26 years as Penn State's head coach, he helped the team produce 48 individual eastern champions, seven eastern team titles, five individual national champions, and one national team title. While boxing is no longer an NCAA-sanctioned sport, Houck's contributions to the school and the sport shouldn't be forgotten.

1. Gene Wettstone (men's gymnastics, 1939–76). Known as "Mr. Gymnastics," Wettstone was the dominant figure in his sport and, in some ways, remains a dominant presence. The numbers alone put him at the top—nine national team titles, 35 national individual titles, and 13 Olympians. But there's also his international influence. He brought teams from around the world to the United States to compete. During his coaching tenure Penn State hosted more than 15 international matches, including one with the Soviet Union. "I brought the Russians here and nobody had ever seen them in any sport," Wettstone told *The Daily Collegian* in an April 21, 2010 article. And if that weren't enough, Wettstone brought back the Nittany Lion mascot when he wore the suit in 1939—12 years after it had last been worn. For many years he helped select a student each year who would be the Nittany Lion mascot. The best part of his coaching career: He went out on top, with the Lions winning the national title in 1976, his final season.

MOST INSPIRATIONAL ATHLETES

They each had the heart of a lion, so to speak. These athletes, put in alphabetical order, inspired everyone across the Nittany Nation—and beyond.

John Cappelletti (football). If his 1973 Heisman speech doesn't bring tears to your eyes, get yourself checked out. Cappelletti starred at Penn State while he and his family were dealing with his younger brother Joey's battle with leukemia. Cappelletti dedicated the 1973 Heisman to Joey, who would pass away in 1976.

Kortney Clemons (paralympic athlete). He joined the Army in 2001, and in 2005, while he and other soldiers were helping another group of soldiers, a roadside bomb exploded, killing three and wounding others, including Clemons. Because of his injuries, he had to have his right leg amputated. Clemons eventually enrolled at Penn State and worked out with the school's Ability Athletics program. He became a national champion in the 100 meters at the 2006 US Paralympic Games. He also has set powerlifting records. Clemons was the first Iraq War veteran to qualify for the US Paralympic Games.

Mike Jacober (men's lacrosse). In late March 2005 Jacober's parents and younger brother were flying up to Penn State from Florida to watch Jacober play against Fairfield. The plane, a single-engine piloted by Jacober's father, crashed near the Penn State campus, killing the three family members on board. Remarkably, Jacober, a senior captain on the team, missed just one game. When he returned, the Lions won their last seven regular season games and received a bid into the NCAA Tournament.

Gary Klingensmith (football). Starting halfback and leading rusher in 1963—even though he was deaf. He rushed for 450 yards and three TDs in 1963. In 2010 Joe Paterno talked about Klingensmith during a press conference and said how Klingensmith always watched the center and could tell when the play was going to start. Paterno also recalled a story of when Penn State played at Ohio State and, on the first play, Klingensmith was offsides. After the game, reporters asked him why he was offsides, as he had never been offsides that season. "This is the biggest crowd I ever played in front of and I wanted to make sure they knew who the deaf kid was," Klingensmith said, according to Paterno.

Kari Lucas (softball). From nearby Penns Valley, Lucas walked onto the Penn State team and played in 44 games as a freshman. Shortly after the season ended, she was diagnosed with leukemia. Lucas vowed to come back and play the next spring, and she met that goal, starting in two games! She finished her career in 2007.

Chris Mazyck (football). Was a sixth-year senior defensive tackle on the 1994 Big Ten and Rose Bowl champion team—and he played that season with six slugs in his body from when he was shot in 1991. In March 1991 Mazyck was shot at point-black range at his family's home in South Carolina by a stranger he had asked to leave his porch an hour earlier. He had played as a freshman for the Lions in 1990, but he would spend 1991 and 1992 recovering from the wounds. He returned to help the Lions in their first two seasons in the Big Ten.

Brian Milne (football/track and field). Diagnosed with Hodgkin's disease in high school, Miline had a tumor the size of a grapefruit removed from his chest. He went on to be a strong fullback on the 1994 Big Ten and Rose Bowl title team. He is best remembered for scoring three touchdowns, including the game-winner, in the comeback win over Illinois. He won the national title in the discus in 1993 while still undergoing chemotherapy treatments.

Rohan Murphy (wrestling/powerlifter). At the age of four, Murphy had both of his legs amputated due to birth defects. That didn't stop him from wrestling in high school and, eventually, trying out for the Penn State wrestling team. He went 3–5 in two seasons (2004–05 and 2005–06) with the Nittany Lions. Like Clemons, he took part in Penn State's Ability Athletics program and has excelled in powerlifting.

Adam Taliaferro (football). He is probably the best known of these athletes because of the amount of lives he has touched and the image in 2001 when he walked onto the Beaver Stadium field less than a year after suffering a paralyzing spinal cord injury. Taliaferro suffered the injury in 2000 when he tackled Ohio State's Jerry Westbrooks. Taliaferro's helmet hit Westbrook's knee, causing the injury. He had surgery but was given just a 3 percent chance of walking again. After eight months of rehab, he had learned to walk, and so he walked out to the Beaver Stadium field on September 1, 2001, prior to the season opener against Miami. It was a scene no one will forget.

Joe Tepsic (football). Fought at Guadalcanal during World War II and was wounded in hand-to-hand combat, he played on the 1945 team as it opened its season just a few months after the war had ended. Tepsic was an inspiration to his team and fans. In his first game he scored two TDs, including one on a 52-yard run. He played just the one season, opting to play baseball for the Brooklyn Dodgers, who offered him a contract.

TOP COMEBACKS FROM INJURIES
:: BY DR. WAYNE SEBASTIANELLI

As head team physician for Penn State athletics, Dr. Wayne Sebastianelli has seen many athletes at their low points—suffering from recent injuries with the long road of rehab awaiting some of them. He's also seen many of those athletes come back and have great success following all their work to return to action. Here are, in alphabetical order, Dr. Sebastianelli's ten most memorable comebacks from injury.

Ki-Jana Carter (football, 1994). During the 1994 season Carter sustained a complex MCP dislocation of his right thumb during our game against Temple. While the game was still going on, he was taken to Temple University, where his thumb was surgically repaired. Following the surgery, within two weeks he was participating again, wearing a protective splint. Because of his quick recovery and ability to hang onto the ball, he was able to help us beat Michigan in Ann Arbor. We were well on our way to an undefeated season and Big Ten championship.

Matt Gaudio (men's basketball, 1995–96). Matt sustained an ankle sprain that resulted in an osteochondral fracture of his left ankle. In early December he underwent arthroscopic debridement that removed the loose piece. Following approximately two weeks of ankle rehabilitation, he returned to the court and helped us earn a bid to the NCAA Tournament.

Jaime Jaax (women's swimming and diving, 1997–01). This young lady was a superb diver who underwent multiple procedures for both shoulders due to multidirectional instability. Her recovery and dedication to diving was excellent. She ended up having success in the Big Ten and national standings, including becoming a Big Ten champion and a first-team All-American in 1999.

Zack Mills (football, 2002). During his sophomore season Mills was the starting quarterback while we were playing at Wisconsin. He sustained a second-degree AC separation in his throwing shoulder. Without any significant medication or alteration in his equipment, he tolerated the discomfort and led us to a 34–31 road win against the Badgers.

Alyssa Naeher (women's soccer, 2009). Alyssa was a tremendous soccer goalie who sustained a PCL tear approximately six to eight weeks prior to the start of her senior season. She rehabilitated, competed well with the brace on, and helped us win the Big Ten title again. She had a 0.84 goals-against average and was the Big Ten's Defensive Player of the Year.

Aleksander Ochocki (fencing, 2009). Aleksander sustained a stress fracture of his right fifth metatarsal (the long bone on the outside of the foot that connects to the little toe), which normally can be a season-ending injury or a minimum of six to eight weeks of recovery. He sustained the injury three weeks prior to the NCAA Championships. After his injury was surgically repaired with an intramedullary screw, he won an individual national championship and helped us win the national title.

Marco Rivera (football, 1993). The offensive guard sustained multiple dislocations of his right shoulder, requiring surgical stabilization following his sophomore year. He underwent surgical stabilization using a Bankart/capsular shift procedure. He started the next two seasons, including for the 1994 Big Ten title team. He also had a successful NFL career, which included a Super Bowl win with the Packers in 1997. He never had any issues with his shoulder again.

Michael Robinson (football, 2005). After leading us to a Big Ten title, Michael, unbeknownst to many, sustained a significant grade-2 AC separation of his right (throwing) shoulder early in the second half against Florida State in the Orange Bowl. Michael's will to win and mental toughness allowed him to continue to compete through the rest of the three-overtime game and lead us to a win over the Seminoles.

Brad Sciolli (football, 1996). Brad sustained an ACL tear to his right knee during a spring practice. He required surgical reconstruction and missed the entire 1996 season. His recovery was excellent. Within nine months he was playing again. After playing tight end in 1997, he went on to become first-team All-Big Ten as a defensive end in 1998.

Janae Whittaker (women's gymnastics, 1998). During her junior season Janae sustained an injury that resulted in an ACL, MCL, and patellar dislocation, with patellar tendon rupture. She underwent multiple procedures in order to reconstruct and repair her knee, including primary MCL and patellar tendon repair followed by the ACL reconstruction. Her recovery was excellent, and she was able to compete her senior year without any issues. The team now gives out the Lynn Crane and Janae Whittaker Attitude Award to the individual who displays a consistently upbeat attitude both in and out of the gym.

Jason Yeisley (men's soccer, 2006–07). Jason sustained a fifth metatarsal stress fracture during his sophomore season in 2006 that caused him to miss all but seven games. The next year, he sustained a severe injury to his right knee, including to his ACL. He took a medical redshirt in 2008. During his recovery he suffered a stress fracture in his left foot that required intramedullary screw fixation. Following those three surgeries, he returned in 2009 to score eight goals and had five assists. He became the Big Ten Offensive Player of the Year and was a nominee for national player of the year honors.

GREATEST FRESHMAN SEASONS

Dick Vitale calls them Diaper Dandies. They're those special college athletes who come right in and have an immediate impact during their freshman seasons. Here are our top ten greatest freshman seasons by a Penn Stater.

10. Jamelle Cornley 2005–06 men's basketball. Cornley was the first player in program history to win Big Ten Freshman of the Year. He averaged 11.4 points and 5.7 rebounds per game, and he helped lead a late-season run that landed the Nittany Lions in the NIT.

9. Curtis Enis 1995 football. The Big Ten Freshman of the Year in 1995, Enis rushed for 683 yards on only 113 attempts (6.04 yards per carry) in leading Penn State to a 9–3 record.

8. Maggie Lucas 2010–11 women's basketball. Lucas's long-range shooting helped the Lady Lions reach the NCAA Tournament for the first time since 2005. Lucas drilled 112 3-pointers, breaking Kelly Mazzante's previous team record of 102. She led the Lady Lions in scoring, averaging 15.8 points per game, and was named the Big Ten's Freshman of the Year and Sixth Player of the Year.

7. Suzie McConnell 1984–85 women's basketball. McConnell was named Atlantic 10 Freshman of the Year in a season when she averaged 12.6 points and 9.7 assists per game. Her assist production was third in the nation at the end of the regular season, and her performance in the Lady Lions' run to the conference title earned her MVP honors of the A-10 Tournament.

6. Megan Hodge 2006 women's volleyball. Hodge's award haul would have been worthy of a career for most. She was a first-team All-American, National Freshman of the Year, Big Ten Player of the Year, and, obviously, Big Ten Freshman of the Year. Her 551 kills were the sixth-highest single-season total in program history.

5. Cary Kolat 1992–93 wrestling. After winning four PIAA state championships, Kolat continued that success at Penn State. In his first season with the Lions he posted a 22–5 record, winning Big Ten Freshman of the Year, and advanced to the NCAA Championship round at the 134-pound class before losing 6–4 to North Carolina's T. J. Jaworsky.

4. Kelly Mazzante 2000–01 women's basketball. Mazzante was not only the top freshman but also one of the top players in the nation during the 2000–01 season. She won a share of the National Freshman of the Year honor (sharing the award with Duke's Alana Beard). She led the Big Ten in scoring with an 18.8 points-per-game average. She also was named third-team All-American.

3. Jesse Arnelle 1951–52 men's basketball. Arnelle began his dominant career by averaging 18.9 points per game and grabbing 254 rebounds as he led the Nittany Lions to their second overall NCAA Tournament appearance and their first in 10 years.

2. Christie Welsh 1999 women's soccer. Welsh scored what was then a team-record 27 goals in help leading Penn State to the Final Four. That season she won the following awards: Big Ten Freshman of the Year, first-team All-Big Ten, Big Ten Player of the Year, National Freshman of the Year, and first-team All-American.

1. D.J. Dozier 1983 football. Immediately putting his name among Penn State's great running backs, Dozier became the first—and still *only*—freshman in the history of the program to rush for more than 1,000 yards (1,002 yards; 5.8 yards per carry). He also led the team with seven touchdowns. He caught 19 passes for 189 yards and had one receiving touchdown in what was his first of four consecutive seasons of leading Penn State in rushing.

TOP REC HALL MOMENTS

Built in 1928, Penn State's Recreation Building, or commonly known as Rec Hall, started a run as being the focal point of activity on the Penn State campus. Several of Penn State's indoor athletic programs either currently call or have called Rec Hall home. The building has hosted 21 collegiate championship events, along with concerts, the school's largest student fundraiser—THON—and major speeches. Once, nearly every sport participated either in the building or in the vicinity, including football at Beaver Field. Today five Penn State teams still compete at Rec Hall. Outside, one of the most photographed sites in Pennsylvania, the Nittany Lion shrine, stands guard. Here are Rec Hall's most memorable moments.

10. Penn State basketball defeats Virginia—December 5, 1973. The game was played in front of what will forever be the largest Rec Hall crowd to watch a basketball game. On the day it was announced that John Cappelletti won football's Heisman Trophy, 8,600 fans packed Rec Hall to watch the Nittany Lions' basketball team host Virginia. "Cappy" was in attendance and was given a standing ovation. He might have been fortunate to be inside the building, as many fans were turned away. The number of fans admitted inside violated several fire codes, and they exceeded the legal fire limit by 1,400. However, on the court, Penn State's Ron Brown was the one who was on fire, scoring 36 points with 24 coming in the second half in a 96–68 rout over the Cavaliers. In commenting on the night, Brown said, "The crowd was beautiful."

9. Another victory and another Lady Lions' volleyball trip to the Final Four—December 13, 2008. The dynasty that is the Penn State women's volleyball program added to its legend on this late Saturday afternoon in the championship game of the NCAA regionals. A crowd of 4,036 rowdy members of the Nittany Nation witnessed No. 1 Penn State sweeping No. 8 California, 3–0, to advance to its (at the time) seventh Final Four. Megan Hodge had a match-high 13 kills on her way to winning Most Outstanding Player of the region. The contest was tense early in the first set when Cal achieved its largest lead of the day, 7–1. Penn State would rally to win the set 25–21 and then took the next two by scores of 25–21 and 25–17.

8. Reid's Rec Hall ride—March 1, 1967. The two best teams in eastern wrestling met on this Wednesday night. A record crowd of 7,900 packed Rec Hall for the Nittany Lions' match with Lehigh. With Penn State leading 15–12, the win came down to the final bout between heavyweight Mike Reid (yes, the same Mike Reid who would win All-American football honors) and the Engineers' Butch Paquin. Paquin's stalling tactics did not succeed against the eventual EWL champion, as Reid won, 5–3. The crowd erupted with the chant "We're number one! We're number one!" as many of them stormed the floor and carried Reid off on their shoulders. "Every one of our boys went out there and fought with everything he had," Penn State coach Bill Koll said. "A coach can't ask for anything more. We outfought, outconditioned, and outhustled Lehigh. That's truly an accomplishment."

7. Atlantic 10 champions Again—March 10, 1990. The Lady Lions' basketball team was technically the visitor at Rec Hall as it played St. Joseph's in the A-10 Tournament championship game. Rec Hall was the host site for the tourney, but because PSU was the third seed, it wore the traveling blue uniforms and sat on the visitors' bench. The Lady Lions did, however, have the home crowd help them against the top-seeded Hawks. The first half was tightly contested, with State leading 31–29 at the break. Seven minutes into the second half, the mostly Lady Lion–partisan crowd was whooping it, those on the Penn State bench were exchanging high fives, and the game was essentially over when PSU sprinted out to a 53–38 lead. State would take the conference's automatic bid to the NCAA Tournament with a 84–60 victory, winning their first Atlantic 10 Tournament since 1986. Center Kathy Phillips's 15-point effort propelled her to the tournament MVP award as the Lady Lions were victorious in all 15 games played on the Rec Hall hardwood that season.

6. A super concert—November 5, 1966. With all the sporting events Rec Hall has hosted, it is easy to forget that for a period in time it was the primary concert and show venue for the Centre Region. Rec was able to book the best. On a dismal November day on campus—in the afternoon, the Nittany Lion football team lost, 12–10, to rival Syracuse—the Nittany Nation was in need of something positive. So attention turned to the much-hyped two-show concert at Rec Hall that night featuring the top female singing group the Supremes, fronted by the dynamic Diana Ross. "We had roughly 14,000 tickets to sell for two shows," Interfraternity Council (IFC) Social cochairman Skip Lange said. "We pre-sold 10,000 to the men in fraternities . . . the other 4,000 tickets sold out in 45 minutes." The Supremes had the No. 1 hit single "You Can't Hurry Love" that year. Ross, Mary Wilson, and Florence Ballard, all decked in white-sequined gowns, had the place jumping as they performed their hit songs. The success of the Supremes concert allowed the IFC to then book Bill Cosby and the Temptations for Rec Hall shows in 1967.

5. The beast of the East tops the best in the nation—December 3, 1986. Iowa is to wrestling as the New York Yankees are to baseball: It is the gold standard of the sport. Perhaps the greatest wrestler of all time, Dan Gable, coached the Hawkeyes, and the afternoon before the meet, his Penn State counterpart, Rich Lorenzo, liked the Lions' chances. "We have more confidence than we've ever had. In the past we've talked about beating Iowa; now the guys really do believe we can beat Iowa," Lorenzo said. That was the hope of the large crowd that flowed into Rec that night. The *Daily Collegian* estimated the crowd to be more than 7,500, and *Sports Illustrated* figured it was even higher, reporting more than 8,000 were in attendance, with several hundred more being turned away. The match that sent the crowd into a frenzy was at the 158-weight class. Iowa's John Heffernan was favored against State's Duane Peoples. Peoples was leading late in the third and final period when Heffernan escaped to tie the match, 4–4. Later, Peoples held on to Heffernan's leg and, with time running out, kept driving until he got a takedown to pull off the upset. Penn State went on to topple the top-ranked Hawkeyes, 27–15, on an evening that is regarded as one the greatest moments in the history of the program.

4. It took 26 years, but the Lions go dancing again—March 7, 1991. For those who follow the fortunes and, yes, the misfortunes of the Penn State men's basketball program, you know that going to the NCAA Tournament is a rarity. Entering the 2011–12 season, the Nittany Lions have made only nine appearances in the NCAA Tournament. Three of those nine occurred between 1952 and 1955, and following a first-round exit in 1965, the Nittany Lions did not go back for the next 25 years. They were probably not going back in 1991 either. Penn State finished the regular season 17–10, and being the third-place team in the Atlantic 10 most likely meant another trip to the NIT would be forthcoming. Then, a great run of basketball followed, with wins in the Atlantic 10 Tournament over sixth-seed Duquesne and second-seed Temple. Those games were played at the Palestra in Philadelphia. Because of the way the A-10 tournament was formatted at the time, the highest remaining seed hosted the championship game at its arena. With fourth-seed George Washington the other survivor of the week in Philly, it meant Rec Hall would be the site where the championship would be decided with the NCAA automatic bid on the line. A crowd of 7,103 packed Rec Hall, with many students interrupting their spring break to return to campus to watch history. The Nittany Lions raced out to an 18–6 lead before the game was five-minutes old. The lead would swell to 31–12. GW would make things close in the second half, but at the end the Lions prevailed, 81–75. The fans stormed court. Lion forward DeRon Hayes perched himself atop the basket opposite the student section celebrating the team's accomplishment. James Barnes led Penn State with 20 points and Freddie Barnes's 18 helped him take tournament MVP honors.

3. Men's gymnastics team wins national championship—April 14, 2007. Host sites for championship events are determined months and sometimes years in advance. Rare is the instance when a championship site also is the regular home venue for one of the participants. But that was the case at the 2007 NCAA Men's Gymnastics National Championship at Penn State. This was the third time Rec Hall hosted the event, and the Nittany Lions began the championship as the third seed. PSU had to rally in its final competition, as it began the rings event in fourth place. Tommy Ramos's score of 9.725 led the Lions to a season-high 38.450 for the rings. That was just enough to give Penn State the victory by 0.200 points over second-place Oklahoma.

2. National champs of the mat—March 28, 1953. It was Penn State's first NCAA wrestling championship, and until the 2010–11 season, it had been the last wrestling national title an eastern school had won. The two-day NCAA Championship Tournament held at Rec Hall drew approximately 15,000 fans, a record at that time. Penn State's 21 points were six better than defending champion Oklahoma. The Nittany Lions' lone individual champion was Hud Samson. Samson usually wrestled at the heavyweight division but dropped down to the 191-weight class for the NCAAs. In the finals he earned his second pin of the tournament by getting the fall against West Chester State Teacher's College's Charles Weber. Overall, Samson was responsible for eight of the Lions' 21 team points.

1. Martin Luther King—January, 21, 1965. At the height of the civil rights movement, Dr. Martin Luther King Jr. addressed a Rec Hall crowd estimated to be at 9,000. His major topics of the night focused on voter registration, housing, and job discrimination. In a press conference prior to the speech, he praised the work of college students across the country, saying, "The student generation may well play the most significant role in bringing about a sociological change." He concluded the evening with the same closing he used in his "I Have a Dream" speech at the Lincoln Memorial—"With this faith, we will be able to speed up the day when all of God's children all over this nation, black men and white men, Jews and Gentiles, Protestants and Catholics, will be able to join hands and sing in the world of the old Negro spiritual, 'Free at last, free at last, thank God almighty, we are free at last.'"

WHAT MADE REC HALL SPECIAL :: BY DAN EARL

Before Penn State's basketball teams moved to the spacious Bryce Jordan Center in 1996, they played in the cozy confines of Rec Hall. Former Lion point guard Dan Earl was one of those players who had the opportunity to play in both venues, and though the BJC is state of the art, Earl still has some fond things to say about the venerable gym on the west side of campus.

5. Old. This sounds weird, but now everything is new. Locker room. Gear—it wasn't Nike; it was old grays and blues. It was in good condition but still had that "old" feel.

4. Location. It was easily accessible—close to the heart of campus.

3. Décor, smell, "feel." It was just like Palestra. I am from outside Philly, so I played in Palestra a lot, and the same builder constructed Rec Hall. People felt like they were "going to a game!"

2. Extremely loud. Rec Hall had great acoustics. I remember not even being able to communicate play calls and so forth. It was the loudest gym I have ever played in. I especially remember wins over Purdue [in 1994 when Boilermakers were ranked No. 7] and Miami [in the NIT]. Those were big wins. It was extremely hot as well.

1. Fans right on top of you/on the court. They were packed in like sardines. There was bleacher seating, no room between sideline out of bounds and fans, a short distance between bench and fans and scorer's table, and so forth. It was truly a great place to play—and opponents *hated* it!

ATLANTIC 10 MEMORIES

Penn State has not played an Atlantic 10 conference basketball game since 1991. However, that was the conference affiliation of the Nittany Lions when Matt attended "Dear Old State." (The Lions played their final A-10 season when David was a freshman.) Though short on national exposure, the A-10 experience did provide some entertainment on those cold central PA winter nights. Also, Penn State had some good teams. Yes, for those too young to remember, PSU had a quality hoops program during this period. The Lions were consistently in the upper echelon of the conference, culminating in 1991 with their winning the Atlantic 10 tournament championship. In its final Atlantic 10 game Penn State defeated George Washington, 81–75, to receive an automatic bid to the NCAA Tournament. For this list of Atlantic 10 memories, I want to focus on some other moments that I experienced either as a member of the media or from the stands.

6. Tom Penders's tan. The 1988 Rhode Island Rams had one of those special seasons—feel-good stories for individual members of the team, a trip to the Sweet 16, and nearly a trip to the Elite 8 as they lost, 73–72, to Duke in the NCAA Tournament. For their February 25 visit to Rec Hall, the lasting image was head coach Tom Penders's rather unusual tan. Considering it was in the middle of winter and Rhode Island is not exactly Key West, the bronzed Penders seemed a bit out of place. Sitting courtside amongst my fellow student fans, the RIU coach certainly heard the chants about his tan. Immature for sure, but it was all in fun. Penders had the last laugh, however, as the Rams won, 77–69.

5. ESPN short circuits the Atlantic 10 Tournament. Rec Hall hosted the 1990 Atlantic 10 women's basketball tournament, and the Atherton Hotel played host to the tournament's hospitality suite. Now as a young member of the media, who was I to pass up all the perks that accompany a hospitality suite? With the women's tournament nearing a full slate of action in the upcoming days, on the night of March 8 the championship game of the men's tournament was being played at Temple's McGonigle Hall, with the Owls hosting Massachusetts. Several media members and conference officials were watching the ESPN broadcast during the hospitality party when, midway through the second half, the cable network cut away from that game to join an opening-round contest from one of the "larger" conferences. It wasn't as if the A-10's game was a rout; quite the contrary: It was tightly contested with Temple eventually winning, 53–51. ESPN eventually rejoined the game with just a few minutes remaining. The faces of the Atlantic 10 officials showed that they were not pleased about their treatment from the "Worldwide Leader in Sports."

4. Beating Temple. Temple has been the top dog of the Atlantic 10 since the conference's inception. Though often outmanned, during the 1980s Penn State would, with regularity, give the Owls all they could handle. There was a 73–70 overtime loss at Rec Hall in 1987. The following season, with the Owls ranked No. 1 in the nation, Penn State lost a 50–49 nail-biter at McGonigle. In December 1988, at the same venue, the Nittany Lions lost, 50–48. Penn State was close but could not finish against the juggernaut Owls. Finally, on December 9, 1989, the Lions got the best of John Chaney's team. It was a Saturday night and the lines outside of Rec Hall swelled with fans wanting to get inside the old building, anticipating that this would be the time. Penn State won the game, 61–59, to start the season 4–0. When the final buzzer sounded, fans swarmed the court to celebrate the win. A guy boosted by one of his friends began cutting pieces of the net and tossing them down to the crowd. It was as if PSU had won the NCAA Tournament. More than 20 years later, I still have a piece of the net that was cut down that night.

3. John Calipari is put in his place. The 1990 Massachusetts Minutemen were the surprise of the Atlantic 10. The previous season UMass finished with a 10–18 record. When the John Calipari–coached team beat Penn State in Amherst, 64–52, on January 6, that game was the second of what would be a six-game win streak. That loss was a bit of a shock to Penn State, and the Nittany Lions were looking for payback when the Minutemen visited Rec Hall 12 days later with that win streak on the line. Penn State won, 64–52, but for me the most memorable part of the evening occurred during the postgame press conference. Calipari started going into a rant about the officiating. (Coaches tend to shy away from criticizing the referees for fear of a fine from the conference and/or subtle retribution from the officials in the next game.) As Calipari continued to voice his displeasure about that night's referees, the Massachusetts sports information director, either looking to protect his coach or embarrassed by the remarks, shouted from the back of the room, "That's enough!" Calipari meekly went on to the next question.

2. Spring break at the Palestra. When some students opt for the warmth of Florida on spring break, I would head to Philadelphia and the Palestra. That was the regular site for the first three rounds of the Atlantic 10 Tournament. It's a perfect setting if you are basketball fan: the University of Pennsylvania campus, one of the greatest college basketball arenas in the country, and, nearby, plenty of options to get a cheesesteak. Plus, with Temple and St. Joseph's part of the conference, you could enjoy a good flavor of Big Five basketball.

1. The Chaney and Macon Show. Temple may have been the Nittany Lions' nemesis, but there also was a great deal of mutual respect. During my time as a student I had a chance to see one of college basketball's legendary coaches on a regular basis, and those years coincided with the career of one of the greatest Owls, Mark Macon. My favorite moment occurred after Macon's last game at Rec Hall, on February 13, 1991. It was a 69–59 Owl victory. Chaney and Macon were center stage in the media room. The two cracked jokes and needled each other like a well-rehearsed comedy team. Chaney has had both his good and bad moments with the media, so watching this good moment was enjoyable.

TOP TEN PENN STATE WRESTLERS
:: BY JEFF BYERS

Here are the top wrestlers in PSU history, according Jeff Byers, longtime play-by-play voice of Penn State wrestling.

10. John Hughes (1992–96). National champion in 1995 and three-time All-American.

9. Sanshiro Abe (1993–96). National champion in 1996, four-time All-American, and Olympian.

8. Jeremy Hunter (1997–2000). National champion in 2000 and three-time All-American.

7. Greg Elinsky (1984–87). Penn State's first four-time All-American, also a two-time national runner-up.

6. Phil Davis (2005–08). National champion in 2008 and four-time All-American.

5. John Fritz (1972–75). National champion in 1975 and three-time All-American.

4. Jeff Prescott (1989–92). Two-time national champion in 1991 and 1992 and three-time All-American.

3. Jim Martin (1986–89). Penn State's career-leader in victories with 155, national champion in 1988, and four-time All-American.

2. Kerry McCoy (1993–95, 97). A two-time national champion in 1994 and 1997 and a two-time Olympian.

1. Andy Matter (1970–72). Penn State's first two-time national champion (in 1971 and 1972), and best career win percentage in team history with 96.7 percent (59–2).

TOP PENN STATE WRESTLING MOMENTS
:: BY JEFF BYERS

Next to football, wrestling likely has the most revered history than any other sport at Penn State. It's filled with memorable moments and people. In 1999 Jeff Byers, the longtime voice of Penn State wrestling, became the first broadcaster to win *Wrestling Insider Newsmagazine*'s Journalist of the Year Award. He also was the National Wrestling Media Association's Broadcaster of the Year in 2006. Byers gives his top ten moments in Nittany Lion history.

10. Lynch's run. Scott Lynch wins the national title with a heavily taped knee. Lynch gave the Nittany Lions a huge boost by competing in the 1984 NCAA Tournament. The hope was that, despite his significant knee injury, he could produce a couple of wins. Lynch turned in a heroic performance and captured the national title.

9. Taking down the Hawkeyes. On December 3, 1986, arguably the largest crowd ever at Rec Hall witnessed the Nittany Lions defeat top-ranked Iowa, 27–15. Every seat was filled, the track was packed, and there were fans sitting up to the mat on either side. Although basketball crowds have been listed as larger, this writer contends that more fans could not possibly fit into Rec Hall than the amount that was there that day.

8. Historic third. In 1998 John Lange made history at the NCAA Tournament. Lange had his sights set on winning a national title, but they were quickly dashed with a 15–5 loss to David Wells of Cal-Poly. Lange turned around and won seven consecutive matches, including a pin over Wells, to become the first wrestler ever to lose his opening match and then win seven straight to place third.

7. Taking down the Hawkeyes—on the road. Penn State was the first opponent to win at Iowa's Carver-Hawkeye Arena. Since the arena had opened in 1982, no opponent had walked out with a victory over the Hawkeyes. On February 6, 1988, Penn State edged Iowa, 19–18, to become the first team other than Iowa to win in that facility.

6. Heart of the Matter. Andy Matter becomes Penn State's first two-time national champion. Matter capped a brilliant career by setting a new precedent—winning a second national title for the Nittany Lions in 1972. He went undefeated in his dual-meet career and also was a three-time EIWA champion.

5. Penn State wins its first-ever Big Ten championship in dramatic fashion. The Nittany Lions crown five individual champions and use a major decision by heavyweight Cameron Wade in the fifth-place bout to edge Iowa by a single point in the 2011 Big Ten Championships. In a conference that has been dominated by Iowa and Minnesota, the title marks a major breakthrough for the program.

4. A hiring for the ages. Penn State hires Cael Sanderson. Just the announcement of the hiring brought newfound prominence to the Nittany Lions' program, changed the scope of support, and sent expectations skyrocketing. It is safe to say it was the most celebrated hiring in the history on Penn State athletics.

3. Martin's run. In 1998 Jim Martin won a national title after battling through broken ribs. With pressure against his cracked ribs, Martin claimed the championship over Iowa's Brad Penrith.

2. Penn State captures its first NCAA Championship in 1953 at Rec Hall. The title is the signature moment of the university's first century of wrestling, as the Nittany Lions become the first school east of the Mississippi to win the championship. Hud Samson wins an individual title with a pin in the finals to give the home crowd its signature moment of the program's finest hour.

1. Penn State wins second NCAA title. With five All-Americans (all top-three finishers), the Lions set a school record with 107.5 points to outdistance Cornell by 14 points for the 2011 championship. Quentin Wright captures the national title at 184 pounds to cap the championship run. The title is won in Philadelphia in front of a record crowd for the NCAA Tournament.

GREATEST ALL-TIME PENN STATE BASKETBALL PLAYERS

For those of us who follow Penn State basketball, there are constant reminders that the program is a second-class citizen to top-dog football. But this does not mean PSU has been deprived of talent. There have been great players throughout the years who have provided thrills and excitement in Rec Hall and the Bryce Jordan Center, including those who are the best of the Penn State best.

10. Mark Dumars (1958–61). Probably the greatest Nittany Lion to never appear in a postseason game, Dumars was twice named honorable mention All-American by the UPI (1959 and 1960). During the 1960 season he poured in 31 points in a game against West Virginia and later scored 36 against Syracuse.

9. Frank Brickowski (1978–81). Penn State's greatest NBA player has to appear on a list of great Nittany Lion hoopsters. In his final two seasons he led the Nittany Lions in scoring with 11.4 points per game in 1979–80 and 13 points per game in 1980–81. He also led the team in 1980 with 7.8 rebounds per game. In the only postseason game of his career, he scored 16 points in a 53–49 loss at Alabama in the NIT. As a 12-year NBA player, he averaged ten points, highlighted by his 1993 season with the Milwaukee Bucks, when he averaged 16.9 points.

8. Dan Earl (1993–99). Earl continued a strong chain of Nittany Lion guards in the late 1980s through the early part of the new millennium. In 1996 he was named second-team All-Big Ten as the Lions spent most of the season ranked in the AP top ten, had a second-place finish in the Big Ten standings, and the fifth seed in the East Region of the NCAA Tournament. When he finished his Penn State playing career, his 574 assists were second all-time. In addition, he scored 1,256 career points.

7. John Amaechi (1992–95). From Great Britain to Vanderbilt to Penn State, Amaechi was certainly well traveled by the time he started playing for the Nittany Lions. Big John's first season also was the program's first year in the Big Ten. In his three seasons at Penn State, he scored 1,310 points (15.6 ppg average) and grabbed 745 rebounds (8.8 rpg average). He was the man in the middle as Penn State improved its conference win total from two wins in 1993 to a .500 record (9–9) by his senior year of 1995. That season Amaechi led Penn State to the NIT Final Four and became the first Penn Stater to be named first-team All-Big Ten.

6. Freddie Barnes (1988–1992). Rare is the Penn State basketball player who gets to experience playing in the NCAA Tournament. After all, heading into the 2011–12 season the Nittany Lions had been on that big stage only nine times. Even rarer is the player who plays in four consecutive postseason tournaments. Freddie Barnes is in that elite PSU company. As a freshman, he cracked the starting lineup during the 1989 season, and a fun run was under way. He helped lead Penn State to the brink of an NCAA tourney bid that season, as the Lions were four points short against Rutgers in the Atlantic 10 championship game. They nearly made it to the Big Dance the following season when they won 20 regular-season games. Barnes finally earned a trip to the NCAA Tournament in 1991, and Penn State upset UCLA in the opening round. After he played his final game against Pitt in the 1992 NIT, he was the school's all-time assists leader (600) and was third on the all-time scoring list (1,342).

5. Jamelle Cornley (2005–09). With a large wrap supporting his injured right shoulder in the opening round of the 2009 NIT, Cornley played through that pain, determined to end his career a winner. The heart and soul of the Lions, he scored 23 points in a 71–62 win at Florida that sent the Nits to Madison Square Garden. In the NIT championship win over Baylor, he had 18 points in taking MVP honors for the tournament. He had to deal with injuries more than once while playing for Penn State on his way to scoring 1,579 points and grabbing 755 rebounds.

4. Pete Lisicky (1994–98). Opposing defenses were forced to respect the outside shooting threat of Lisicky. In the NCAA Tournament season of 1995–96, he drilled 89 3-pointers, shooting 47.1 percent from beyond the arc. The next season, he averaged 16.3 points and was named second-team All-Big Ten. His Penn State career concluded with him holding the No. 2 spot on the all-time scoring list, and at the start of the 2010–11 season he was the school's leader in career 3-pointers (332) and most 3-pointers in a game (9).

3. Joe Crispin (1997–01). It is probably safe to say that Joe Crispin never met a spot on the floor for a shot that he did not like. If he was open, there was a decent chance he was jacking up a shot—and enough of these shots went in to make Crispin the second-leading scorer in school history with 1,986 points and a career 15.6 ppg average. He ran the point on two NIT Final Four teams and the 2001 NCAA Sweet 16 squad. There are many great Crispin moments to choose from, but two of the best came during the 2001 season: scoring 31 points in an upset win at Kentucky and his 3-pointer in the closing seconds of the Big Ten Tournament quarterfinal that helped give Penn State a 65–63 win over second-ranked Michigan State.

2. Talor Battle (2007–11). As of this writing, Battle is the all-time leading scorer in Penn State history (2,213 points) and the only player in Big Ten history to have 2,000 points, 500 rebounds, and 500 assists. He is just one of three players in NCAA Division I history to post at least 2,000 points, 600 rebounds, and 500 assists. The legend of Talor Battle was cemented during the 2009 NIT championship season. He became only the fifth Penn Stater to be named first-team All-Big Ten. His 635 points are the fifth-highest single-season total in school history, and he set the school record for assists in a season with 189. In 2011 he led the Nittany Lions back to the NCAA Tournament after a 10-year drought. He scored 25 points in the Big Ten Tournament semifinal game against Michigan State that essentially put Penn State into the Big Dance, and he scored 23 points against Temple in his only NCAA Tournament game—which ended up being a heartbreaking 66–64 loss to the Owls.

1. Jesse Arnelle (1951–55). He is now the program's *second* all-time leading scorer (2,138), and is still the all-time leading rebounder (1,238). Arnelle accomplished all he did while playing in the greatest era of Penn State basketball, as the Lions went to three NCAA Tournaments (1952, 1954, 1955) and advanced to the 1954 Final Four. He also owns five of the top-six single-game efforts, topped by pouring in 44 points in a 1955 win over Bucknell. Not counting consolation games, Arnelle averaged 18.5 points in those NCAA Tournament appearances. On top of that, he is the only Nittany Lion to ever earn first-team All-American honors.

Honorable Mentions: Calvin Booth (1996–99); Carver Clinton (1964–66); DeRon Hayes (1989–93).

FAVORITE LADY LIONS :: BY LISA SALTERS

Lisa Salters's basketball career ended as a Lady Lion, and her broadcast career began with the Lady Lions. Salters played on the 1985–86 and 1986–87 Penn State teams that went a combined 47–15 and won an Atlantic 10 Tournament championship. She decided to hang up her sneakers prior to her senior season and put on the headphones as the color commentary for the Lady Lions' radio broadcast. Here are Salters's favorite Lady Lions—in alphabetical order—of all time.

Bethany Collins (1985–88). She scored 1,186 points and grabbed 757 rebounds in her career. She is now the head coach of the girls' basketball team at State College Area High School.

Helen Darling (1997–2000). She is the only Lady Lion to score 1,000 points, grab 600 rebounds, and have 700 assists. Darling led the NCAA in assists in 1999–00 with a 7.83 average. She was first-team All-American and Big Ten Player of the Year in 2000, as she led the Lady Lions to their first trip to the Final Four.

Lisa Faloon (1984–97). She scored 1,162 career points. In the first season of the 3-point line in 1986–87, she made 54.8 percent of her attempts, which is still the team career record.

Kahadeejah Herbert (1982–85). She is the leading rebounder in team history with 1,103 and is one of only two Lady Lions with 2,000 career points and 1,000 rebounds.

Vickie Link (1984–87). She scored 1,514 points and grabbed 943 rebounds in her career. Her 306 rebounds in a season (1985–86) is the second all-time in Lady Lion history.

Kelly Mazzante (2001–04). She is the all-time scoring leader in Big Ten history (male or female), with 2,919 points. She also was a two-time first-team All-American and Big Ten Player of the Year.

Suzie McConnell (1985–88). She finished her career as the NCAA's all-time assists leader (1,307) and also scored 1,897 points, which is the sixth all-time for the Lady Lions.

Joanie O'Brien (1983–86). The team's most outstanding player award is named the Joanie O'Brien Award. O'Brien was known more for her leadership than any numbers she put up. She helped the Lady Lions to three seasons of 20 or more wins during her four-year career. She ranks in the top 20 on the team's career assists list.

Vanessa Paynter (1984–87). She had one of the best freshman seasons when she scored 324 points in 1983–84. She also ranks in the top 20 of the team's career steals record, with 182.

Susan Robinson (1989–92). She is the second all-time leading scorer in team history with 2,253 points and was the national player of the year in 1992. Robinson joins Herbert as the only two Lady Lions with 2,000 points and 1,000 rebounds.

PSU MEMORIES :: BY LISA SALTERS

As a broadcast journalist, Lisa Salters has covered some of the biggest stories over the past 20 years and has been nominated for a Sports Emmy Award for her work on ESPN's *E:60*. As a Penn State student in the mid-1980s, she definitely made the most of her college experience, what with classes, playing some basketball, and starting her career. Here are some of her top PSU memories.

10. The Dance Marathon.

9. Cheesesteaks from CC Pepper's.

8. Grilled Stickies from The Diner.

7. Grapenut ice cream from Meyer Dairy.

6. Trying out for the women's basketball team—and making it.

5. Beating Rutgers in 1987 when the Scarlet Knights were ranked No. 2 in the nation.

4. Rene Portland making us run. Some members of the team got in some trouble, so the coaches woke us up at 5 a.m. to run at the track. Then there was one practice when Rene was so upset she said, "It looks like you guys don't want to learn the plays, so just run until I get back." We ran for about an hour.

3. That's gotta hurt. We used to practice with some guys, and this one guy tried to intercept a pass I threw, and he broke his nose when he didn't catch it.

2. Laying out in the sun on Old Main Lawn during the spring thaw.

1. The 1986 national championship football team.

TOP MOVIES THAT REFERENCE PENN STATE

Both literally and figuratively, Penn State, the former farm school, is probably as far from Hollywood as any place. But that doesn't mean Tinseltown has completely ignored our humble Happy Valley. Here are five movies that put Penn State—even if it was for a brief moment—on the big or small screen.

5. *The Paper.* Toward the end of this 1994 comedy about a day in the life of reporters and editors at a New York City daily newspaper, editor Henry Hackett (played by Michael Keaton) tells a police detective that one of the kids the police mistakenly arrested for murder was a tailback set to go to Penn State. We wonder how Keaton felt saying that, as he grew up near Pittsburgh.

4. *Jerry Maguire.* Two for the price of one here as two stars from the 1994 football team—Ki-Jana Carter and Kerry Collins—had cameos in the 1996 Tom Cruise movie about a sports agent with a heart.

3. *Groundhog Day.* With a movie that takes place in Punxsutawney, there just had to be some reference to Penn State. At the restaurant Bill Murray's character always goes to, he tries to convince Andie MacDowell's character that he is, in fact, reliving the same day over and over again. He tells her all he knows about the people there, including Bill, a waiter for three years since he left Penn State and had to get work—"He likes the town, paints toy soldiers, and he's gay."

2. *Rudy.* In a movie that is the quintessential film for Notre Dame fans, there is some sense of pleasure that comes with hearing the Blue Band playing "The Nittany Lion" when Rudy's father enters Notre Dame Stadium to see his son and the Irish play—wait for it—Georgia Tech. The Blue Band's appearance happened because some of the movie was filmed during Penn State's 1992 visit to South Bend.

1. *Something for Joey.* What else could top this list but the one movie that is all about Penn State? The 1977 made-for-TV film was about Nittany Lion Heisman-winner John Cappelletti and the relationship he had with his younger brother, Joey, who had leukemia. Marc Singer played Cappelletti and Paul Picerni played Joe Paterno. The film was nominated for two Emmy awards and a Golden Globe.

WHICH FILM/TV FICTIONAL COACH WOULD BE A GREAT REPLACEMENT FOR JOEPA?

Let's face it, Joe Paterno will probably not coach Penn State forever—or maybe he will. Sometime within the next "four or five years" he may decide to retire. There have been a number of names bantered about over the past 20 years for Paterno's replacement. The names include assistants on the Nittany Lion staff, former assistants who are now head coaches elsewhere, and head coaches with Pennsylvania ties. What has been missing from the discussion are the fictional coaches—probably because they aren't real. But still, these coaches give the most inspiring pregame speeches that dwarf anything Knute Rockne spouted. They have the perfect play that enables their teams to pull out a last-second victory. If TV and movie coaches could be in the running for the Penn State job, here are our top candidates.

5. Hayden Fox—*Coach*. He won the national championship at Minnesota State and then followed it up with back-to-back Super Bowl championships with the Orlando Breakers. Fox also would appeal to the rural section of Nittany Nation, with his penchant for spending time outdoors, mostly reflecting on top of a fire tower in the woods. He is often confused with Cal Poly's and former Ampipe High School head coach Nickerson, who wasn't nice to some player who looked like Tom Cruise, but he made amends later.

4. Ed Gennero—*Necessary Roughness*. If Penn State is looking for somebody to maintain the football team's reputation of "Success with Honor," they might want to look to Ed "Straight Arrow" Gennero. He was a successful college coach who came out of retirement to attempt to right the ship of the scandal-plagued program at Texas State. Working with walk-ons, due to the NCAA stripping away TSU's scholarships, he overcame those challenges to end his first season with a tie over Kansas and an upset win over top-ranked Texas. And he did all that with Kathy Ireland as his kicker!

3. Eric Taylor—*Friday Night Lights* (TV). There are some strong similarities between Taylor and Paterno: Both were assistant coaches who specialized in developing quarterbacks. Taylor eventually was elevated to head coach of Texas's Dillon High School over coaches that had more seniority on the staff (sounds familiar). High school football is king at Dillon, where a single loss could put a coach's job in jeopardy. Taylor succeeded in that pressure cooker by winning the state championship in his first year. Want some college experience? His high school success caught the attention of Texas Methodist University when

Taylor accepted the position as quarterbacks coach following his high school title. In fact, he was so respected in the college community that he was able to get troubled running back Brian "Smash" Davis a scholarship to Texas A&M despite the fact that Davis had not played for nearly a year because of a leg injury.

2. Coach Klein—*Waterboy*. Another coach who had a similar path as Paterno's (minus the victories). Coach Klein was the successful innovative offensive coordinator at the University of Louisiana, but he lost the power struggle with fellow assistant Red Beaulieu to take over when Coach Cavanaugh retired. Klein would become the head coach of South Central Louisiana State, but he lost that offensive touch, eventually finding success with a dominant defense (I think we have seen this a few seasons at Beaver Stadium). SCLSU earned a date in the Bourbon Bowl against Klein's former team, and during this game Klein was able to regain his dominant offensive schemes to lead the Mud Dogs to victory.

1. Tony D'Amato—*Any Given Sunday*. You want Paterno-style loyalty to veteran players? You want the flexibility to eventually open things up with a spread offense? You want one of the greatest pregame speeches in football history? If you answered "Yes!" then you have to go with D'Amato. He was the head coach of the AFFA's Miami Sharks, where he won two league titles. He is currently coaching the expansion Albuquerque Aztecs.

CHARACTERS OF THE STATE

Like most communities and sport fan bases, Penn State can lay claim to several unique characters. These people have garnered enough media attention over the years that they have reached celebrity status in their own right. Some can be found roaming Beaver Stadium on a fall Saturday afternoon, and others have been Penn State and State College living institutions that link generations of students and regular visitors to Happy Valley.

5. The Willard Preacher. Two men have been known as the Willard Preacher—first Clarence Cope and later Gary Cattell. They took to the Penn State campus outside of the Willard Building to spread the Word of God. The two have had to deal with taunts from passers-by and intense debates from atheists. If you attended Penn State anytime from the mid-1970s to the present, chances are that at least once you witnessed the Willard Preacher delivering his daily sermon.

4. The Ticket Man. Known for sporting his white lab coat adorned with blue paws, Steve Keesey has been a fixture at Penn State football games since attending school here in the mid-1970s. He also lays claim to having one of the largest private inventories of PSU football tickets that he makes available for sale.

3. Mike the Mailman. He may be the most engaging mail clerk you will ever meet. Mike Herr first manned the post office near the HUB in 1978. The banter he makes with his customers has made Herr a favorite with the public, as he is often the recipient of cookies, pizza, and other gifts.

2. Ernie and the Phyrst Phamly. The band first hit the stage in 1969, and for a good number of years was fronted by Ernie Oelbermann, who also owned the Phyrst Bar from 1968 to 2000. For those in the know, the band was *the* live act to see on a Saturday night. The audience participated in songs such as the "Unicorn Song" and the themes to the *Brady Bunch* and *Gilligan's Island*. Of course, there was the band's staple "Saturday Night." Ernie has been retired for a number of years, and a falling-out in 2009 between the Phyrst and some of the active band members led to a split, with some members becoming the Family Brew and performing Saturdays at the Brewery. The Phyrst countered with some new band members who perform under the old Phyrst Phamly name. Now it is a matter of choice of where "you'll kick off your shoes and . . . suck some brews."

1. The Big Ugly Guys. I challenge anybody to find a televised Penn State football game over the past five years in which the fans wearing the ugly football helmet masks, jerseys, and shoulder pads did not receive decent airtime. Along with the guy wearing the rubber Joe Paterno mask, this group has become the unofficial mascots of the team. Whether they're dancing in the northwest corner of Beaver Stadium or roaming the stands, these guys have become part of Penn State's "Great Show."

MEMORABLE PERSONALITIES :: BY STEVE JONES

Besides calling some of the greatest moments in Penn State history, Steve Jones, the voice of Penn State football and men's basketball, has met some interesting people along the way. Here are the ten most memorable personalities he's come across.

10. Jack Ham, Dick Jerardi, Jeff Tarman, and Roger Corey. No one in this business is luckier than I am to work with people such as these who are not only great at their jobs but also the best people you could possibly ever meet.

9. Gil Santos, John Grant, and Fran Fisher. My mentors. I learned so much from each of them. They are great guys who each did so much to try to make me better.

8. Talor Battle. In the last four minutes of a game he owns it and has the personality to go with it. When Penn State beat Illinois in the Bryce Jordan Center in 2009, he hit the game-winner with .03 seconds to go. I asked him during the postgame show what ran through his mind, and he said, "I was thinking that Dick [Jerardi] and you said I was the best player in the country in the waning moments." You don't get guys like that on the postgame show very often.

7. John Shaffer. He never will get the credit he deserves. He lost one start in high school and in college. That start was the 1986 Orange Bowl for the national championship. He did not play well and stood up like a man in the postgame and said that. He was destroyed in the *Miami Herald* by writers who didn't understand the meaning of the term "student-athlete." Entering the 1986 season, he had to endure a poll as to who the starting quarterback should be. In games at Alabama (13 for 17) and Notre Dame (15 for 18), he was great—and no one remembers it. I do. Today, he continues to be a great success.

6. Joe Crispin. He was always counted out by everyone except himself. Sure, he took some shots that made even me say, "You have to be kidding me." But he had swagger and he backed it up.

5. Matt Gaudio. Injuries bothered him, but when he played, he made an incredible difference. He was a great interview, but his most memorable moment was going chest to chest with Glenn Robinson of Purdue in Rec Hall and basically telling Robinson that he didn't care about his reputation—he was in "our" house. That is an attitude Penn State basketball has always begged for.

4. Michael Robinson. In 2001 Penn State played at Virginia and lost on a controversial call. Michael was a true freshman and was on the trip because he was from Virginia. He sat across from me on the bus on the way to the airport to go home. He looked at me and said, "Steve, when I get my shot, this will never happen." In 2005 he got his shot—enough said.

3. Barry Switzer. In early December of 1985 Penn State basketball played at Oklahoma. We arrived in time for the Oklahoma-SMU football game. I was given one-on-ones with Switzer and all of their players after the game, including Brian Bosworth. When the Orange Bowl between Penn State and Oklahoma happened, Switzer was walking in the lobby and, for some reason, recognized me. I asked him if he would mind giving a few minutes on my talk show. He said, "Sure, why not." The first caller said, "I can't believe I'm talking to Barry Switzer!"

2. Bear Bryant. Penn State played Alabama in 1981 and the Tide stayed in what was once the Holiday Inn in Burnham. The day before the game I went down to a press conference. I could not understand a word Bryant said during the interview, but I remember him shaking my hand and saying, "Thanks for your time son."

1. Joe Paterno. I think that is rather obvious. Simply the best.

THRILLING ENDINGS

Penn State has had quite a few of those special game-ending moments that fans remember for the next 20 to 30 years and beyond. Here are our top ten moments that shook the Nittany Nation with joy and still live in our memories.

10. "We are back"—October 8, 2005. After suffering losing seasons in four of the past five years, Penn State was ready to announce to the college football world that it was back to being a national power. All it had to do was beat No. 6 Ohio State in a primetime showdown at Beaver Stadium. Penn State brought a 5–0 record and No. 16 ranking into the game. ESPN's *College Gameday* set up shop outside the BJC for the weekend, and Lee Corso (never a Penn State advocate) did his best to antagonize Nittany Lion fans by picking Ohio State to win. With the Lions holding a 17–10 lead, Penn State fans grew nervous in the final 90 seconds of the game as Ohio State marched into Nittany Lion territory attempting to tie the contest. Defensive end Tamba Hali then sacked Buckeye quarterback Troy Smith, forcing a fumble. Lion tackle Scott Paxson recovered, sending the Beaver Stadium crowd into a frenzy. Penn State was indeed back as a national title contender.

9. Talor Battle sinks Illinois—March 5, 2009. The 2008–09 season was a special one for Penn State basketball: The year ended with the Lions winning the NIT Championship. When the Lions played their regular season home finale against No. 23 Illinois, they still had dreams of making the NCAA Tournament. The Fighting Illini built a 10-point lead in the second half, but Penn State began to chip away, closing the gap to 63–62 with time running out. Before his heroics, Talor Battle nearly became the goat when he allowed himself to get tied up as Illinois forced a jump ball. The alternate possession gave the ball to the Illini. Penn State fouled Mike Davis, who missed the front end of a one-and-one. Battle got the ball and drove the length of the court. His running lay-up danced around the rim and dropped in with 0.3 seconds remaining. The student section stormed the court, and Penn State had a win that, at the time, appeared to have propelled the Lions into the NCAA tourney.

8. Goal line stand turns away the Fighting Irish—November 15, 1986. For the second consecutive week, Penn State's defense was pushed to the brink of allowing a team to end the Lions' hopes for a perfect season and national championship. On a dreary afternoon at Notre Dame Stadium, the defense rose again to the challenge. Trailing 24–19, the Fighting Irish drove to the Nittany Lion 6 with less than two minutes to go. On first down, Lion safety Ray Isom dropped

Irish wide receiver Tim Brown for a three-yard loss. Then Bob White sacked quarterback Steve Beuerlein for a nine-yard loss. Notre Dame just missed a touchdown on third down when Lion defensive back Gary Wilkinson broke up a pass intended for Notre Dame's Joel Williams. Finally, on fourth down, running back Mike Green caught a pass in the flat, but his knee touched the ground at the 13, ending the threat. Penn State maintained its No. 2 ranking and kept its national title hopes alive.

7. Joe Crispin sends Penn State to the NCAA Tournament—March 9, 2001. The 2000–01 Nittany Lion basketball team produced one of the greatest seasons in the program's history. The team made it to the Sweet 16 for the first time since 1955. However, without some Joe Crispin magic in the Big Ten Tournament, Penn State may have been playing in the NIT again. In the quarterfinals against No. 2 Michigan State, the Lions solidified their case to go to the Big Dance. With under 22 seconds left, Penn State held a one-point lead when Crispin drained a 3-pointer to make the score 63–59. Michigan State's Jason Richardson countered with a trey of his own. The Spartans were forced to foul Crispin with 5.7 seconds remaining. Crispin hit both free throws, and the Lions eventually hung on for the 65–63 win. Two days later they had their names called on Selection Sunday to go dancing.

6. Penn State comeback at Illinois clinches first-ever Big Ten title—November 12, 1994. Penn State was rolling through the Big Ten in its second year in the conference. With All-Americans at nearly every starting position on offense, the Nittany Lions were scoring as many points a game as their basketball counterparts. With a chance to win the Big Ten title, Penn State traveled to Illinois and looked terrible from the start, at one point trailing 21–0. The Nittany Lions rallied and closed the gap to 31–28 with 6:07 remaining when they started a drive from their own four. They methodically moved the ball deep into Illini territory—the drive was lengthy and time consuming. With 57 seconds remaining, fullback Brian Milne plunged into the end zone from two yards out, his third touchdown of the day, and Penn State had come all the way back to lead 35–31. Kim Herring's interception with two seconds remaining ended Illinois's final chance to pull off the upset.

5. Kevin Kelly prolongs, puts an end to Orange Bowl marathon—January 3–4, 2006. The game that would never end finally did around 1 a.m. after four hours and three overtimes. People who wanted to see Joe Paterno and Bobby Bowden face each other one more time got their money's worth. The fun began with the score tied 16–16 and 32 seconds remaining. Penn State's freshman kicker Kevin Kelly missed a 29-yard field goal and the game went into overtime.

In the first OT both FSU's Gary Cismesia and Kelly missed field goals. The teams exchanged touchdowns in the second OT. In the third overtime, Cismesia missed a 38-yarder, and Kelly was given a third chance to win the game. It was not pretty, but his 29-yarder hugged the right upright and went through, and Penn State won their fourth Orange Bowl, 26–23, and capped an 11–1 season.

4. Craig Fayak's field goal takes down No. 1 Notre Dame—November 17, 1990. With the game tied at 21 and Penn State facing a fourth-and-2 from the Notre Dame 37 with 2:35 left, Joe Paterno decided to punt the ball. But this wasn't Joe being the "too conservative Joe." He knew Notre Dame couldn't afford a tie if it wanted to have a shot at a national title. The gamble paid off, as Darren Perry intercepted Notre Dame's Rick Mirer and ran the ball back to the Irish 19. Freshman Craig Fayak kicked the game-winner with four seconds remaining, and the Nittany Nation—both those in South Bend and also back in Happy Valley—celebrated into the night.

3. Extra Jayhawk gives Penn State an extra chance—January 1, 1969. Penn State was fighting for national respect as it took a 10–0 record into its Orange Bowl matchup with No. 6 Kansas. But with less than two minutes left, Penn State trailed 14–7. The Lions took over at their own 49 with 1:16 remaining. Quarterback Chuck Burkhart hit Bob Campbell, whose momentum carried the ball all the way to the 3 with 66 seconds to go. Three plays later Burkhart, on a keeper, scored with 15 seconds left to make the score Kansas 14, Penn State 13. The Lions then went for the win on a two-point conversion. Burkhart's pass to All-American tight end Ted Kwalick was too high and fell incomplete. Kansas began celebrating what it thought was an Orange Bowl title, but the officials began signaling that something was wrong with the play—the Jayhawks had 12 defenders on the field. Given a second chance to win the game, Campbell scored on a sweep play. The Nittany Lions won, 15–14, and finished the season 11–0.

2. The Miracle of Mount Nittany—September 25, 1982. It is arguably the greatest game ever played at Beaver Stadium—No. 8 Penn State vs. No. 2 Nebraska. The Cornhuskers trailed for most of the game but took their first lead at 24–21 with 1:18 remaining. The Lions began their final drive from their 35. They moved to the Nebraska 33 with 52 seconds left. Facing a fourth-and-11, quarterback Todd Blackledge completed a pass to Kenny Jackson for a first down. On a second-and-4 at the Nebraska 17, Blackledge threw to tight end Mike McCloskey at the Cornhusker 2. Now from a Penn State perspective and what the officials called, McCloskey got a toe in-bounds for a completed pass. Nebraska thought McCloskey was out of bounds. Penn State took advantage of the fortuitous call as Blackledge hit backup tight end Kirk Bowman in the back of the end zone for the winning touchdown. The victory propelled Penn State to its first national title.

1. National champs again!—January 2, 1987. The stats show that heavily favored Miami had outgained Penn State 445 yards to 162 and had 22 first downs to Penn State's eight. Yet it was the Nittany Lions who led 14–10 in the 1987 Fiesta Bowl as the Hurricanes, with Heisman quarterback Vinny Testaverde, lined up for their final play with 18 seconds left—a fourth-and-goal from the Penn State 13. Testaverde threw to his left toward the end zone, linebacker Pete Giftopoulos intercepted the pass—Testaverde's fifth INT—clinching the national championship for Joe Paterno and Penn State. With Miami arriving in Arizona in battle fatigues and talking trash during the course of the week and even into the game, the contest took on a good vs. evil tone. To the delight of many, good prevailed.

HEARTBREAKING LOSSES

The fact that Penn State has enjoyed having so many great teams also means that it sets itself up for some heartbreaking losses that end seasons or cost teams chances at a national title.

Here are ten games that Penn State fans probably would like to forget, but they will always be remembered.

10. November 20, 1993—Field hockey team loses to North Carolina on penalty shots. The 1993 Penn State field hockey team had one of those special seasons. It won the Big Ten title and was on the verge of winning the national championship. Ranked No. 1 in the nation for most of the year, the Nittany Lions reached the semifinals against North Carolina with a 20–1 record. This was the third time in four years that Penn State and the Tar Heels met in the semifinals—North Carolina prevailed by 1–0 scores in both 1990 and 1991. This time it was supposed to be different. During the regular season Penn State defeated North Carolina, 2–0.

In the rematch, held on a neutral field at Rutgers, the teams battled to a 1–1 tie to force overtime. After two scoreless overtime sessions, penalty shots would determine which team would advance to the finals. Penn State missed on all three of its shots, whereas North Carolina made all three of theirs, abruptly ending the Lions' thrill ride that lasted much of the fall semester.

9. March 7, 2009—Men's basketball loses at Iowa in double OT. It was the final game of the 2009 regular season. A Penn State win would have clinched sole possession of second place in the Big Ten and all but guarantee an at-large bid in the NCAA Tournament. The Lions had already won ten games in the conference, including wins over Purdue and at Michigan State. They also had just completed a sweep of Illinois two days earlier, when Talor Battle made a last-second shot for the win at the BJC.

Unfortunately, an Iowa team with only four conference wins got the best of Penn State in double overtime. The Lions trailed by nine points with less than two minutes to go. They were able to rally and tie the game, and they had a chance to win it, but Battle missed a 3-point try in the closing seconds of regulation. The game eventually went to a second overtime, and with 54 seconds left, Iowa's Jake Kelly shot a 3-pointer that went off the backboard, hit the rim, ricocheted back to the glass, and dropped in for what proved to be the game-winning bucket. The 75–67 loss dropped Penn State into a tie for fourth place and, due to tiebreakers, the sixth seed in the Big Ten Tournament. The Lions beat Indiana in the first round but lost to Purdue the next night. On Selection

Sunday their bubble burst as they were not picked to be in the NCAA Tournament. However, they made the best of their consolation NIT bid, winning the tournament for the first time in school history.

8. December 1, 2001—Football team blows lead, game, and bowl bid at Virginia. After opening the season 0–4, the Nittany Lions season began to turn around. They won five of six, including getting head coach Joe Paterno his 324th victory to break Bear Bryant's record. But because of the terrorist attacks on September 11, the Lions had to make a trip to Virginia on December 1 to play a game that was originally scheduled for September 13. They were 5–5 with a chance at a winning record and a bowl bid. Penn State jumped out to a 14–3 lead midway through the second quarter. After Virginia kicked a field goal to make the score 14–6, Penn State quarterback Zack Mills had the Lions driving deep into Cavalier territory when the game swung on a controversial no-call. On a third down from the Virginia 8-yard line Mills scrambled, but Cavalier linebacker John Duckett caught him from behind. As he was going down, Mills fumbled the football. Virginia cornerback Art Thomas scooped up the ball and raced 92 yards for the touchdown. Replays would show that Mills's knee was down before the ball came out and Penn State should have retained possession. Late in the third quarter the Cavaliers scored on a 16-yard run by Alvin Pearman that led to Virginia's 20–14 win, sending Penn State home with no bowl appearance and a second consecutive losing season.

7. October 15, 2005—Another trip to Ann Arbor, another game marked by dubious officiating. Nittany Nation had suffered through four losing football seasons in five years. In 2005 Paterno began his and the program's turnaround with a stellar recruiting class, highlighted by top prospects Derrick Williams and Justin King. The week prior to the Michigan game, Penn State announced its return to football prominence with a 17–10 win over Ohio State. The Nittany Lions brought a perfect 6–0 mark into Michigan Stadium.

Trailing 21–18 late in the fourth quarter, Nittany Lion quarterback Michael Robinson led the Lions on an 81-yard drive. He capped it with a three-yard touchdown run that gave Penn State a 25–21 lead with 53 seconds remaining. Wolverine Steve Breaston returned the ensuing kickoff to the Michigan 41. A few plays later, Michigan head coach Lloyd Carr called a timeout. The officials added two seconds to the clock, saying that too much time had run off after the timeout was granted. With six seconds remaining, Michigan QB Chad Henne took the snap from the Penn State 10 and threw incomplete to Breaston. When play was stopped, there was one second left on the clock. On the next play Henne hit wide receiver Mario Manningham for the winning score. Michigan won 27–25.

6. March 15, 1991—No. 1 Lady Lion basketball team is upset in the second round of the NCAA Tournament. Lady Lion head coach Rene Portland had turned the Penn State women's basketball program into a national power. Portland spent the early part of her PSU coaching career battling regional bias. Southern teams, especially elite programs such as Tennessee, Old Dominion, and Louisiana Tech, received favorable regular-season rankings that translated into higher seeds in the NCAA Tournament. By 1991 Portland had won that battle. After winning the Atlantic 10 Tournament, the Lady Lions were ranked No. 1 in the country, having won 18 games in a row and posting an overall record of 29–1. Penn State was the top seed in the East Region and earned a first-round bye.

The Lady Lions played James Madison in the second round at Rec Hall, where Penn State hadn't lost in two years. Penn State scored the game's first 11 points and led by 12 at halftime. The momentum changed in the second half, however, and with 12:14 remaining in the game, the Dukes' Brandy Cruthird hit a pair of free throws, giving James Madison its first lead, 49–47. The game remained tight, and with 18 second left, Penn State had the ball, trailing 73–71. With time running out, Penn State guard Tanya Garner attempted a 3-pointer for the win, but James Madison's Jeanine Michaelson blocked the shot. The game ended, giving James Madison one of the biggest upset wins in NCAA Tournament history. It would take another nine years for Penn State to finally reach its first Final Four.

5. December 2, 2005—No. 1 seed women's soccer team loses in NCAA semis on penalty kicks. The Lady Lion soccer team was the top seed of the East Region of the 2005 NCAA Tournament and began a march to a national title. Wins over Bucknell, West Virginia, Texas A&M, and Santa Clara put Penn State into its third Final Four. Against Portland, the game was scoreless after regulation and two overtime periods. Penalty kicks would determine who would play UCLA for the championship. Penn State made three penalty kicks and Portland made four, so the Pilots advanced and ultimately won the national championship.

4. November 8, 1997—Michigan derails run to the national championship. Three years after winning its first Big Ten title, the Penn State football team was poised to win it again and play for another national championship. The Nittany Lions had held the No. 1 ranking early in the season and had a signature come-from-behind win over Ohio State in October at Beaver Stadium. At 7–0, the Lions hosted fourth-ranked Michigan. The game was essentially over before it started. Michigan kicked a field goal on its opening drive. Then its defense sacked Lion quarterback Mike McQueary two times during Penn State's first three plays. From there a flood of Wolverine scoring highlighted the first half, as Michigan led 24–0 at halftime and would go on for a 34–8 win.

3. November 8, 2008—Iowa's last-second field goal ends dreams of a national championship. With three games remaining in the regular season, Penn State figured to have a birth the BCS title game all wrapped up. The Lions had taken care of what appeared to be the toughest part of their schedule—winning at Wisconsin and Ohio State and then thrashing Michigan at home. A road game at Iowa and two home games with Indiana and Michigan State to close out the season should not have been a problem. The Nittany Lions did take care of the two home games; however, the road trip to Iowa ended any hopes of another national championship for Paterno.

A sluggish start put the Nittany Lions behind early, but they rebounded to lead 23–14 at the start of the fourth quarter. An Iowa touchdown cut the lead to two at 23–21. Penn State then drove into Iowa territory to put the game away. It faced a third-and-24 from the Hawkeye 37 when quarterback Daryll Clark threw an interception and Iowa took over at its 15-yard line. After moving the ball to midfield, the Hawkeyes faced a third-and-15. On a bang-bang play, Lion defensive back Anthony Scirrotto broke up a pass while making contact with the wide receiver at nearly the same time. Scirrotto was flagged for pass interference, and the Hawkeyes kept the drive going. Iowa eventually moved into field goal range, and with time for one more play, Hawkeye kicker Daniel Murray booted the game-winner from 31 yards out.

2. November 6, 1999—The game that launched a thousand losses (not really, but it sure seemed like it). This was the most memorable loss in Beaver Stadium history. Penn State was undefeated and ranked second in the nation, thanks to impressive wins at Miami and against Ohio State. In previous seasons Minnesota had put a scare into Penn State, but the Lions always prevailed. On a beautiful, sunny Saturday afternoon the two teams went back and forth almost from the start. The Lions led 23–21 when Minnesota took possession for its final drive. It appeared as if the Gophers' valiant effort would fall short when they faced a fourth-and-16 from the Penn State 40. One more stop and Penn State was one step closer to a national championship. Gopher quarterback Billy Cockerham launched a pass downfield, and the ball deflected off wide receiver Ron Johnson and was inches from falling to the turf incomplete when the Gophers' Arland Bruce caught it, giving Minnesota a first down in field-goal range. The Gophers ran the clock down, and on the final play of the game, Dan Nystrom nailed the 32-yard game-winning field goal.

The 24–23 loss set off a terrible chain of events for the Nittany Nation. The Lions would go on to lose their next two games before winning in the Alamo Bowl. Some say the loss triggered the program's "dark times," when it had four losing seasons over the next five years.

1. January 1, 1979—Alabama 14, Penn State 7. The defining image of the Sugar Bowl will last forever in the minds of fans of both the Nittany Lions and Crimson Tide—'Bama linebacker Barry Krauss's stuffing Lion running back Mike Guman on fourth-and-goal at the 1-yard line late in the fourth quarter. The play kept the Tide in the lead, 14–7. For Penn State, this was to be the year that righted all the wrongs, when the Lions had been snubbed by pollsters of the past. In his 13th season Paterno had finally brought Penn State to the top of the college football world, achieving its first-ever No. 1 ranking from both the Associated Press and UPI Coaches polls. No. 1 Penn State against No. 2 Alabama were battling it out in the Sugar Bowl for the title.

Trailing 14–7 midway in the fourth quarter, Penn State recovered an Alabama fumble on the Tide 19, putting the Lions in great shape to tie or win the game. Penn State eventually set up for first-and-goal from inside the 5-yard line. On first down, Guman carried for a minimal gain. Second down was an incomplete pass to Fitzkee. After a third-down plunge by Matt Suhey that nearly got into the end zone, Penn State had fourth-and-goal from the 1-foot line. Guman leapt, Krauss leapt, Guman was denied, and Alabama won the national championship.

HONORABLE MENTIONS:

October 1, 1977—Kentucky's 24–20 win at Beaver Stadium was the Nittany Lions' only loss of the season, and—thanks to the backroom deals of bowl representatives, which was the norm for this era—it kept Penn State out of a major bowl.

January 1, 1986—Oklahoma's 25–10 win over No. 1–ranked Penn State denied another national championship.

March 9, 1989—The Nittany Lions lost to Rutgers, 70–66, in the championship game of the Atlantic 10 Tournament and lost the automatic bid (their only chance of making the Big Dance) to the NCAA Tournament.

March 23, 2001—Appearing in the Sweet 16 of the NCAA Tournament for the first time in 46 years, Penn State lost to Temple, 84–72. Four months earlier the Nittany Lions defeated the Owls, 66–60. A win over Temple would have pitted Penn State against Michigan State, who the Lions had defeated, 65–63, in the Big Ten Tournament—so at the start of the day, a trip to the Final Four was not a far-fetched scenario.

MEMORABLE WEATHER GAMES :: BY JOE BASTARDI

State College could be considered the weather capital of the world, of sorts. That's because it's home to AccuWeather and also the fact that Penn State turns out a number of meteorologists. Joe Bastardi may be best known for the weather forecasts he gave at AccuWeather for 32 years. He certainly could be the only meteorologist to earn a varsity letter in wrestling, which he did at Penn State.

Bastardi has appeared on everything from *The O'Reilly Factor* to *The Colbert Report*. He has tremendous passion for weather and sports, so why not ask him to select some of the most memorable weather games Penn State has played in at Beaver Stadium over the past 40 years (in chronological order). By the way, Bastardi says his fantasy weather game would be a snowfall during a late-season battle of unbeatens—and at night!

10. November 10, 1973—vs. North Carolina State. It was the year of Cappelletti's winning the Heisman, and an undefeated PSU team had to deal with a tougher-than-forecasted N.C. State team led by Lou Holtz. One to two inches of snow had fallen from early season snow squalls the night before, and though the snow was melting off as the game progressed, the field was still sloppy. Temperatures in the mid-30s didn't help either. The result was a PSU win, 35–29.

9. September 21, 1974—vs. Navy. When I say, "Wind," you say, "Rain." A cold front came through just as the game was starting, and the first half was spent in a driving cold rainstorm that left the field a quagmire. In spite of outgaining Navy almost 5 to 1, costly fumbles and missed field goals left us on the short end of a 7–6 game. It figures—all that water had to favor Navy.

8. September 12, 1981—vs. Cincinnati. It was a great day—until the nasty thunderstorm hit at the end of the game. Why is this in here? Well, I was working that morning at AccuWeather and took the thunderstorm out of the forecast. And if you think all you-know-what broke loose at the end of the game with the thunderstorm, well you should have seen what happened to me Monday morning at work when the Grand Poobah of AccuWeather, Joel Myers, came in. Fortunately, I had Elliot Abrams to console me. However, this does raise the question: What do we do when thunderstorms hit in the middle of the game and there are 107,000 people out in the open? I say, run the ball up the middle—it has worked for Joe for years. Penn State won, 52–0.

7. October 16, 1982—vs. Syracuse. It was a miserable Homecoming with temps near 40, howling northwest winds, and showers of rain and snow. It joins some other October games I have listed as reasons for why even though I do not believe that humans are causing global warming, I wish we were. We should not have to deal with such things in October, even here, and especially at Homecoming. Penn State won, 28–7.

6. November 26, 1982—vs. Pitt. What a year, eh? Pitt head coach Foge Fazio came here thinking he was going to stop us from winning the national title. But the second half turned ugly as temps dropped toward freezing and some light snow and freezing drizzle followed what had been periods of rain beforehand. It was not the worst day, but it was one that had me fantasizing about my dream game and a heavy snow. Penn State won, 19–10.

5. November 16, 1985—vs. Notre Dame. Heavy rains and a recently sodded field made for a debacle—not so much for the Lions, we won the game handily, 36–6—but for the field coming apart during the game. It was one of the great gloomy weather games I have ever seen. I think this was the game JoePa mentioned on TV that he hoped some Catholics were praying for PSU. My mom called me up and asked me to tell Joe she was—like I could really do that.

4. November 21, 1987—vs. Notre Dame. The Ice Bowl. We won this game, arguably the most brutal game weather-wise in PSU history. The strong front came through the night before, and temps were in the upper teens at game time, with howling winds and frequent snow flurries. My brother, at that time an assistant coach at Trenton State, came up with his future wife, Barbara, a PSU grad. We stayed the whole game and froze. Neither one of us was going to be the first to give in and leave. A tribute to the stubbornness and stupidity of both of us—something that was so bad that we had to bond over it. However, I knew then and there that my brother had found the one woman in the world who he could possibly be happily married to, as she never let on that she wanted to leave. We won the game, 21–20, and I knew my brother had found his wife.

3. November 18, 1995—vs. Michigan. Darn if only the foot and a half of snow had not hit earlier in the week, I could have had it—the fantasy game. As it was, the game occurred after the major mid-November storm that started the winter of 1995–96. Inmates from Rockview came in to shovel out the stadium, but with all the snow in the stands, snowball fights broke out left and right during the game, with snowballs raining down onto the field. It seemed as if only divine intervention could stop the snowball fights—either that or thunder from JoePa, who walked out onto the field and yelled at the crowd to stop. Like

Moses parting the Red Sea, the snowballs being tossed onto to the field did stop. However, they continued in the stands. Penn State won, 27–17.

2. October 19, 1996—vs. Iowa. Misery personified in the form of Tim Dwight galloping around a field with rain and wet snow falling and temps near 40 degrees. My in-laws were up—some from Houston, Texas—and were treated to what Big Ten weather can be like in October. Fortunately for me, I stayed home and babysat my son, Garrett, and watched the debacle in the warmth of my home. The snow that was on the ground in the morning had melted, but 13 years later, in October, history repeated itself, which is our next event. Penn State lost, 21–20.

1. October 17, 2009—vs. Minnesota. Central PA looked like a battleground the morning of Homecoming, as a 3–6 inch wet snowstorm, the earliest heavy snow ever, took down many trees and resulted in one the ugliest messes in PSU history as far as getting people to the game. The weather during the game: light rain and a little wet snow with temps in the mid to upper 30s—and snowball fights from the snow that was still around. Penn State won, 20–0.

Honorable mention: September 21, 1991—vs. Brigham Young. Here is an honorable mention that only if you wrestled here and loved the weather you could possibly stick in. A crisp, calm night with an early frost in outlying areas meant that the stadium with more than 96,000 became a heat island! This led to a "circulation" at the top of the stadium, with the flags there blowing counter-clockwise even though the wind was calm all around the stadium. I was explaining to people around me that this is similar to a warm-core tropical system, where the rising air in the middle was creating the circulation. Most of them had absolutely no interest at all in what I was saying. But this, combined with the antics of the Nittany Lion, played by ex-PSU wrestler Tim Durant, makes this 33–13 blowout of BYU one of my favorite games. The Lion met Cosmo the Cougar before the game and hit him with a textbook fireman's carry. Cosmo got up, but then Tim blasted him with a double-leg takedown. So I am watching this, screaming, "Hit him with a headlock!" Finally, he let Cosmo up, and the Cougar scampers away. It was the perfect combination of my two passions, weather and wrestling—and at a football game.

GREATEST PENN STATE FOOTBALL PLAYERS FROM PENNSYLVANIA

It is only natural that the flagship school in the Keystone State should have a "Lions" share of homegrown talent. Check the Pro and College Football halls of fame and you will find a strong Pennsylvania presence. For our list of Penn Staters from PA, we included six players who won multiple first-team All-American honors, three Maxwell Award winners, a couple of Butkus and Bednarik Award honorees, and, of course, one Heisman Trophy winner.

10. Jack Ham. 1968–70 LB—Johnstown, Bishop McCort H.S.

9. Kerry Collins. 1991–94 QB—West Lawn, Wilson H.S.

8. LaVar Arrington. 1997–99 LB—Pittsburgh, North Hills H.S.

7. Mike Reid. 1966–69 DT—Altoona, Altoona H.S.

6. Ted Kwalick. 1966–68 TE—McKees Rock, Montour H.S.

5. Dennis Onkotz. 1967–69 LB—Northampton, Northampton H.S.

4. Keith Dorney. 1975–78 OL—Macungie, Emmaus H.S.

3. Bruce Clark. 1976–79 DT—New Castle, New Castle H.S.

2. Paul Posluszny. 2003–06 LB—Aliquippa, Hopewell H.S.

1. John Cappelletti. 1971–73 RB—Upper Darby, Monsignor Bonner H.S.

GREATEST PENN STATE FOOTBALL PLAYERS FROM MARYLAND

A little more than 100 miles south of State College is the state of Maryland. Over the decades that proximity has allowed the Nittany Lions to stock their roster with players from the Old Line State. Although there might not be as many All-American Penn Staters who came from Maryland, there still are several impact players who have come north of the border to play in the Happy Valley.

10. Pete Speros. 1979–82 OG—Potomac, St. John's College H.S. (Washington, DC)

9. Rogers Alexander. 1982–85 LB—Riverdale, DeMatha H.S.

8. A.J. Wallace. 2006–09 CB—Waldorf, McDonough H.S.

7. Charlie Pittman. 1966–69 RB—Baltimore, Edmondson H.S.

6. Richie Anderson. 1990–92 RB—Sandy Spring, Sherwood H.S.

5. Steve Smith. 1983–86 FB—Clinton, DeMatha H.S.

4. Mark Robinson. 1980–83 S—Silver Spring, John F. Kennedy H.S.

3. Zack Mills. 2001–04 QB—Ijamsville, Urbana H.S.

2. Derrick Williams. 2005–08 WR—Greenbelt, Eleanor Roosevelt H.S.

1. Aaron Maybin. 2006–08 DE—Elicott City, Mount Hebron H.S.

GREATEST PENN STATE FOOTBALL PLAYERS FROM NEW YORK

On the north border of the Commonwealth of Pennsylvania is the state of New York. Owner of the nation's largest city and being one of the most populous states, New York, naturally, is home to some fine football talent. The Empire State claims three Division I-A programs—Army, Buffalo, and Syracuse. Buffalo is still relatively new when it comes to D-I football, Army has seen better days, and Syracuse has had long stretches on irrelevancy since Joe Paterno became the Nittany Lions' head coach in 1966. Even in the days when the Orangemen and Lions were battling for eastern supremacy, Penn State was still able to get their share of NY talent to head south to Happy Valley.

10. Kevin Baugh. 1980–83 WR—Deer Park, Deer Park H.S.

9. Jesse Arnelle. 1951–54 E—New Rochelle, New Rochelle H.S.

8. Bill Dugan. 1977–80 OL—Hornell, Hornell H.S.

7. Bob Campbell. 1965–68 RB—Vestal, Vestal H.S.

6. Alan Zemaitis. 2002–05 CB—Rochester, Spencerport H.S.

5. Tom Rafferty. 1972–75 OG—Manlius, Fayetteville-Manlius H.S.

4. Jimmy Kennedy. 2000–03 DT—Yonkers, Roosevelt H.S.

3. Sean Farrell. 1978–81 G—Westhampton Beach, Westhampton Beach H.S.

2. Steve Suhey. 1942, 1946–47 LB—Cazenovia, Cazenovia H.S.

1. Shane Conlan. 1983–86 LB—Frewsburg, Frewsburg H.S.

HEAD COACH

Joe Paterno. 1966–Present—Brooklyn, Brooklyn Prep

GREATEST PENN STATE FOOTBALL PLAYERS FROM NEW JERSEY

For most of the history of Penn State football, Nittany Lion coaches have viewed the state of New Jersey as basically an extension of the Commonwealth of Pennsylvania. The Lions regularly cross the Delaware River and raid Jersey of its top high school talent. So besides Bruce Springsteen, Bon Jovi, and *The Sopranos*, the Garden State also has produced many great Penn Staters.

10. Bruce Bannon. 1970–72 LB—Rockaway, Morris Hills H.S.

9. Lou Benfatti. 1990–93 DT—Denville, Morris Knolls H.S.

8. Pete Harris. 1977–78, 1980 S—Mount Holly Township, Rancocas Valley Regional H.S.

7. Tamba Hali. 2002–05 DL—Teaneck, Teaneck H.S.

6. Walker Lee Ashley. 1979–82 DE—Jersey City, Snyder H.S.

5. Greg Buttle. 1973–75 LB—Linwood, Mainland Regional H.S.

4. Andre Collins. 1986–89 LB—Cinnaminson, Cinnaminson H.S.

3. Kenny Jackson. 1980–83 WR—South River, South River H.S.

2. Dave Robinson. 1960–62 LB—Mount Laurel Township, Moorestown H.S.

1. Lydell Mitchell. 1969–71 RB—Salem, Salem H.S.

GREATEST PENN STATE FOOTBALL PLAYERS FROM OHIO

On the western border of the Keystone State is Ohio. It may come as a shock to those who reside in Buckeyeland that not every high school football player dreams of playing for Ohio State. The Nittany Lions have been able to pry some top talent from Ohio—talent that would be major factors in winning national championships and Big Ten titles.

10. Jeff Hartings. 1992–95 OL—St. Henry, St. Henry H.S.

9. Lance Mehl. 1976–79 LB—Bellaire, Bellaire H.S.

8. Mike Michalske. 1922–25 OL—Cleveland, West Tech H.S.

7. William T. "Mother" Dunn. 1903–06 LB—Youngstown, Youngstown H.S.

6. Michael Zordich. 1982–85 LB—Youngstown, Chaney H.S.

5. Daryll Clark. 2006–09 QB—Youngstown, Ursuline H.S.

4. Todd Blackledge. 1980–82 QB—Canton, North Canton H.S.

3. Curtis Enis. 1995–97 RB—Union City, Mississinawa Valley H.S.

2. O.J. McDuffie. 1989–92 WR—Gates Mills, Hawken H.S.

1. Ki-Jana Carter. 1992–94 RB—Westerville, Westerville South H.S.

GREATEST PENN STATE FOOTBALL PLAYERS FROM DELAWARE AND WEST VIRGINIA

Of the six states that border Pennsylvania, Delaware and West Virginia have had the least impact in contributing talent to the Nittany Lion roster, partly due to the limited population of both states and, in the case of West Virginia, a rabid following of the flagship school—West Virginia University. Over the past ten years, Penn State has begun to bring more Delawareans to Happy Valley. As for West Virginia, there have not been many that have gone to PSU, but one of the all-time greats hailed from the Mountain State.

9. Andrew Szczerba. 2008–present TE—Wilmington, DE, Salesianum H.S.

8. Eric Latimore. 2008–present DE—Middletown, DE, Middletown H.S.

7. Justin Brown. 2009–present WR—Wilmington, DE, Concord H.S.

6. Mike Meade. 1978–81 FB—Dover, DE, Dover H.S.

5. BranDon Snow. 2002–06 FB—Newark, DE, Newark H.S.

4. Gary Hayman. 1971–73 RB—Newark, DE, Newark H.S.

3. Ross Hufford. 1920–22 E—Hillsboro, WV, NA

2. Devon Still. 2008–present DT—Wilmington, DE, Howard Tech H.S.

1. Curt Warner. 1979–82 RB—Pineville, WV, Pineville H.S.

WHY JOE PATERNO IS A GREAT COACH
:: BY LOU HOLTZ

Lou Holtz may be friends with Joe Paterno, but he's also coached against him several times, so he knows firsthand why Paterno has become one of the greatest coaches in college football. The two went against each other when Holtz coached North Carolina State from 1972 to 1975, and they met seven times when Holtz was at Notre Dame (1986–96). Both beat each other on their ways to winning national titles—Paterno and the Lions bested Holtz and the Irish in 1986; Holtz returned the favor in 1988. Now an ESPN analyst, Holtz gives his top five reasons why Paterno is so good at what he does.

5. Bland. The team's uniform, his dress, the way he deals with media—it's all the same. There's no showboating from him or the players.

4. Focus. There are only two things that are important to him—family and Penn State football. He's not about golf, tennis, traveling—it's singularly those two things.

3. Durability. To be at one university for this long is unprecedented, and even Bobby Bowden found out how hard that is. I remember in 1986, talking before a game, I said, "How long you gonna coach?" He said, "Four years." In 1987 I asked him the same question. He said, "Four more years." If you ask him today, it's "Four more years."

2. Consistency. Seldom having bad years—had a few in there, but consistency for that many years, especially considering changes in society—is extremely impressive.

1. In-Game Coaching. He's the best I ever competed against. He had a great game plan going in and he executed it. His teams didn't beat themselves: They played intelligently, had low penalties, and were good fundamentally. Throughout the years his teams have been always the same.

TOP FOOTBALL NICKNAMES

Nicknames have been a part of sports since, well probably since organized sports became part of the American culture in the mid- to late 1800s. Penn State has had quite a few players who have had interesting nicknames as well. Here, we want to focus on original nicknames, not some hybrid of a player's name, so you won't find anything such as M-Rob, L.J., D-Will, or Poz on this list. In addition to individual players, we included nicknames for two defensive positions and one special defensive unit.

15. "The Reading Rocket" Lenny Moore. Moore is obviously not from Shamokin, not that there is anything wrong with being from Shamokin.

14. "Scrap" Tom Bradley. Known for his, well, scrappy play on special teams in 1977 and 1978, he is now known for producing dominating defenses as the Lions' defensive coordinator since 2000.

13. "The Foot" Ted Kemmerer. A punter on the 1952 team, his 52 punts for 1,904 yards helped earn him his nickname and helped Penn State go 7-2-1. And on that same team there was . . .

12. "The Toe" Bill Leonard. A State College native, he led the Lions in scoring in 1952 with three field goals and 21 PATs.

11. "Riverboat" Richie Lucas. Lucas earned the nickname for his daring style of play. It also led to an un-Penn State–like publicity photo of Lucas dressed like a riverboat gambler, circa late 1800s, holding a royal flush.

10. "Salt" Matt Millen. And . . .

9. "Pepper" Bruce Clark. Millen and Clark pushed each other in the weight room and on the practice field to become two of the best defensive linemen in Penn State history. Clark, however, has to share his "Pepper" nickname with John "Pepper" Petrella, who was one of the Lions' star running backs on the 1939 and 1940 teams.

8. "Light Horse" Harry Wilson. All-American running back in 1923 and in the College Football Hall of Fame, he earned his nickname for his performance against Navy in 1923. In that game he had a 55-yard interception return for a TD, a 95-yard kickoff return for a TD, and 72-yard run off of a fake reverse for a third trip to the end zone. The Lions won, 21–3.

7. "Upper Darby Iceman" John Cappelletti. Cappelletti was cool before George Gervin became cool.

6. William "Mother" Dunn. The first great Nittany Lion, Dunn was a center for Penn State from 1903 to 1906. According to *The Penn State Football Encyclopedia*, he earned his nickname when he was leading fellow freshmen across campus one day in 1903 when an upperclassman said, "There goes Mother Dunn leading his chickens." And if there's "Mother," there's . . .

5. "Dad" Lloyd Engle. He was an outstanding offensive tackle from 1910 to 1912. And if the last name looks familiar, yes, he's an uncle of Rip Engle.

4. "Seven Mountains." The name given to the team's seven-man defensive line in 1940 also is the name for the mountain range near State College. The line included All-American linebacker Leon Gajecki, defensive ends Lloyd Parsons and Tom Vargo, tackles Carl Stravinski and Frank Platt, and guards Mike Garbinski and Wade Mori. The unit led the Lions to their best season in 19 years, going 6–1–1.

3. "Hero." It is the strong safety position. When Rip Engle was the head coach, many schools referred to the strong safety as the "monsterback." Engle wanted a name that was not dehumanizing. He wanted something noble, thus the Heroback was born. Joe Paterno kept the tradition for the next two decades after replacing Engle in 1966.

2. "Dobre Shunka" Jack Ham. Dobre Shunka is Polish for "good ham." It also can mean All-American linebacker.

1. "Linebacker U." Penn State has had great linebackers for nearly as long as it has played football. However, when Joe Paterno became head coach, the Nittany Lions started producing All-Americans on a nearly annual basis.

SALT AND PEPPER :: BY BRUCE CLARK

Bruce Clark and Matt Millen formed one of the most feared and dominant defensive-tackle combinations in college football in the late 1970s. Clark came from the western part of Pennsylvania and Millen came from the eastern part. Off the field the two formed a strong friendship that lasts today. On the field they led a Penn State defense that helped the Nittany Lions reach their first No. 1 ranking. Clark, who is still Penn State's only winner of the Lombardi Award—which he won in 1978 as the nation's outstanding lineman/linebacker, becoming the first junior to win the trophy—recalls some special times with Millen.

6. Recruiting trip. We first met at the Big 33 game and talked about the possibility of us playing together. We decided to take the same recruiting trip to Penn State the same week to see if it was a perfect fit for the both of us. I was the Best from the West and he was the Beast from the East. We had a $5 bowling pass and were put in a dorm room. So we sat in this room not being entertained and doing pushups all night. That's when the competition started. That was the worst recruiting trip I ever went on—but it was by far the most honest trip. I got an academic interview and I met other student-athletes. It felt like home.

5. Start of a beautiful friendship. Our freshman year we'd walk up the street and put cars on the curb and then walk down and take the cars down from the curb. There wasn't much to do at Penn State. We got in trouble for silly stuff. We just hit it off.

4. "Salt and Pepper." Some newspaper reporter came up with that. They saw how well we worked together and pushed each other academically and athletically. Plus, it was after the Brian Piccolo movie came out. But Matt, I didn't understand. He was actually Pepper and I was Salt. He would always be getting into trouble. I told him, "You can't cut on Joe Paterno. You can't say you're not running when everybody else is running." That's the reason they took his captaincy away our senior year. I said, "We have to be leaders on this team. We have to lead by example." He said, "Oh, you big kiss-ass. I've been putting up with [Paterno's] s*** for four years." He was a rebel without a cause.

3. Competitive streaks. We kept things competitive on the field, which made us all great as a team. He would ask, "How many sacks you getting today?" I would say, "I'm getting two sacks." He would say, "Well, I'm getting three sacks." He said he was getting ten tackles and I would say I was getting 12. We pushed and motivated each other.

2. 1978. That was such a great year for us. We were part of a lot of firsts here. You think about 1978 and what we could have accomplished. We had the No. 1 offense and had the ball at the four-inch line [in the Sugar Bowl] and couldn't score! Matt and I ask why they didn't put us in. We could have gotten a yard. We should have never lost that game.

1. End of the Road. Everyone was looking forward to our senior year, but Matt gets hurt one week and he misses six games. I thought, "This isn't how the story is supposed to end. He's not supposed to get hurt." I end up getting hurt the next week and thought, "Well, maybe this *is* the way the story is supposed to end." He's in one bed at the Hershey Medical Center and I'm in the other, and there's a candy striper taking care of us. I thought, "It's not a bad way to end. It wasn't exactly what we wanted, but we'll both finish school with a great Penn State education. We'll be okay." We both got drafted and the rest is history.

THE BIGGEST SHOES TO FILL

One of the more unenviable tasks there can be is to be "the next guy." Replacing great players comes with extra scrutiny and comparisons to the predecessors' achievements. Some athletes were able to make the transition successfully, whereas others buckled under the weight of expectations.

10. Kelly Mazzante. When her Penn State career concluded in 2004, Mazzante was the all-time leading scorer in Lady Lion and Big Ten history.

> **Shoes filled by Jennifer Harris.** The change ultimately proved to be the start of the darkest days in Lady Lion history. Harris did contribute in her 22 starts, averaging 10.4 points per game, but the controversy about her sexual orientation and subsequent lawsuit against head coach Rene Portland, athletic director Tim Curley, and the university led to Portland "resigning" in 2007.

9. Mike Reid. In 1969 the defensive lineman was a first-team All-American, winner of the Outland Trophy and Maxwell Award, and was part of the Nittany Lions' back-to-back undefeated teams of 1968 and 1969.

> **Shoes filled by Frank Ahrenhold.** 1970 was a transition year. The Nittany Lions' 31-game unbeaten streak ended in the second game of the season with a 41–13 loss at Colorado. Penn State would finish 7–3, but the players voted to decline a bid to play in the Peach Bowl. For Ahrenhold, he would have a strong senior season in 1971, as his 107 tackles were second best on the team. The Lions would complete an 11–1 season by trouncing Texas, 30–6, in the Cotton Bowl.

8. Joe Crispin. His four-year career as a starter concluded by leading Penn State to the Sweet 16 of the 2001 NCAA Tournament and, at the time, the distinction of being the second-leading scorer in program history.

> **Shoes filled by Brandon Watkins.** The junior generated productive stats, averaging 13.3 points and 4.1 assists per game in 2002, but the team success was not there. In addition to the NCAA Tournament appearance in 2001, Crispin also led the Nittany Lions to two NIT Final Fours. In each of Watkins's two years as a starter, the Lions went 7–21.

7. Suzie McConnell. After her senior season of 1988, McConnell was the all-time career-assists leader (a record she still holds), and during her career the Lady Lions had four consecutive 20-win seasons.

Shoes filled by Dana Eikenberg. The Lady Lions were in capable hands with Eikenberg. A four-year starter, she ran the point as Penn State achieved its first-ever No. 1 ranking, won a pair of Atlantic 10 titles, and posted an 84–29 record during her career. And, like her predecessor, she led the team in assists for four consecutive years.

6. LaVar Arrington/Courtney Brown. Arrington won the Butkus Award in 1999 as the best linebacker in the country and was a two-time All-American. Brown was the force on the defensive line and set school sack and tackles for losses records.

Shoes filled by Aaron Gatten/Bob Jones. Gatten was a fifth-year senior linebacker in 2000, and Jones started two years at defensive end. Replacing two dominant All-Americans was certainly a challenge at the start of the millennium. The play of Gatten and Jones probably would have been fine if they were complementary roles surrounded by impact players, but with no impact players to be found, Penn State finished 5–7 in 2000 and 5–6 in 2001.

5. Shane Conlan. He was one of the all-time greats at "Linebacker U," whose play in the Fiesta Bowl for the 1986 national championship exemplified his career in leading Penn State to victory.

Shoes filled by Keith Karpinski. This was another transitional period that did not stand up well to the predecessor. The Nittany Lions' defense overall suffered a drop-off that played a part in an 8–4 record in Karpinski's junior season and, unfortunately, the first losing season for Penn State in 50 years, when it went 5–6 in 1988.

4. Chuck Fusina. The quarterback set a high bar for his successor. With Fusina, the Lions posted consecutive 11–1 records in 1977 and 1978. In his final season he was the runner-up to Billy Sims in the Heisman Trophy voting.

Shoes filled by Dale Tate. The Nittany Lions had a hangover from the Alabama loss in the Sugar Bowl for most of the 1979 season. Tate led Penn State to a 7–4 record, but a shoulder injury in the regular season finale against Pitt kept him from playing in the Liberty Bowl against Tulane.

3. Michael Robinson. One of the greatest leaders in Penn State history, Robinson became the full-time starting quarterback in his senior season of 2005. He led Penn State to an 11–1 record and the program's second Big Ten championship.

Shoes filled by Anthony Morelli. Although Morelli had the arm and some moments, the expected consistency for his two seasons as starter never fully materialized. Still, he is in good company in the Penn State record book. He left with 5,275 career-passing yards, placing him in fifth place in team history just behind Kerry Collins. His career-completion percentage of 56 percent is better than Todd Blackledge's 51.8 percent.

2. Jesse Arnelle. After more than 50 years since he played his last game as a Nittany Lion, Arnelle is still the greatest Penn State basketball player in school history. He had been the all-time leading scorer with 2,138 points until Talor Battle broke his record in 2011, and is still the leading rebounder in team history with 1,238 boards. Oh, by the way, he also was part of the greatest era in Penn State basketball history, with three trips to the NCAA Tournament, including the school's lone Final Four appearance in 1954 and a trip to the Sweet 16 in Arnelle's 1955 senior season.

Shoes filled by: Bob Ramsey. The 6'7" center was named the starter days prior to the season opener at North Carolina State. Penn State would finish the season 12–14, its first losing season in seven years. In Ramsey's senior season Penn State would finish 15–12.

1. John Cappelletti. When you are the school's only Heisman Trophy winner, your shoes, of course, will be difficult to fill.

Shoes filled by: Woody Petchel. Petchel technically was Cappelletti's replacement, as he was the starting tailback. However, Penn State employed a wingback in their offensive formation that season with freshman Jimmy Cefalo rushing for 328 yards on 53 carries, compared to Petchel's 294 yards on 75 carries. The top rushers on the team were fullbacks Tom Donchez and Duane Taylor. However you slice it, the sum of the parts helped the Nittany Lions go 10–2, including a 41–20 rout over Baylor in the Cotton Bowl.

And the Big One in Waiting: Joe Paterno. Paterno completed his 45th season as Penn State head coach in 2010. It is probably safe to say that no coach from any school will ever eclipse his achievement of having the most wins in Division I college football. It certainly will be an odd—and sad—sight not seeing the black shoes and his rolled up pants roaming the Beaver Stadium sidelines.

TOP ASSISTANTS UNDER JOE PATERNO

Joe Paterno has been the Nittany Lions head coach for more than 45 seasons. What makes Penn State unique is that many of his assistants have stayed in Happy Valley for so long. Some have gone other places and later returned to Paterno and Penn State. Others have had opportunities to leave for head coaching and coordinator positions, yet they opted to stay. Part of Paterno's success has been his ability to build a strong and loyal staff who have seen and done it all. Included are some who may not have served long under Paterno after he became head coach but were his peers as a Rip Engle assistant and stayed with him during the early years and rise to national prominence.

10. Booker Brooks. A 15-year assistant, Brooks, who was the program's first black assistant coach, was in charge of the wide receivers during most of the 1970s. Scott Fitzkee and Jimmy Cefalo were the primary pupils during his time on the coaching staff.

9. Earl Bruce. Bruce was part of Joe Bedenk's staff that Engle had to retain. It proved beneficial to both Engle and his successor, Joe Paterno. Bruce was in charge of the freshman squad until retiring in 1970. He and Paterno formed a strong recruiting tag team on the road in the 1950s. In their book *Joe Paterno: Football My Way*, Mervin Hyman and Gordon White described Paterno as having a knack for "buddying" up to a recruit while Bruce provided the "fatherly" influence.

8. Bob Phillips. Paterno's first appointment to his very first staff, Phillips was on board from the 5–5 1966 season to being in Tempe for the Lions' second national championship. He was in charge of the quarterbacks, developing John Hufnagel and Chuck Fusina into All-Americans and Todd Blackledge into an award-winning signal caller.

7. Jim O'Hara. A holdover from Engle's staff, O'Hara came to Penn State the same year as Paterno in 1950. Bachelor Paterno lived with O'Hara and his wife for 11 years before his 1962 marriage. O'Hara was the defensive coordinator for the 1968, 1969, and 1973 perfect-season teams.

6. Jay Paterno. At times the younger Paterno has been a polarizing figure in Nittany Nation. When Penn State's offense, along with the rest of the team, struggled at the beginning of the millennium, the head coach's son was an easy target in assigning blame. However, JayPa also must be given credit for developing two award-winning quarterbacks in Michael Robinson and Daryll Clark.

Whereas head coach Paterno almost proudly admits that he does not know how to use e-mail, assistant coach Jay Paterno is on the cutting edge of technology, including the use of college football video games to help his players better understand the playbook.

5. Larry Johnson. Many Penn State fans breathed a huge sigh of relief when Johnson turned down the offer to be Illinois's defensive coordinator in 2009 and remain in Happy Valley. He not only has produced some of the school's best defensive lines, but he also is one the staff's best recruiters, handling South/Central Pennsylvania; Maryland; Washington, DC; and Virginia. If you liked Derrick Williams, Navorro Bowman, and Aaron Maybin, you have Larry Johnson to thank.

4. Dick Anderson. Over 30 years on the Penn State staff sandwiched around a stint as Rutgers head coach, Anderson has been in charge of the offensive line during most of that time. He also served as quarterbacks coach from 1993 to 1999, including during Kerry Collins's record-breaking 1994 season.

3. Fran Ganter. An assistant for more than 30 years, Ganter was the longtime offensive coordinator and, at one time, thought to be Paterno's successor. He was named Athlon's Assistant Coach of the Year in 1994 as he mapped out the record-setting Nittany Lion offense.

2. Tom Bradley. Another coach with more than 30 years on the Nittany Lions staff, Bradley was elevated to defensive coordinator in 2000 and has helped keep this unit as one of the best in the nation. Prior to the 2010 season, the Lions had a top-15 total and scoring defense for six consecutive seasons.

1. Jerry Sandusky. He was the linebackers coach for most of the 1970s and became defensive coordinator in 1977. During that time the "Linebacker U" moniker became a calling card for the Nittany Lion defense. His defensive game plans led to the Lions' two national-title victories—the victory over No. 1 Georgia and Heisman-winner Herschel Walker in the 1983 Sugar Bowl and, of course, the upset win over No. 1 Miami and Heisman-winner Vinny Testaverde in the 1987 Fiesta Bowl. In 1991 he backed off from the offer to be Maryland's head coach. Many Penn State followers thought that he would succeed Paterno, but it was Sandusky who retired first following the 1999 Alamo Bowl.

TOP REASONS THAT EXPLAIN PENN STATE'S FOOTBALL SUCCESS :: BY JIM CALDWELL

Jim Caldwell became only the fifth first-year NFL head coach to take a team to the Super Bowl when he accomplished the feat with the 2009 Indianapolis Colts. Prior to becoming the headman in Indy, he was a longtime assistant for Tony Dungy, first in Tampa Bay and then with the Colts. Before the NFL, Caldwell was the head coach at Wake Forest from 1993 to 2000, and in 1999 he led the Demon Deacons to only their third bowl win in school history. The success he earned at Wake and in the NFL does have some roots in Happy Valley. Caldwell joined Joe Paterno's staff in 1986. He was the wide receiver coach during that championship season and eventually became quarterbacks coach before taking the job at Wake. Here are Caldwell's reflections as to why Penn State football continues to have success.

6. Fan commitment. The game-day ride to Beaver Stadium is one of my lasting memories. Heading up from the locker room on the blue buses and seeing what seemed like miles and miles of RVs started to create a buzz of excitement. When the buses made the final turn, we could see fans on both sides of the road, with that buzz rising to a crescendo of enthusiasm that demonstrated how united everyone was around Penn State football.

5. Toughness. Joe Paterno has both mental and physical toughness. Though few can doubt his mental toughness, an example of his physical toughness occurred one time in practice. Joe would like to stand behind the linebackers and challenge both the defensive and the offensive lines by telling everyone what hole the running back was going to run through. Running back Richie Anderson came clean through the line. To avoid a linebacker, Anderson made a move and collided with Paterno, crashing his helmet into Joe's nose. Despite bleeding from his nose, Paterno would not allow the trainers to assist him, only saying, "I've been hit harder" and then returning to the drill.

4. Staying power. Many assistant coaches have long tenures on the Penn State staff. Joe creates an atmosphere in which the coaches have a sense of autonomy and are rewarded for the work they put into their roles. Also, State College is a great place to raise a family; it is such a vibrant town with great primary and secondary schools all in a unique college setting.

3. All walks of life. Joe has the ability to get along with anyone, whether it is a multimillionaire or somebody who is at a different station in life. Wherever he goes, Joe's presence commands the full attention of all those around. During Joe's recruiting visit to Leroy Thompson's home in Knoxville, Tennessee, he totally captivated the family. They could not believe how down to earth he was. Joe sat on the floor and became involved in a heated game of spades with Thompson's younger sister, and he would not leave until the game was completed.

2. Fresh and hungry. Joe was ahead of the curve in his ability to keep his team fresh and hungry. A key to the 1986 national championship was that he held almost all of the returning fifth-year seniors out of spring practice. This had two benefits: The veteran players got some needed rest, and it allowed us to strengthen the team's depth by getting the younger players more practice time and experience. By the start of fall practice, the seniors were well rested and hungry for success. We used the same strategy [in 2009] with the Colts. We have a great group of veterans, and we monitor their workload throughout the year to ensure that they are not overworked. But we work our younger players hard to develop our depth when injuries beset us.

1. Structure. The structure at Penn State is designed to win championships. Joe has the ability to crystallize, focus, and reduce things to the lowest common denominator. Penn State wins consistently because he and his staff are great teachers of the basic rudiments of football—fundamentals and techniques. He also is intense, focusing all his energies on that week's opponent, and he has little time to look ahead. Joe has a saying he likes: "Take care of the little things, and the big things will take care of themselves." We put that quote on the wall in our [Indianapolis Colts] locker room.

PENN STATERS WHO COACHED ELSEWHERE

Whether it is a former player or an assistant making their way up the coaching ranks, there have been several success stories for coaches who have their roots in Happy Valley. Here are our top ten success stories of coaches who had ties to Penn State.

10. Greg Schiano. Schiano spent six seasons on Joe Paterno's staff—1990 as a graduate assistant and from 1991 to 1995 coaching the Nittany Lions' defensive backs. Prior to the 2001 season he became head coach at Rutgers and has built up a perennial doormat program into one of the top teams in the Big East. All his hard work in New Jersey paid off in 2006 when the Scarlet Knights finished 11–2, including a win over Kansas State in the Texas Bowl (the first bowl win in school history). Rutgers finished that season ranked No. 12 in the AP poll (14 spots ahead of Penn State), and Schiano won National Coach of the Year honors.

9. John Hufnagel. Penn State's former All-American quarterback parlayed his playing career in the Canadian Football League into a successful coaching career. He was named head coach of the Calgary Stampeders prior to the 2008 season. He led Calgary to a 13–5 record as the Stampeders won the Grey Cup. Hufnagel won the 2008 CFL Coach of the Year award. The following season, he had Calgary back in the title game, but his team fell short of a repeat, losing 28–27 to Montreal.

8. Suzie McConnell-Serio. After her playing career concluded as one of the greatest players in Lady Lion basketball history, a gold medal–winning Olympian, and first-team All-WNBA team member, McConnell continued her winning ways as a head coach. At any level McConnell-Serio has proven to be a winner. During her 13 years as head coach of Oakland Catholic High School, she averaged 24 wins a season and won three state championships. She won 2004 WNBA Coach of the Year award when she guided Minnesota to a second consecutive playoff appearance. She became head coach at Duquesne University in April 2007, and in 2008–09 became the first coach in school history to lead the team to a 20-win season. She followed that with 20-win seasons in 2009–10 and 2010–2011.

7. Ed DeChellis. This is not a typo—we are recognizing what DeChellis did for his work at East Tennessee State. When he was named the Nittany Lions' men's head basketball coach following the 2002–03 season, it marked his second stint at Penn State. During his first tour in Happy Valley he was an assistant on Bruce Parkhill's staff for nine seasons and assisted Jerry Dunn in his first year as head coach in 1995–96 before becoming head coach at East Tennessee State. DeChellis took over a last-place program and built it into a Southern Conference power, winning three division titles and the 2002–03 tournament championship, giving the team an automatic bid into the NCAA Tournament.

6. Paul Pasqualoni. A former Penn State backup linebacker (1968–71), Pasqualoni would eventually become one of the greatest head coaches in Syracuse history. During his tenure (1991–2004) he led the Orangemen to four Big East titles. He took Syracuse to nine bowl games (6–3 record), including the 1992 and 1997 Fiesta Bowls and the 1998 Orange Bowl. He had a record of 107–59–1, and his win total is the second most in school history. After several seasons as an assistant coach in the NFL, he was named head coach of the University of Connecticut's football program in January 2011.

5. Galen Hall. Another coach who has had multiple roles and stays at Penn State, the former Nittany Lion quarterback would eventually become the offensive coordinator at Oklahoma in 1966. His wishbone offense racked up yards and points for most of the 1970s. Hall would earn his first college head coaching job in 1984 when he replaced Charley Pell (who was forced out due to NCAA violations) at Florida three games into the 1984 season. Hall won all eight games he coached that year, and the Gators finished No. 3 in the AP poll but were not recognized as SEC champs and did not go to a bowl due to NCAA probation. In 1985 Hall led the Gators to a 9–1–1 record, including an SEC best 5–1 mark, but once again probation prohibited a bowl appearance and official recognition as conference champ. That season, Hall's Gators were ranked No. 1 in the AP poll that was issued on November 5, one spot ahead of his alma mater. The following week Florida lost to Georgia, and Penn State assumed the top spot for the remainder of the regular season.

4. Kerry McCoy. One of the greatest wrestlers in Nittany Lions's history, McCoy has led two schools to NCAA success as a head coach. He spent three seasons at Stanford (2005–08), taking over a team that was 6–8 the season prior to his arrival and leading the Cardinal to a 19th-place finish at the 2008 NCAA Championships, the second-highest finish in school history. Following that season McCoy returned to the East Coast as head coach at the University of Maryland. In his first season he led the Terps to the ACC championship and won ACC Coach of the Year. Maryland also tied for 10th at the NCAAs, tying the best finish in school history. In 2009–10 his Terps went 19–4, setting a team record for wins in a season.

3. George Welsh. The former Rip Engle (1963–65) and Joe Paterno (1966–72) assistant, Welsh would leave Penn State for a long head coaching career at Navy and Virginia. In nine seasons at Navy he led the Midshipman to a 55–46–1 record (31–15–1 in his final five seasons). His 1978 squad won the Holiday Bowl, 23–16, over BYU for the program's first bowl victory in 20 years. In 1982 Welsh took over at the University of Virginia, where he won two ACC championships. In 1990 he had the Cavaliers on the brink of a national championship. Virginia took over the No. 1 ranking in the AP poll on October 16 and held that ranking for two more weeks before losing to Georgia Tech. The season ended with a 23–22 loss to Tennessee in the Sugar Bowl. How important was Welsh to UVA football? Prior to his arrival in Charlottesville, the Cavaliers had never been to a bowl game. They went to 12 during Welsh's 19 seasons as head coach.

2. Brian Hill. Hill was an assistant on Bruce Parkhill's first three Penn State basketball teams (1983–86). He started his NBA coaching career in 1986 as an assistant for Mike Fratello in Atlanta. He became head coach of the Orlando Magic in 1993. During his three-plus years in Orlando he guided the Magic to a 191–104 record. His tenure with the Magic included back-to-back Atlantic Division titles, two consecutive Eastern Conference Finals appearances, and the 1995 Eastern Conference championship, which led to the franchise's first appearance in the NBA Finals. He is the ninth-fastest coach in NBA history to 100 victories (achieving the mark in game 149).

1. Jim Caldwell. Caldwell joined Joe Paterno's staff in 1986 as the wide receiver coach, and he later transitioned to quarterback coach. Following the 1992 season he was named the head coach at Wake Forest. He led the Demon Deacons to a 23–3 win over Arizona State in the 1999 Aloha Bowl, only the third bowl victory in school history. He became an NFL assistant coach in 2001 with the Tampa Bay Buccaneers and head coach Tony Dungy. He followed Dungy to Indianapolis in 2002, and when Dungy resigned after the 2008 season, Caldwell was elevated to head coach. In his first year the Colts went 14–2, winning their second AFC Championship since moving to Indianapolis. Caldwell became the fifth rookie head coach to take a team to the Super Bowl.

OUR FAVORITE COLLEGE FOOTBALL ANNOUNCERS

They are the added ingredients that make watching or listening to college football fun. The announcers provide opinion, insight, and humor to the television or radio broadcasts. They are the people who you can't wait to hear what they will say next. Whether watching from the comfort of your home, enjoying the tailgate atmosphere in a stadium parking lot with a satellite dish mounted to the top of an RV, or listening on your headphones to the radio call while watching from inside the stadium, the announcers and analysts play an important and entertaining role in the game-day experience.

7. Kirk Herbstreit. Speaking of *Gameday*, Herbstreit has been an analyst on ESPN's "must see TV" college football preshow since 1996. Along with his ability to throw a subtle zinger to cohost Lee Corso, we appreciate how "Herby" is able to explain the things he sees on game film that are the reasons for a team's success. He added to his responsibilities in 2006, giving himself an extremely busy Saturday. He still cohosts *College Gameday*, and now he also is the color analyst for ABC's primetime college game. Several times a season the locations for the two shows *are not* in the same place, meaning Herbstreit must get to a jet following the ESPN show and fly to the site of the ABC game. It was Herbstreit who, in 2005, stated that Penn State had the best student section in the country. That one line led the school's continuing marketing campaign proclaiming Penn State football at Beaver Stadium to be "The Greatest Show in College Football." For that alone, Herbstreit earns a spot on this list.

6. Beano Cook. He is one of the greatest college football historians who has a knack for instantly recalling specific details about games and events that took place decades ago (even before Joe Paterno took a low-paying assistant coach position at Penn State). A former sports information director at Pitt, Cook first came to national prominence in 1982 when he became the lead analyst on ABC's college football studio show. Four years later he joined ESPN. Prior to the 1987 Fiesta Bowl game that had Penn State against Miami for the national title, Cook was one of the few in the national media who successfully predicted that double-digit underdog Penn State would defeat the Hurricanes. He still maintains that Penn State should have been awarded the 1994 national championship, just as he can make a strong case in defense of Texas winning the 1969 title (despite the Nittany Lions' second consecutive perfect season). Some of the best of Cook can now be found during his weekly online ESPN.com chats. Some fans chatting online have even offered Cook tickets.

Not only does Cook give great insight into current college football topics, he also offers his opinion on his beloved Pirates and another favorite subject of his, the USC Song Girls.

5. Brent Musburger. In the 1970s he was the host of the iconic *NFL Today* on CBS. He was CBS's lead announcer for the NBA and college basketball, and is credited with coining the term "March Madness." No matter what the sporting event, when you hear Musburger's long-running opening catch phrase, "You are looking live at . . . ," you get the feeling the contest about to take place might be just a little extra special. Since 1990 he has announced college football games for both ABC and ESPN. He narrated the opening montage featuring Joe Paterno that aired prior to the 2008 Penn State–Ohio State game, which was replayed multiple times during the remainder of that season. His in-game interview with Paterno during the national broadcast of the 2010 Blue-White Game, which concluded Penn State's spring football practice, gave great insight into the upcoming season and the revelation that for many years Penn State has asked several SEC schools to be part of a series of scheduled games—all but Alabama rejected those offers by refusing to play a road game in Beaver Stadium. I guess that puts a chink in the SEC superiority armor.

4. Chris Fowler. The host of ESPN's *College Gameday*, Fowler occasionally will serve up a reminder that he has ties to Penn State. His father was a faculty member at State during the 1970s, and Fowler will reference those times by recalling a specific game he attended at Beaver Stadium or showing a picture from his childhood of himself decked out in Penn State gear. He is great at controlling all the moving parts of the two-hour live show, which, by the way, is on location each week and not in a comfortable studio setting. When one of those weeks involves a return trip to the Happy Valley, he has the opportunity to renew acquaintances with Joe Paterno. "I really value the time I get to spend with Joe," he said. "My dad knew him when he as a faculty member. Penn State football meant a lot to me."

3. Keith Jackson. If you mention the phrase "Whoa Nellie!" to any college football fan over the age of 35, it won't take long before the name Keith Jackson is linked to those words. As lead television announcer on ABC, Jackson was the national voice of college football during the 1970s and through most of the 1990s. The little quirky phrases intertwined with his strong play-by-play description are what made him a fan favorite. He provided the television soundtrack to so many great Penn State games during the seventies and early eighties. He was the man behind the mic calling the Nittany Lions' 1982 national championship victory in the Sugar Bowl over Georgia.

2. Fran Fisher. *The* voice of Penn State football. Fisher had two stints as a member of the Nittany Lions radio broadcast crew. He joined the network in 1966 (Joe Paterno's first season as head coach) and in 1970 was named play-by-play announcer. He witnessed the Lions rise from disrespected regional power to one of the country's elite football programs. In addition to calling the action on game day, Fisher hosted the weekly show *Joe Paterno's TV Quarterbacks* for 18 years. The show ran on PBS stations across Pennsylvania. When he counted down the clock of the Sugar Bowl against Georgia, Fisher boomed into the microphone, "Penn State's National Champions! Penn State's the National Champions! What a tribute to this team, what a tribute to its coach!"—that was supposed to be his last game on the radio network, as he retired after that season. However, he remained a strong ambassador for Penn State, and when the play-by-play position opened after the 1993 season, he was asked to return and describe the action of the new conference Penn State had recently joined. He picked up where he left off and lent his voice to the 1994 team that won the school's first Big Ten title. In 1999 he retired for good, and his final game that year ended with another Nittany Lion bowl win (24–0 over Texas A&M in the Alamo Bowl).

1. Steve Jones. Personal note from Matt Pencek: I had the opportunity to work for Jones as an intern for two years. I was able to see firsthand on a daily basis the amount of preparation he puts into each broadcast. Back in the day, prior to the Internet, Jones would calculate specific statistics he liked to use in his broadcasts. My favorite was "basketball free-throw percentage in the final four minutes of close games." Although that may seem like a lot to spit out, it did provide another layer to how players performed in clutch situations. He would manually calculate this stat via the printed play-by-play sheets of each game that the statisticians provided. Even though he had multiple responsibilities, he also had time to listen to my early high school football play-by-play tapes and offer detailed feedback. This was something I did thank him for, but I probably never expressed how much that meant to me as I was trying to make my way in the broadcast field. So yes, I do have a bias on this one, but for those who have listened to Jones announce more than 25 years of Nittany Lions' basketball and serve as the lead announcer for football games since 2000, you know the guy does call a great game. He has a sense for adding that one little phrase at the end of a call that usually makes it bound for ESPN *SportsCenter*—"2K for LJ," highlighting the run in which Larry Johnson surpassed the 2,000 rushing-yard mark in 2002, being a good example. Like his predecessor, Fisher, Jones also is a recognizable ambassador for the school.

... AND THOSE ANNOUNCERS WE DON'T LIKE

Whether it is a body of work or just one game, these are the broadcasters who run the gamut of being a minor annoyance to having us turn down the TV volume and turn up Steve Jones and Jack Ham on the radio.

5. Jimmy Cefalo. So how does a former Nittany Lion great, somebody who hosted the commercial version of *TV Quarterbacks* in 1985, someone who has done many great things for the university and charities across Pennsylvania get on a list of negativity? One game—and unfortunately for Jimmy it just so happened to be "The Game of the Century." Cefalo was a color commentator on NBC's broadcast of the Fiesta Bowl National Championship Game against Miami, played on January 2, 1987. Perhaps if it was not a game of great significance, then Cefalo's transgressions would have been forgiven and forgotten. However, this is a game that many a Penn State fan has either in their DVD or VCR tape collection, and it is replayed at least once a year on ESPN Classic. It was almost comical how Cefalo would praise Hurricane quarterback Vinny Testaverde's arm strength on passes that would end up being Penn State interceptions. He celebrated the boorish behavior of Miami's Jerome Brown. But the biggest flaw on his part in the broadcast occurred seconds after Joe Paterno was thrust on the shoulders of his players as the Nittany Lions won the title. Before one congratulatory word for Penn State, Cefalo was droning on and on and on and on about the wonderful season Miami had in 1986. He had to be interrupted from this diatribe by fellow commentator Bob Griese, who chimed in and reminded everyone that Penn State was the team that won the game. Jimmy, you seem like a good guy, but for your commentary in the signature game in Penn State history, we have to throw a penalty flag on you for this one.

4. Mike Tirico. You would think that with all the good that Joe Paterno has done for the university and college football that he would be given the benefit of the doubt in certain situations. Not so with Syracuse grad and ESPN announcer Mike Tirico. Let's go back to the night of September 23, 1995 in the New Jersey swamplands of Giants Stadium. With Penn State leading Rutgers 52–34 late in the fourth quarter, Paterno called a pass play intended to be a hit over the middle to the tight end. As he began to drop back, backup quarterback Mike McQueary saw wide receiver Chris Campbell break open. Instead of going for the short pass, McQueary launched a bomb that Campbell hauled in for a 42-yard score with 58 seconds remaining. Rutgers coach Doug Graber thought Paterno was running up the score, and so did Tirico. The ESPN announcer blasted Penn State and stated he would never let his kid play for Joe Paterno because of this injustice to sportsmanship. The only thing Paterno was guilty of was attempting to give his backup QB some experience in a game. Maybe it was Paterno's domination of his alma mater over the years that had Tirico's ire on this night. But whatever the case, if your kid is not allowed to play for a coach who values academics and prides himself on running a program with class, I guess the kid could always play for Jackie Sherrill.

3. Craig James. Several times during his broadcast career, James has made snide little comments about Penn State. He apparently does not like Penn State—several people in the media don't like Penn State, just as one or two authors of this book don't like Pitt. But what happened on November 6, 2006, definitely crossed a line into extreme bad taste and bad announcing. Penn State was in Madison, Wisconsin, and Badger head coach Bret Bielema used the rules at the time to his advantage by having his team intentionally onside kick short of the required ten yards multiple times so as to run the remaining seconds off the clock and deny Penn State the opportunity to attempt one more drive before halftime. After a few choice words for the officials, Joe Paterno trotted to his team's locker room. As studio analyst for ABC's coverage, James described the scene this way for the viewing audience: "JoePa goes in at halftime, and I mean the camera crew is following him, and JoePa's Geritol that he had too much of this morning kicks in. Must have, must have had some bad beans in his soup last night. Man, JoePa's fired up ready to get after him. Way to go, Coach Bielema, give it to the old fart." A fist pump and a smile accentuated this comment. This also was the game when Paterno injured his leg when he was unable to avoid a sideline collision. James, who was forced to apologize on air later in the evening, said, "I continue to be a big fan of this guy for all these years." That did not fly with Penn State communications director Guido D'Elia. "Craig James has always had a problem with Penn State," D'Elia said. "He's never been neutral when it comes to Penn State. It's insulting for him to spin that on our fans that he's always liked Penn State and Coach." This is just another chapter for James in a book that is lowlighted by being part of the SMU team that received payments from boosters that eventually forced the NCAA to impose the "Death Penalty" on the school.

2. Lee Corso. For whatever reason, Corso seems to relish the subtle shots he directs at Penn State. He loves to deal in generalities. Like in 1994 prior to the Michigan game, Corso predicted the Wolverines would win because Penn State had not played anybody all year. In fact, the Nittany Lions had routed 14th-ranked USC, 38–14, in the second game that season. The Trojans would end the season ranked 13th. When Penn State was set to meet Tennessee in the

Outback Bowl concluding the 2006 season, Corso said Tennessee's southern speed would be too much for too slow Penn State. Now one thing you can't say about the 2006 Nittany Lions was that they were slow, especially with the likes of Derrick Williams and Justin King. Corso had that one wrong as well. At the 2005 Penn State–Ohio State game, at that time a rare visit to Beaver Stadium from the *Gameday* crew, Corso donned the Brutus Buckeye mascot head for his traditional end-of-broadcast pick, much to the disappointment of the crowd on hand. There are many more instances like this that could easily fill multiple pages. Although there's nothing outrageous like the James incident with Corso, he is the guy we like to hate. I think he enjoys that role. He does it with humor, and I think maybe, just maybe, it is part shtick, unlike . . .

1. Mark May. May is a bitter, bitter, bitter former Pitt Panther. Basically take everything said about Corso, delete the humor and shtick stuff, and you have ESPN analyst Mark May. Penn State's schedule has been a favorite target of May's, and with the teams Penn State plays, it is difficult to defend. However, it's not like Penn State has had to stoop to playing MAC teams on the road like Pitt agreed to do in 2005, losing at Ohio, 16–10, in two overtimes. And the Nittany Lions do not have the embarrassment of playing in the weakest of the BCS conferences. Normally the highlight of any May tirade is that his co-analyst, Lou Holtz, usually has a good one-liner that puts him in his place.

AN ALL-AMERICAN EDUCATION

When one attends college, you know you'll be taking classes that will help you in your future career. But going to college also means a chance to take courses that will expand your knowledge in subject matters that have nothing to do with your major. And Penn State, like most schools, offers some interesting courses to attend.

10. AN SC 215 (Animal Science 215)—Pets in Society. "Introduction to the varied roles that companion animals play in human society and their impact on human activity and well-being." Can a Nittany Lion be considered a "companion animal"?

9. HRIM 311 (Hotel, Restaurant, and Institutional Management 311)—Wine Appreciation. "I am not drinking any *$@!(@&# Merlot!"

8. HIST 113 (History 113)—Baseball in Comparative History. For a final exam, find out if there's a way Roger Maris and Hank Aaron can have their home run records back.

7. ANTH 478 (Anthropology 478)—Cannibalism. "Explores the cultural institution of cannibalism, uses of the 'cannibal' label, and cannibalism's meaning among those who practiced it." As a side effect, taking this class could turn you into a vegetarian.

6. FRNSC 201W (Forensic Science 201W)—Principles of Crime Scene Investigation. In case you were wondering, neither Marg Helgenberger, David Caruso, nor Emily Procter are guest lecturers.

5. INART 200 (Integrative Arts 200)—The Popular Arts in America: Elvis Presley—The King of Rock and Roll. If you take this around lunchtime, bring a peanut butter-and-banana sandwich for the professor.

4. E SC 123S (Engineering Science 123S)—Catastrophic Failures. This course actually explores "design deficiencies through the study of case histories of a number of famous failures." In Ann Arbor they call it the Rich Rodriguez Era.

3. PPATH 120 (Plant Pathology 120)—The Fungal Jungle: A Mycological Safari from Truffles to Slime Molds. You probably don't want to make this your 8 a.m. class after a night out at the bars.

2. FOR 497D (Forestry 497D)—Chainsaw Safety, Maintenance, and Operation for Timber. If Stanford ever pays a visit to Penn State with its Tree mascot, things could get ugly.

1. COMM 498E (Communications 498E)—Big Ten Network. For the final exam, create alternate endings for the 2005 Michigan and 2008 Iowa games.

TRADITIONS NO MORE :: BY LEE STOUT

Whereas Penn State has maintained many traditions over the years, some items also have faded away. Penn State's retired historian and Librarian Emeritus, Special Collections, Lee Stout ranks the top ten things you don't see happening at Penn State anymore.

10. I have to get back to my dining hall. A dramatic change made possible by the Internet as well as student food preferences is the revolution in the "board" part of "room and board." In days gone by, students who lived in dormitories on campus were assigned to a dining hall in the union building of their dorm complex. The meal plan was simple: You paid for 21 meals a week, and it was up to you if you ate them or not. But class schedules notwithstanding, the only place your meal ticket was accepted was in your assigned dining hall. If you had a third-period class in Reber Building and you ate in Findlay in East Halls, get ready to hustle back if you wanted lunch. The "snack bars" in union buildings were usually only open in the evening, so the only place you could grab lunch on campus was the HUB, but it was cash on the barrelhead. Of course, you could go downtown to eat, but there, too, you were paying the check for a meal your parents had already covered in the payment for your room and board. Today, with Lion Cash and meal-plan points, students can eat almost anywhere, on or off campus, whenever they want.

9. Arena registration. Another relic of the pre-Internet era was "arena registration." It required two to three days for all students to move through, in the earliest days, the Armory, then Rec Hall, and finally the IM Building to sign up for courses. You entered by class and alphabetical cohort, filling out various IBM punch cards and collecting more cards for the classes you wished to take if your preregistration had not delivered an acceptable schedule. Each academic department had a representative at a table on the floor, arranged around the edge of the gym in a large rectangle. Students entered this arena at predetermined times and began trading cards with the department reps for desired class sections. If you were lucky, you might emerge in a couple of hours with a reasonable schedule. If the class sections you wanted were full, however, you either settled for ones you could get into or sat and waited for someone else to drop a class card back in the hopper. You might be there for all three days if you were really determined. It could be an ordeal to say the least—students had little or no access to advisers during the process, and they were on their own to figure out a good selection of courses. As computers and network technology advanced, the entire registration process has been revamped a number of times. Today, registration is far less painful, and the results are usually much more satisfactory. Students no longer have to waste hours "on the floor" trying to put together a schedule of classes.

8. Giving your prof a postcard with your bluebook at finals—what's a "bluebook" anyway? Before the advent of computers and modern telecommunications networks, taking tests and receiving your grades at the end of the semester was a far less complex matter. In the 1960s machine-scored multiple-choice tests were a relatively new innovation on campus. Most exams were done the old-fashioned way: You hand-wrote your answers in an exam booklet. The little blue examination books could be purchased almost anywhere, in various sizes—from 8 to 24 or even 36 pages for big essay tests. Given their color, they were known almost everywhere as "bluebooks," as were the exams themselves. "I've got a bluebook tomorrow at 8 a.m." was a common complaint of coffee-swilling students "pulling all-nighters." Exams given during the term were always handed back in class, but final exams and the resulting final grades would often be a mystery until the Registrar's Office mailed out those grade reports a couple of weeks later. If you couldn't stand the anxiety, you left a self-addressed postcard clipped to your final exam bluebook, with spaces for the prof to fill in the exam grade and the final grade. When the grading was done, the prof dropped the postcards in the mail and you would find out your grades a week or so before the official report arrived. Needless to say the Internet has changed the grading process completely, and although their use is less common today, you can still buy bluebooks at bookstores.

7. Walking to class and everywhere else. The pre–World War II campus was a pretty compact affair. There were basically no buildings west of Atherton Street or east of Shortlidge Road. By the 1960s a lot had changed—South, Pollock, Nittany, and East Halls had pushed thousands of students further east, and Beaver Stadium now rose in the cow pastures beyond them. With the calendar change to terms in 1960, 75-minute periods became the rule, and for many students the walk from East Halls to Hammond, for example, was longer than anything previous generations of students had endured. The new calendar helped by providing 20-minute breaks between class periods. You could just about make it across campus in that amount of time. Why the rush? Everyone walked; riding a bicycle was just not cool and there was no bus service. If you lived in a fraternity on Hamilton Avenue, for example, your walk would be even longer and you rarely returned to the house until classes were over for the day. Students didn't need gyms or treadmills to exercise—they pounded out the miles every day on foot.

6. The isolation of campus—once you got here, you stayed here. In 1855 the closest train station was Spruce Creek, 22 miles away. By the early 1900s two trains a day stopped in Lemont for travelers from the east. Once in Lemont, you caught Harvey's Stage, which dropped you at "Co-op Corner," where the Corner Room is today. Travelers from the west arrived on one of two trains a day in Bellefonte, where you changed to the Bellefonte Central for an hour-long ride to the station on College Avenue. From there you would walk across College Avenue to Co-op Corner, the center of the village at that time. By the 1930s train service had been largely replaced by bus service. Before World War II few students had cars, and even through the 1960s most students were still not driving their own vehicles to college. Besides, the roads into State College were mostly two lanes and slow going. This isolation gave Penn State students a unique sense of camaraderie. You had to make your own fun here; there was no easy way out of "Happy Valley" for students. Interstate highways, Megabuses, and frequent air travel were still 10, 20, 30, or more years into the future for Penn Staters.

5. Fraternity and dormitory housemothers. The housemother, hostess, or chaperone, as they were variously called, inspired a level of decorum and order in a fraternity or dormitory. In women's dormitories there had always been an adult woman present to oversee the protection of the coeds. Women's physical education head Marie Haidt lived in McAllister Hall for a time, and Dean of Women Charlotte Ray lived in the Women's Building in the 1930s and 1940s, for example. When women occupied sorority houses on campus, from 1928 through the late 1940s, they had hostesses living in as chaperones. Men were under much less control. Fraternity housemothers only came to Penn State in the 1950s. A new IFC "dating code," issued in 1954, mandated that chaperones would have to be present whenever women were visiting fraternities for study dates, dinner, or parties. Although faculty, staff, parents, and older alumni could serve as chaperones at parties and socials, most fraternities hired housemothers to meet the need at other times. Generally an older widow with grown children and a college education, a housemother could work part time or live in the house full time. Their primary role was to serve as a hostess for visiting coeds, parents, and alumni; to raise the level of civilized behavior among the boys; and to keep an open door for anyone with a problem. By 1970, with the demise of in loco parentis, they had largely disappeared. As one student put it then, "I had a grandmother at home; I didn't want one at college, too."

4. Parietals—hours and signing out for women. Although colleges have always been concerned for the safety of their students, the fairly abrupt passing of in loco parentis, the idea that the college acted in the place of the parents, in the early 1970s brought many changes in colleges' relationship to students.

A major one was in how schools treated women, and Penn State was no exception. Parietal rules were literally "the regulations governing the visiting privileges of members of the opposite sex in campus dormitories" according to the dictionary. Up until about 1970 this meant all but the public areas of women's dorms were off-limits to men, and even those public areas were closed to men "after hours." Curfews were imposed on women students—by the 1960s they were supposed to be in their dorms by 11:30 p.m. Sunday through Thursday and by 1:00 a.m. on Friday and Saturday. When women left the dorm to go out in the evening, they had to sign out, indicating where they'd be and when they expected to return. Although women could attend fraternity parties and legitimate social events, going to a male student's apartment was forbidden. Many women got around this problem by signing out to the open-all-night College Diner. This all ended in 1970, when the same housing rules men had were applied to women. They could then move off campus to apartments after their freshman year. This change had an impact beyond the social life of students. The rule requiring women to live all four years in the dorm had artificially held the number of women students at the number of available beds. With the lifting of the restriction, women's enrollments began to increase dramatically. Today, more than 44,000 women are registered Penn State students, about 46 percent of the total enrollment.

3. Dressing up for class and football games. Freshman customs reinforced the tradition of men wearing ties and jackets to class. By the 1930s, photographs show, students had become a bit more casual; nonetheless, wearing a tie and jacket to class was still common. Women's rules were, if anything, stricter. Slacks for women attending class or other campus events were not common even in the early 1960s. Blue jeans were restricted to casual in-dorm wear only, except for the occasional blue jean dance. These rules for women even prohibited smoking outside the dorm or leaving with your hair in rollers. Later in the sixties classroom wear became more casual, and with the era of student activism and psychedelics, it became "anything goes." Before that, members of fraternities, in particular, could be seen attending football games and other events in suits and ties, with their dates in dresses and heels, in anticipation of postgame cocktail parties at the houses. Today, one rarely sees a tie and jacket in class, even on a professor, and Coach Paterno may be one of the few people still wearing a tie to a football game.

2. Freshman customs—dinks and all that. Perhaps the earliest custom was the prohibition of freshmen from using the front door of Old Main, which was reserved for the use of the president and the faculty, whose offices in the original Old Main flanked it. The first freshman customs rules appeared in the student handbook in 1904, and the No. 1 rule was to always salute the president. Dinks, the famous green beanies, came along in 1907. Freshmen were required to wear a black tie and buttoned coats. They wore a nametag for the first two weeks, had to speak to all other freshmen, know the songs and yells, and attend all class meetings. They were forbidden to cross Old Main lawn, walk on any grass, or sit on the wall along College Avenue. They were not permitted to use tobacco, associate with women except for house parties and recognized dances, or grow facial hair. They were always to carry a match for an upperclassman's smoke and give way to upperclassmen. Violators faced a student tribunal and maybe a "molasses feed" for the most egregious malefactors. Customs largely disappeared during and after World War II, but they were revived in 1950. By the mid-1960s, however, they were a relic of the past.

1. Class scraps. New students had always been hazed by their elders in one way or another. Beginning in the 1880s and lasting for about 30 years, Penn State entered the "scrap era." These battles between the freshman and sophomore classes were common at American colleges and probably dated back to the eighteenth century. Initially, there was the flag scrap, the cider scrap, the class-supper scrap, the picture scrap, and the poster scrap; later there was the pushball scrap, tie-up scrap, tug-of-war, and a few others. Typically, these were spontaneous events with the freshmen trying, for example, to sneak off campus for a class dinner or class picture and the sophomores doing their best to stop them. Faculty had to put up with the sudden disruptions of class, but most had lived through them in their own undergraduate years and, thus, understood and tolerated the passion. As Penn State grew, however, the numbers of students participating reached dangerous levels. Some fractures and contusions were common, but in 1907 a student died in a scrap. They soon faded away, replaced by the gentler regimen of freshman customs.

TOP PITTSBURGH VS. PHILADELPHIA MOMENTS :: BY JEFF BYERS

Besides being the voice of Penn State wrestling, Jeff Byers is a die-hard fan of everything Pittsburgh—well, except for the Pitt Panthers, of course. From Pirates to Steelers to Penguins, the man nicknamed "Ironhead" loves the *Steel* City. Here are his top Pittsburgh sports moments when a team from the 'Burgh took on one of those hated cross-state teams from the City of Brotherly Love.

5. Start of something good. In 1989 the Penguins and Flyers squared off in the postseason against each other for the first time. State College felt like it was in a civil war for this electrifying series as banners for each team were hanging from seemingly every apartment building while students donned jerseys. Even though the Pens ultimately lost the series that was for the Patrick Division Final, that series established Pittsburgh as a legitimate contender and laid the groundwork for its Stanley Cup championships in 1991 and 1992. The signature win for the Pens came in Game 3, a 4–3 victory in overtime.

4. On the air. History was made in a Pirates victory over the Phillies. In 1921 the beloved Buccos downed Philadelphia, 8–5, at Forbes Field. It was the first time ever that a radio audience heard baseball on a commercial radio station. Harold Arlin called the action on KDKA, and the romance of broadcasting and baseball—and of Pittsburgh beating Philadelphia—was born.

3. The dynasty begins. In 1974 the Steelers were still searching for their first Super Bowl ring (they now have six, which is exactly six more than the Eagles have). The key to launching them to that first Super Bowl victory later that season was undoubtedly the 27–0 victory over their cross-state rivals. Well, it may not have been key, but it sure was fun. The Steelers' defense dominated the game with Mel Blount's 52-yard interception return for a touchdown, putting the exclamation point on a long afternoon for the Eagles. The loss is one, it could be argued, from which the Eagles franchise has never recovered. (I'm not saying it's a good or strong argument, but it's one that could be made nonetheless.)

2. January 18, 2009. Although Pittsburgh and Philadelphia did not meet that day, Steelers fans reveled in the results of the conference championship games. Only because of the Eagles' ineptitude (again) to win in the NFC title game, Pittsburgh fans were denied a chance to prove their team's supremacy on the ultimate sporting stage. Instead, Pittsburgh fans had to settle for watching their team beat the rival Ravens while the Eagles handed the Cardinals the NFC bid to the Super Bowl. The Steelers, of course, went on to defeat the Cardinals for a sixth Super Bowl title—did we mention that is six more than the Eagles have?

1. On their way to another Cup. Because sports fans are largely a "what have you done lately" crowd, I'm putting the most recent postseason clash at the top of the list. In 2009 the Penguins came back from a 3–0 deficit to beat the Flyers, 5–3, to win Game 6, and to clinch the opening-round playoff series en route to the Stanley Cup. Making the Eastern Conference quarterfinal win all the more satisfying was that Sidney Crosby sliced the Flyers' defense during the series for four goals and four assists, which especially irritated Philadelphia fans. Penguins' fans rejoiced, as it set the tone for a great playoff run that ended with the Cup coming back to its Pittsburgh home.

TOP PHILADELPHIA VS. PITTSBURGH MOMENTS :: BY SCOTT HENRY

State College is almost perfectly placed between Philadelphia and Pittsburgh, so whenever the professional teams from those two cities play each other, especially if it's a playoff game, the campus becomes divided. Forget "We Are . . . Penn State"—this is Philly Fans vs. 'Burgh Fans.

Scott Henry, who graduated from Penn State in 1991, grew up in the Lehigh Valley, just a little north of Philly. He is cofounder of Orange Lion Productions, which he started after working for more than six years at ESPN. During his 20-year career, he has won five Emmy Awards and a Peabody Award for his work in nonfiction programming. Here are his top five moments that caused the Philly faithful to celebrate on College or Beaver Avenue.

5. September 30, 1978—Phillies 10, Pirates 8. Phils' hurler Randy Lerch hit two home runs as the Phillies clinched their third consecutive division crown over the rival Bucs on the second to last day of the season.

4. November 12, 2000—Eagles 26, Steelers 23 (OT). Down 23–13 with less than four minutes left on the road, Donovan McNabb led the Eagles down the field twice for a TD and then a tying field goal at the end of regulation. The Birds won the coin toss in overtime, and McNabb drove them down again, setting up David Akers for the winning field goal attempt. It resulted in a high-decibel, "It's goooooooooooooood!" call from longtime Eagles' play-by-play voice Merrill Reese.

3. April 29, 1989—Flyers 4, Penguins 1. We watched Game 7 of the Patrick Division Final in the living rooms of our Beaver Avenue apartments, but the real action was the taunting on the balconies after every big play. Flyers' backup goalie Ken Wregget—who didn't know until the morning of the game that he would start—made 39 saves to end the Penguins' season.

2. April 18, 1987—Mike Schmidt 500th HR at Pittsburgh. Schmidty not only hits his 500th career home run but also the three-run blast off of Don Robinson came with two outs in the top of the ninth and the Phillies trailing 6–5. The homer gave Philly an 8–6 win. I unfortunately listened to it on the Pirates' radio broadcast; only later did I see the highlight and hear the still famous "Michael Jack Schmidt" call from Harry Kalas.

1. May 4–5, 2000—Flyers 2, Penguins 1 (5 OTs). Who was still awake? Actually just about everyone in Happy Valley (it is college, after all). Keith Primeau scored at 12:01 of the fifth OT of Game 4 of the Eastern Conference Semifinals, sparking delirious celebration and an eventual Flyers series win in six games.

Honorable Mention: June 8, 1989—Phillies 15, Pirates 11. The Pirates jumped out to a 10–0 first-inning lead in Philadelphia, causing Pirates announcer Jim Rooker to say, "If the Pirates lose this game, I'll walk home." Months after the 15–11 *Phillies* victory, Rooker paid up—walking from Philadelphia to Pittsburgh in 13 days for charity.

TOP TEN PENN STATE-PITT GAMES

They used to play every year, but now it looks like it will be years, if ever, that the great Keystone State Cat Fight resumes. Now, Penn State doesn't even have their season-ending pretend rivalry with Michigan State anymore thanks to Big Ten expansion. The Lions used to have a *real* rivalry at the conclusion of the year when it would battle the Pitt Panthers. With any good rivalry, there has to be some animosity, such as Pitt refusing to play at Penn State, resulting in 28 consecutive games played in the Pittsburgh from 1903 to 1930. Fights, accusations of recruiting shenanigans, and, for a glorious period from 1976 to 1986, having a direct impact on the national championship almost every year highlighted (or lowlighted, depending on your perspective) the rivalry.

10. Kissing one extremely ugly Western Pennsylvania sister—November 19, 1983. The 1983 season was one of disappointment for Penn State. As defending national champions, the Nittany Lions started the year 0–3, including an embarrassing 14–3 loss to lowly Cincinnati. They did rebound, winning six of their next seven heading into the game at Pitt Stadium. For the Panthers, it was a solid first ten games. With Dan Marino's departure to the NFL, Pitt responded with an 8–2 record and No. 17 ranking in the nation. This game was one wild and entertaining contest, with plenty of offense and five lead changes. However, the ending had a little bit of controversy sprinkled in with a feeling of dissatisfaction for both sides. With just over one minute remaining, Penn State led 21–17 when Pitt quarterback John Congemi hit wide receiver Bill Wallace on a 23-yard touchdown pass. The extra-point made it Pitt 24, Penn State 21. Lion quarterback Doug Strang quickly drove his team to the Panther 40-yard line. On third-and-16, Pitt jumped offsides, but the clock mistakenly continued to roll for another six seconds while play was stopped. "The official came over to me and said the clock is wrong," Penn State coach Joe Paterno said, "so it's a dead-ball foul and there should be six more seconds on the clock. They couldn't move the clock up to 19 seconds." The officials decided to keep the time on the field due to the inability to correct the scoreboard clock. Later on the drive, running back D.J. Dozier gained four yards to the Pitt 19—the clock on the scoreboard showed 00:00 and the Panther fans were chanting "Goal posts! Goal posts!" thinking the game was over and victory secured. To the shock of Pitt fans, Penn State kicker Nick Gancitano trotted onto the field, thanks to those extra seconds of time on the officials' clock, and kicked a field goal that made the final score 24–24. It was one of the rare times that Paterno opted for a game-ending tie instead of calling a play in an attempt to win the game.

9. Turkey Day muck—November 27, 1919. The Penn State-Pitt game played Thanksgiving Day 1919 took place at Pittsburgh's Forbes Field. "Field" is being too kind to describe the conditions because this one was played in what was basically a quagmire of mud. However, the conditions did not hamper the Nittany Lions. They opened the scoring on what was considered to be at the time one of the greatest plays in Penn State history. The Lions appeared to be in punt formation deep in their own territory. Pitt had a ten-man rush in an attempt to block the kick, but punter Harold Hess avoided the Panthers and flipped a short pass to Bob Higgins, who ran untouched down the right sideline for a 92-yard score. The play set a record for longest pass play in Nittany Lion history that still stands today. Pitt's offense didn't muster much of a challenge, as Penn State won, 20–0, to snap a six-game losing streak to the Panthers.

8. Another LaVar leap—September 11, 1999. After a brief interruption of the series, Pitt returned to the Penn State schedule in 1997, the start of a four-game arrangement. Penn State won the first two matchups, which were played in September instead of late November. In 1999 the Lions were ranked No. 2 in the nation, with wins over Arizona and Akron. Pitt would be on its way to an unremarkable 5–6 season, but on this day it challenged Penn State all game long in a contest that perhaps foreshadowed the Nittany Lions' late-season collapse. The game was tied 10–10 early in the fourth quarter, when Penn State running back Eric McCoo rushed seven yards for the go-ahead score. Pitt would not go away and tied the game with 4:34 remaining, as quarterback John Turman hit receiver Julius Dixon on a 42-yard touchdown pass. The Lions would regain the lead, 20–17, on a field goal, when the Panthers began their final drive. There were plenty of nervous fans in Beaver Stadium as Pitt moved inside Penn State territory and then continued the drive to the 25-yard line. Perhaps Pitt coach Walt Harris became a little greedy as he called for another pass play and it didn't work out well. David Fleischhauer sacked Turman for a ten-yard loss. Now with time for only one more play, Pitt kicker Nick Lotz faced a 52-yard attempt instead of an easier 42-yarder. Needing to dial up some extra distance, Lotz had to kick more of a line drive, and this played into Penn State linebacker LaVar Arrington's strength. The year before, against Illinois, Arrington made all the highlight replays in the country with his vault over the Illini offensive line to deny running back Elmer Hickman on a fourth-and-1 play. Arrington used his "Jordanesque" abilities again and blocked Lotz's try. The win did not impress the voters, however, as they dropped Penn State to No. 3 in the AP poll that week.

7. Tisen Thomas to the rescue—November 24, 1990. With the continuous part of the series nearing an end (each team would have one more home game), Penn State entered the regular season finale on a roll. After dropping their first two games (Texas and USC), the Nittany Lions had won eight in a row, including a thrilling 24–21 upset win over No. 1–ranked Notre Dame the week before in South Bend. Pitt was in the pits, sporting a poor 3–6–1 mark. However, the Panthers did not play like a losing team on this late Saturday afternoon. Using some trickery, Pitt took a 17–16 fourth-quarter lead when wide receiver Darnell Dickerson caught the ball behind the line of scrimmage and, on the option pass, hit Olanda Truitt for a 63-yard touchdown. Penn State had allowed Pitt to hang around all game long and now trailed for the first time in the contest. However, Pitt's momentum and lead did not last long. On the following kickoff Nittany Lion returner Tisen Thomas took off for 59 yards, bringing the ball to the Pitt 35. Quarterback Tony Sacca would later hit David Daniels on a screen pass that resulted in a 16-yard touchdown and the final score of a 22–17 Penn State win.

6. Redemption for Ray Tarasi—November 25, 1989. This game lacked offense but not high drama. For the third week in a row Joe Paterno was quick with the hook at quarterback, replacing ineffective Tony Sacca with Tom Bill in the second quarter. Bill was in "game manager" mode, leading the Nittany Lions to a 13–10 advantage. The lead looked safe with less than six minutes to play, and the Panthers having the ball at their own 14. That's when things became interesting. The Panthers quickly dug out of that hole when quarterback Alex Van Pelt hit Henry Tuten on a 54-yard pass. A few plays later, on first-and-10 from the Lions' 14, running back Adam Walker went off tackle and into the end zone for an apparent touchdown. The smack talk the Pitt fans on the sidelines gave to the Penn State players would go for naught, as the play was called back on a holding call. Pitt had to settle for a tying field goal. Now with the ball late in the fourth quarter, in probably the finest performance of his limited Penn State career, Bill converted two third-and-10 plays with passes to David Daniels and later to Leroy Thompson. Bill drove the Lions to the Pitt 32. Penn State ran twice for 12 yards and, in so doing, ran time off the clock. JoePa called a timeout with 17 seconds remaining and sent out Pittsburgh-area native kicker Ray Tarasi. Four weeks earlier Tarasi missed a game-winning 18-yard field goal in a 17–16 loss to Alabama. The season before against Pitt, Tarasi missed one field goal, had another blocked, and was benched in favor of Henry Adkins for a key fourth-quarter try in a 14–7 loss. This time, however, Tarasi was perfect on his attempt, his third field goal of the day, and the Lions had a 16–13 victory.

5. Extra! Extra!—November 22, 1975. It was a nightmare game for Pitt kicker Carson Long. Midway in the second quarter, Pitt's Elliott Walker had a 37-yard touchdown run up the middle as the first score of the game played at Three Rivers Stadium. Penn State's Tom Odell blocked Long's extra-point try, leaving the score at 6–0. Early in the fourth quarter the Panthers were still clinging to that 6–0 lead when Long missed a 51-yard field goal try. The crack in the door remained opened, and the Nittany Lions were going to bust through. Steve Geise's 28-yard touchdown run-off left tackle tied the game 6–6, with Chris Bahr's extra-point pending. Bahr nailed it, and Penn State led 7–6. With less than three minutes to go, Pitt had driven to the Lions' 6-yard line but could get no further. Long came out for the field goal try that would regain the lead for the Panthers, but his kick went wide right. Penn State's offense could not do anything against Pitt's "D," and Bahr, who also served as the punter, booted the ball to the Panther 40. Pitt had 37 seconds for one more chance at victory. A Matt Cavanaugh to Karl Farmer pass play brought the ball to the Penn State 25. With the clocked stopped at nine seconds remaining, Long had *yet another* chance to win the game for Pitt. His try dropped short of the goalpost, and Penn State had their tenth win in a row over the Panthers. For Long, the day wasn't all lost: Just hours before the game he became a father when his wife, Peggy, gave birth to a baby girl.

4. Ending 20 years of frustration—November 25, 1939. Penn State was able to release two decades worth of frustration in a domination of Pitt, winning 10–0 in a game that wasn't even as close as the score indicated. Bill Smaltz's one-yard plunge late in the first quarter opened the scoring. Although the Lions threatened in the second and third quarters, they could not put any more points on the board. Penn State's final points were scored midway in the fourth when John Patrick kicked a 24-yard field goal. The Lions racked up 17 first downs, and their defense kept Pitt bottled up on its half of the field for most of the game. The player of the game, according to both head coaches, was center Leon Gajecki, who played the entire 60 minutes and was a major force for the defense that pitched the shutout. The win broke a 14-game losing streak to the Panthers.

3. National championship derailed—November 28, 1981. For the final two weeks in October 1981 Penn State was ranked No. 1 in the AP poll. Then it lost 17–14 at Miami, and Pitt assumed the top spot for the remainder of the season heading into the finale. Pitt seemed destined to play for the national championship when it jumped out to a 14–0 first-quarter lead. Panther quarterback Dan Marino was looking to put the game away on the first play of the second quarter, but his pass into the end zone was intercepted by Roger Jackson. Mike Meade's two-yard touchdown run capped an 80-play drive that followed, and the Lions offense had taken off for what would be a very productive afternoon. A Todd Blackledge eight-yard quarterback keeper for a score had the game tied 14–14 at the half. The Nittany Lions would score 34 points in the second half, highlighted by two spectacular touchdowns. In the third quarter Penn State had the ball at the Pitt 41. Blackledge connected with wide receiver Kenny Jackson at the 10, and instead of allowing his momentum to take him out of bounds, Jackson pivoted toward the middle of the field and ran into the end zone. In the fourth quarter Marino was intercepted by Mark Robinson, who, despite losing a shoe on the play, raced 91 yards for a score on a soggy sock. The 48–14 Penn State win prevented Pitt from playing for the national championship. "I never dreamt this could happen," said Panther tight end John Brown. "When it rains, it pours, and it really rained on us today."

2. Onward to the National Championship—November 26, 1982. The roles were reversed from our No. 3 game that occurred a year earlier. Pitt was the 1982 preseason No. 1 ranked team. After bouncing between No. 1 and No. 3 during September and October, the Panthers were again atop the polls in early November when they were upset at home 31–16 against unranked Notre Dame. After suffering a midseason loss at Alabama, the Nittany Lions had rebounded and were ranked No. 2 prior to the season finale at Beaver Stadium against the Panthers. This time it was Penn State eyeing a date in the Sugar Bowl against Georgia for the national championship and Pitt looking to play the spoiler. The Panthers took well to that task, leading 7–3 at halftime. In the third quarter Penn State took the lead for good when Todd Blackledge beat a Pitt blitz to find an open Kenny Jackson for a 31-yard score. In a season that started with the offense being touted as "Air Paterno," it now went back to basics with a strong rushing attack. Penn State would gain 210 yards on the ground against the third-best defense in the nation for that category. Penn State's final score, a Nick Gancitano 29-yard field goal, culminated a 58-yard, eight-play drive, with all the previous plays being running plays. Penn State won 19–10, and fans flooded the field to celebrate and begin to turn their attention to New Year's Day 1983 in New Orleans.

1. The touchdown on fourth down—November 24, 1978. It really didn't seem fair. After years, decades even, of fighting for respect, Penn State finally controlled its own destiny in pursuit of that elusive national championship. The Nittany Lions were ranked No. 1 in the AP poll for the first time in history. They were 10–0, and they were supposed to be heading to New Orleans and the Sugar Bowl to play for the title. Now, late in the fourth quarter they were losing— at home—to Pitt. The No. 15–ranked Panthers had shut down Penn State's offense for most of the game. Penn State quarterback Chuck Fusina did have time to add to his 1978 heroics. The Lions drove to the Pitt 37, when Fusina hit Brad Scovill for 15 yards. Add in a ten-yard roughing-the-passer penalty, and Penn State had a first down at the Panther 12. Three plays later netted eight yards. Joe Paterno and company were faced with fourth-and-2 at the 4 with 5:02 to play. Paterno had the best kicker in college football in Matt Bahr ready to tie the score with a chip shot. However, if the game ended in a tie, then it might as well have been a loss and Penn State would probably not get its chance to play for the national championship. Paterno opted to go for it. The Nittany Lion offensive line blasted a huge hole in the Panther defense, and Mike Guman picked up four yards instead of the two he needed—and, more importantly, ended up in the end zone for the go-ahead score, 14–10. "I never considered a field goal," Paterno said. "I felt we had to win it and not play for the tie." After Rich Milot intercepted Pitt quarterback Rick Tracano's pass, Bahr kicked his NCAA record 22nd field goal of the season. Penn State had the win, 17–10, the perfect regular season, and the No. 1 ranking in tact—and also a date with Alabama for the national championship.

PITT-PENN STATE MEMORIES
:: BY CHET PARLAVECCHIO

Chet Parlavecchio was a second-team All-American linebacker at Penn State in 1981, as he helped the Lions to a 10–2 season that ended with a win over USC in the Fiesta Bowl. However, he forever etched his name in Penn State lore with his, some would call, brash comments prior to the 1981 contest between Penn State and No. 1 Pitt. Hailing from West Orange, New Jersey, Parlavecchio didn't have the strong feelings toward the rivalry that the Pennsylvania kids who went to the two schools had. Still, he left his mark on it and has some unique memories of it.

5. Mark May. Mark May gave me one of the greatest beatings in my lifetime in 1979. I was a sophomore filling in for Lance Mehl, and May gave me a beating. It was so bad that the next day my girlfriend had to dress me. There was healthy respect there on the field, but I hate what Mark May does now on ESPN. He zings Penn State any chance he gets. It's only because he wishes he could have played for Penn State. (Note: This is the only time Parlavecchio used the word "hate" in talking about the rivalry with Pitt.)

4. 1981 pregame—why Thiel? I was on a radio show hosted by Stan Savran, and he was just going on and on about how are we going to stop Pitt. I finally had enough and told him that we're going to win, and not only that, we're going to kick the crap out of them. We're going to win 48–20. I said they hadn't played anybody. We played everybody that year, and they hadn't played anybody. So I said, "Maybe next week they'll schedule Thiel." People ask, Why did I say Thiel of all schools? Well, Rich D'Amico's buddy was up visiting and he played at Thiel. You know what? Joe [Paterno] never said a word. He let it go. He didn't say anything.

3. Jackie Sherrill. When we were down 14–0, I knew we had to do something. Julius Dawkins caught a pass, and I cleaned his clock out of bounds. Next thing I know, [Pitt head coach] Jackie Sherrill was in my face. I went to the sidelines and told Joe that I knew what I was doing, that I wasn't crazy. And wouldn't you know, Roger Jackson intercepts the very next pass. A few months later I'm going to be playing in the East-West Shrine Game, and Jackie Sherrill is the head coach of the East. I thought I would be lucky to get on the field to hold kicks, but he picked me up at the airport and said let's just put all that stuff behind us. I went on to win the MVP of the game. Sherrill said, "Enjoy that one. How many MVPs did Paterno get you?" I said, "You know what Coach, you got a point there."

2. 1981 postgame. My father was allowed in the locker room after the game, and it was one of the great moments in my life. Everyone else was on the bus and I was sitting there with my dad. Coach [Paterno] saw me with my dad and said they'd wait for me. My nose was broken and I was hurting. My dad and I took a walk and stared out onto the field. The stadium was empty and the confetti was blowing. My dad and I just stared at the field. I'll never forget that.

1. The players. The greatest thing about those games were how great the people were that played in those games and the character of those people and what they've become—the Dan Marinos, the Mike Munchaks, the Curt Warners, even the Mark Mays. I think back, and no other rivalry could stand up to that one. I don't care about Alabama and Auburn or USC and UCLA. It still bothers me that they no longer play. It was shameful how easy it went way. It still bothers me.

PENN STATERS BY THE NUMBERS

Plenty of athletes have donned blue-and-white numbered uniforms in more than a century of Nittany Lion sports history, but who is the best player (or, in some cases, players when a tie could not be broken) to represent each number? Below is the best of the best—1 to 99.

#1 Tyra Grant and Bob Higgins. We have two for the price of one for our first number. Grant was a two-time first-team All-Big Ten women's basketball star, averaging 19.3 points per game in her senior season of 2009–10. She finished fourth on the all-time Lady Lions' scoring list. Higgins was the cocaptain on the 1919 Nittany Lion football team and a Walter Camp first-team All-American.

#2 Lauren Caccimani. She was the 1999 women's volleyball co-national player of the year, leading Penn State to three consecutive Final Four appearances and one national championship.

#3 Ivan Contreras. In 1997 he became the first men's volleyball player from an eastern school to win the national player of the year award, as he led the Nittany Lions to the championship game before losing to UCLA in five sets.

#4 Char Morett. As of this writing, the only three-time first-team All-American in Penn State field hockey history, Morett was the captain of the undefeated 1978 team. She scored 50 goals in her career.

#5 Larry Johnson. Johnson's 2,087 yards rushing in 2002 is the greatest single-season performance by a running back in the history of Penn State football.

#6 Alisha Glass. She was a first-team All-American and member of three consecutive women's volleyball national championship teams (2007–09).

#7 Candy Finn. Arguably the greatest women's lacrosse player in school history, Finn also was an outstanding field hockey player. She won three Broderick Awards, which is given to the top female student-athlete in each sport. Finn won two for lacrosse and one for field hockey. As of this writing, she ranks second in career goals and career points in lacrosse.

#8 Tiffany Weimer. She was women's soccer player of the year runner-up in 2004 and 2005 and holds the team record for career goals. Fittingly, her nickname was "Ocho."

#9 Dick Packer. He was a two-time All-American on the Nittany Lions' back-to-back soccer national championship teams in 1954 and 1955.

#10 Matt Bahr. He set the Penn State single-season record for field goals in 1978 with 22. His efforts helped lead the football team to its first-ever No. 1 ranking in the AP and Coaches polls as well as a date in the Sugar Bowl against Alabama for the national championship.

#11 Megan Hodge and LaVar Arrington. Hodge won the 2009 women's volleyball national player of the year award and led the Lions to three consecutive national championships. Arrington made his mark at "Linebacker U" as a first-team All-American in 1999. That season, he also won the Butkus Award as the nation's top linebacker. In 1998 Arrington became the first sophomore in the history of the Big Ten to win the conference's Defensive Player of the Year award.

#12 Kerry Collins. He was the record-breaking quarterback for the 1994 Big Ten, Rose Bowl (and, in our opinion, national champion) Nittany Lions. In that season Collins set single-season records for passing yardage (2,679) and completion percentage (66.7). He was named first-team All-American and won the Maxwell Award (nation's outstanding player) and Davey O'Brien Award (nation's top quarterback).

#13 Kelly Mazzante. She was a two-time women's basketball All-American and, in 2004, became the first player in Big Ten history to be a four-time first-team all-conference selection. She is the leading scorer in Big Ten history (male or female), with 2,919 points.

#14 Todd Blackledge. In 1982 he led Penn State to its first football national championship. He won the Davey O'Brien Award as the nation's top quarterback and also set Penn State records for single-season (22) and career (42) touchdown passes.

#15 Monroe Brown. Following the 1992 basketball season, Brown ranked third in PSU basketball history in career points (1,244). He was a four-year starter and helped the 1990–91 team to a first-round upset of UCLA in the NCAA Tournament.

#16 John Hufnagel. He was a 1972 All-American quarterback. In that season he threw for 2,039 yards and 15 touchdowns.

#17 Daryll Clark. A two-year starter, Clark was a 2009 cowinner of the Chicago Tribune Silver Football, given to the Big Ten's player of the year, and a two-time first-team all-conference quarterback. In 2008 he led Penn State to its third Big Ten title.

#18 Troy Drayton. In 1992 he set the single-season record for receptions by a tight end (33).

#19 Gregg Garrity. He led the 1981 Nittany Lions in receptions (23), and his diving 47-yard touchdown catch from Todd Blackledge in the Sugar Bowl the following season clinched the 1982 national championship. The picture of Garrity's celebration after the score was the cover for the proceeding issue of *Sports Illustrated*.

#20 Eddie Drummond. In a career that spanned 1998 to 2001, he had 71 receptions for 1,132 yards and five touchdowns.

#21 Susan Robinson. One of only two Penn Staters to achieve 2,000 points and 1,000 rebounds, Robinson was the 1992 winner of the Wade Trophy, awarded to the player of the year in women's college basketball.

#22 John Cappelletti. Penn State's only Heisman Trophy winner, Cappelletti earned the award in 1973 by rushing for 1,522 yards and scoring 17 touchdowns as he helped lead the Nittany Lions to a perfect 12–0 season. His acceptance speech at the awards ceremony hardly left a dry eye in the ballroom, as he dedicated the Heisman to his 11-year-old brother Joey, who was battling leukemia.

#23 Lydell Mitchell. When his Penn State career ended following the 1971 season, Mitchell stood atop the team's list for career-rushing yards with 2,934 yards. His senior season was his best, as Mitchell rushed for 1,567 yards, which, at the time, was the most ever by a Nittany Lion in a single season.

#24 Ed Drapcho. A 1957 All-American pitcher, Drapcho went 12–0 with 116 strikeouts and a 1.52 E.R.A. as he led Penn State to the College World Series.

#25 Curt Warner. He was the Lions' all-time rushing leader until Evan Royster broke his record in 2010. Warner finished his career with 3,398 yards and 24 touchdowns. He was at his best against the best, outgaining 1981 Heisman Trophy–winner Marcus Allen, 145 yards and two touchdowns to 85 yards and no touchdowns in the Fiesta Bowl. The next season in the Sugar Bowl and the game that decided the national title, he had 117 yards compared to 1982 Heisman-winner Herschel Walker's 103.

#26 Leon Gajecki. First-team All-American center, Gajecki was the captain of the 1940 Nittany Lion football team that posted a 6–1–1 record.

#27 Pete Harris. In 1978 Harris led the nation with ten interceptions and was named a first-team All-American safety.

#28 Brian Chizmar. Initially a defensive back and later a linebacker, Chizmar led Penn State in tackles (69) in 1987 and recorded 110 tackles in 1989.

#29 Steve Geise. He led the 1976 Nittany Lions in rushing. Geise also ran for 111 yards and a touchdown in the 1977 Fiesta Bowl win over Arizona State.

#30 Helen Darling. As a senior in 2000, Darling led the nation in assists, was a first-team All-American, and led the Lady Lion basketball team to its first Final Four appearance.

#31 Shane Conlan. The sixth two-time All-American in Penn State history, Conlan led the 1986 Nittany Lions in tackles (79). He intercepted two Vinny Testaverde passes in the Fiesta Bowl against Miami—the second interception was returned to the Miami 5-yard line and set up the winning touchdown, helping Penn State claim the national championship.

#32 Suzie McConnell. One the greatest players in the history of Lady Lion basketball, McConnell was the program's first first-team All-American. She set Division I records for career assists (1,307), assists in a single season (355 in 1987), and assists average for a season (11.8 in 1987).

#33 Richie Lucas. 1959 Heisman Trophy runner-up and All-American quarterback, Lucas led the 1959 Lions in rushing (325 yards) and passing (913 yards).

#34 Franco Harris. In a three-year career that spanned 1969 to 1971, Harris rushed for 2,002 yards and scored 24 touchdowns.

#35 Dennis Onkotz. All-American linebacker in 1968 and 1969, Onkotz helped lead the Lions to consecutive 11–0 seasons, including back-to-back victories in the Orange Bowl.

#36 Pete Mauthe. He was the captain of the undefeated 1912 football team that outscored opponents 285–6. In a season that was only eight games, Mauthe had 710 yards rushing and scored 119 points in 1912. He also was the team's kicker and punter, and he kicked a 51-yard field goal in a win over Pitt that remained the team record until 1975. He became the first Penn State player to be inducted into the College Football Hall of Fame.

#37 Walker Lee Ashley. Three-year starting defensive end, Ashley recorded 52 tackles, recovered three fumbles, and forced two others during the 1982 national championship season.

#38 Jon Witman. He was a fullback who led Penn State in touchdowns in 1995 and was a powerful blocking back for the 1994 Big Ten and Rose Bowl champions.

#39 Curtis Enis. Forget about how his Penn State career ended, Enis was one of the more dominant backs the Lions have had in the Paterno era. He was an All-American in 1997, when he rushed for 1,363 yards and 19 TDs. And who could forget his performance in the thrilling win over Ohio State that year when he went off for 211 yards on 23 carries?

#40 Dan Connor. Was named first-team All-American as linebacker in 2007 and also won the Bednarik Award as the nation's top defensive player. Connor finished his career as Penn State's all-time leader in tackles.

#41 Elwood Petchel. He led the Lions to its unbeaten season in 1947. Petchel could run, pass, kick, and play defense. He was a third-team All-American in 1948, when he threw for a then-impressive 628 yards and nine touchdowns.

#42 D.J. Dozier. The first Penn State running back to lead the team in rushing in four consecutive seasons, Dozier also scored the winning touchdown in the 1987 Fiesta Bowl win over Miami that gave Penn State the national title. He finished his career with 3,227 yards, which, at the time, was second only to Curt Warner.

#43 Michael Zordich. He was the starting safety and a captain of the 1985 Lion team that was ranked No. 1 heading into the Orange Bowl against Oklahoma. He also saw plenty of action as a backup during the 1982 season that ended with Penn State's first national title.

#44 Jimmy Cefalo. A 1977 Penn State all-purpose yard leader and team MVP of the 1976 Gator Bowl, he returned two punts for TDs during his senior season.

#45 Sean Lee. Lee finished with 325 career tackles, ranking him fourth on the team's all-time list.

#46 Roger Kochman. Star running back on some of Rip Engle's best teams, Kochman would finish his career with 1,485 yards rushing. He scored the only touchdown in the 1959 Liberty Bowl win. Earlier that season, in the 20–18 loss to Syracuse, his efforts nearly pulled out the win for the Lions. He was named an All-American by US Coaches in 1962.

#47 Josh Gaines. He was a three-year starting defensive end and cocaptain of 2008 Big Ten championship team. During his senior season he had 31 tackles and three sacks.

#48 Booker Moore. Rushing for 2,072 yards and 20 touchdowns in his career, Moore started as a sophomore in 1978 and teamed with Matt Suhey to form a formidable backfield.

#49 Roger Jackson. In 1981 he led the Nittany Lions with five interceptions, including his pick of a Dan Marino pass in the end zone that helped turn the momentum of the game in the Lions' 48–14 win over the top-ranked Panthers.

#50 Jeff Hartings. Two-time All-American offensive guard, Hartings was a mainstay of the 1994 line that gave up only three sacks in leading Penn State to an undefeated season and its first Big Ten championship.

#51 Jim Dooley. A 1952 second-team All-American football center, he helped the Lions pull off upsets over Penn and Pitt.

#52 Calvin Booth. The 1997 Big Ten Basketball Defensive Player of the Year, he was the Lions' leader in career blocked shots with 428.

#53 Glen Ressler. He was an outstanding lineman on offense *and* defense, and in 1964 he became one of the few linemen to ever win the Maxwell Award as college football's player of the year.

#54 Bruce Clark. A 1978 and 1979 All-American defensive tackle, Clark is the only Penn Stater to have won the Lombardi Award as the nation's outstanding lineman/linebacker. He was a standout on the Lion team that played Alabama in the Sugar Bowl that decided the 1978 national championship.

#55 Tim Johnson. A 1986 All-American defensive lineman, Johnson had five sacks that season that helped lead Penn State to the national championship. He had a crucial sack during Miami's final drive in the 1987 Fiesta Bowl.

#56 Lance Mehl. A linebacker who led Penn State in tackles in consecutive seasons in 1978 and 1979, he was a second-team All-American in 1979.

#57 A.Q. Shipley. The 2008 Big Ten Offensive Lineman of the Year, Shipley also won the Remington Award as the best center in college football. He was the leader of the offensive line that helped the Lions win the Big Ten title.

#58 Todd Atkins. Starting defensive end for the 1994 Big Ten champions, Atkins had six sacks that season and was selected second-team all-conference.

#59 Aaron Maybin. In 2008 Maybin led the Big Ten in sacks (12) and tackles for losses (20), helping lead the Nittany Lions to their third conference title.

#60 Matt Millen. A 1978 All-American defensive tackle, Millen made 54 tackles and recorded nine sacks on a Penn State team that played for the national championship. He also blocked a punt and recovered two fumbles that season.

#61 John Nessel. He was the first All-American offensive lineman coached by Joe Paterno. He also helped pave the way for John Cappelletti's 1973 rush to the Heisman.

#62 Sean Farrell. A two-time first-team All-American, Farrell also was a finalist for both the Lombardi and Outland awards during his senior season of 1981.

#63 Todd Moules. He was an offensive guard and cocaptain of the 1985 PSU squad that finished the regular season ranked No. 1 in the country and played Oklahoma in the Orange Bowl for the national championship. He also was a third-team All-American that season.

#64 Earl Shumaker. He was an offensive and defensive guard who blocked for Lenny Moore in 1954 and 1955.

#65 Paul Suhey. Cocaptain and linebacker of the 1978 undefeated team, Suhey was second on the team in tackles with 63. Paterno called him one of the finest captains he ever had.

#66 Steve Wisniewski. He was a three-year starting guard (including on the 1986 national championship team) and two-time All-American in 1987 and 1988.

#67 Greg Buttle. He was a 1975 All-American linebacker. In that season Buttle registered 140 tackles and three interceptions. He was the team's all-time leader in career tackles until Paul Posluszny broke his record in 2006.

#68 Mike Reid. Reid is a 1969 All-American defensive lineman and the only Lion to win the Outland Trophy as the outstanding interior lineman in college football. He also won the Maxwell Award in 1969 as the outstanding player in college football.

#69 Leo Wisniewski. Cocaptain his senior year in 1981, Wisniewski was the Defensive Player of the Game in the 1982 Fiesta Bowl when he led the Lions' defensive effort in holding Heisman-winner Marcus Allen to 85 yards rushing. He had six tackles, including three in which he took Allen down for loss yardage, and he recovered a fumble.

#70 Dave Joyner. All-American offensive tackle in 1971, Joyner also excelled academically and was inducted into the GTE/CoSIDA Academic Hall of Fame in 1991.

#71 Keith Dorney. A two-time first-team All-American in 1977 and 1978, he finished tenth for the Lombardi Award in 1978, the year Bruce Clark won the award.

#72 Tom Rafferty. A 1975 All-American offensive lineman, Rafferty started two seasons and was a backup in 1973 on a line that helped Cappelletti win the Heisman.

#73 Jimmy Kennedy. The 2002 Big Ten Defensive Lineman of the Year, Kennedy had 16 tackles for losses and 5.5 sacks.

#74 Larry Kubin. Defensive end of the late 1970s, Kubin held the team's career sack record of 30 until Courtney Brown broke it. He is still tied for most sacks in a season with 15. His career numbers are even more impressive when you consider that he missed most of his senior season in 1980 with a knee injury.

#75 Charlie Janerrette. Starting tackle on the 1959 team that finished 9–2, he was a second-team All-American. In the Liberty Bowl victory over Alabama, Janerrette was the first African American to ever play against the Crimson Tide.

#76 Steve Smear. Cocaptain defensive tackle of the 1968 and 1969 undefeated teams that won back-to-back Orange Bowls, Smear is often overlooked because he played alongside Mike Reid, but the two formed one of the best defensive-tackle duos in the country.

#77 Chuck Sieminski. A two-way tackle in the early 1960s, he was a second-team All-American in 1962.

#78 Mike Munchak. A 1981 third-team All-American offensive guard, Munchak was part of one of the greatest lines in Penn State history, which included fellow guard Sean Farrell. He made two key blocks in the 1982 Fiesta Bowl that helped Curt Warner in his two TD runs.

#79 Mike Hartenstine. A first-team All-American defensive tackle in 1974, he led the Lions in tackles during the 1973 undefeated season.

#80 Brad Scovill. Leading the 1979 Nittany Lions in receptions (26) and yards (331), Scovill also was the pass-catching tight end on the 1978 squad that played for the national championship.

#81 Kyle Brady. Not only the greatest No. 81, but also one of the all-time great tight ends in Penn State history, Brady was a 1994 All-American, and his blocking and receiving ability were key factors in the school's first-ever Big Ten championship.

#82 Ted Kwalick. The distinction of *greatest* tight end in Penn State history goes to Kwalick, who was Penn State's first two-time All-American (1967–68), capping his career by leading the team in receiving in the Orange Bowl win over Kansas. He finished fourth in the Heisman voting in 1968.

#83 Bruce Bannon. He was a 1972 All-American defensive end and defensive MVP of the 1972 Cotton Bowl, when the Lions routed Texas 30–6.

#84 Jack Sherry. One of the top defensive backs under Rip Engle, Sherry also played offensive end. In 1952, as a sophomore, he had eight INTs, which was a team record.

#85 Sam Tamburo. He was an all-American in 1948 and led the Lions in receiving in 1946 and 1947.

#86 Courtney Brown. The 1999 Big Ten Defensive Player of the Year and All-American defensive end, Brown set school records for career tackles for losses (70) and sacks (33). He was a three-year starter, and each season concluded with Brown being named to the All-Big Ten team.

#87 Ed O'Neill. He was a 1973 All-American linebacker and a captain of that season's undefeated team that eventually won the Orange Bowl. He is tied for seventh on the team's list of tackles in a season, with the 126 he had in 1972.

#88 Greg Edmonds. Penn State's leading receiver in 1969 and 1970, Edmonds had six TD receptions in 1970 that, at the time, was a team record.

#89 Dave Robinson. A star two-way player at the end position on both sides of the line, Robinson also was Penn State's first black All-American in 1962. He recovered three fumbles in one game during a 23–7 win over Maryland in 1962.

#90 Pete Giftopoulos. Starting linebacker on the 1986 national champions, he was second on the team in tackles (71) and made one of the signature plays in school history when he intercepted Miami quarterback Vinny Testaverde's pass in the closing seconds of the Fiesta Bowl to cement the victory.

#91 Jared Odrick. The 2009 Big Ten Defensive Player of the Year and All-American defensive tackle, Odrick also was a first-team member of the All-Big Ten team in 2008, helping lead the Nittany Lions to the conference championship.

#92 Terry Killens. Having switched from linebacker to defensive end prior to the 1995 season, Killens registered 62 tackles that year.

#93 Brandon Noble. A three-year starting defensive tackle, including his sophomore season on 1994's Big Ten and Rose Bowl champions, Noble led PSU in sacks (7.5) in 1996.

#94 Chet Parlavecchio. A second-team All-American linebacker in 1981, he led Penn State in tackles in 1980 and 1981.

#95 Rogers Alexander. An honorable mention All-American linebacker in 1985, he was cocaptain of the 1985 Lions that played for the national title against Oklahoma. He led the team in tackles that season with 102. During his freshman season he caused a fumble in the 1983 Sugar Bowl win over Georgia.

#96 Bob Jones. He was a two-year starting defensive end 2000–2001 and had 35 tackles and three sacks his senior season.

#97 Scott Radecic. A two-year starting linebacker and second-team All-American in 1982, he led Penn State in tackles (71) and interceptions (4) that season to help the Lions win the national title. Against Georgia in the Sugar Bowl, he had a team-high 14 tackles and caused one fumble.

#98 Anthony Adams. A two-year starting defensive tackle, Adams had a combined 126 tackles in 2001 and 2002.

#99 Chris Bahr. A 1975 All-American kicker, Bahr also had a 39-yard punting average. He kicked six field goals of 50 yards or more during his Penn State career.

SATURDAY NIGHT LIVE ALUMNI AND PENN STATE

What do movies featuring *Saturday Night Live* alumni and Penn State have in common? Well, practically nothing. But if you look hard, there are some great quotes from their movies that can easily apply to specific Penn State football events.

10. "We zip in, we pick 'em up, we zip right out again. We're not going to Moscow. It's Czechoslovakia. It's like we're going into Wisconsin." Bill Murray to Harold Ramis in *Stripes*—and Penn State's 2008 statement game at Wisconsin. The Nittany Lions zipped to a 24–7 lead and zipped out of Madison with a 48–7 win.

9. "Even if every man, woman, and child held hands together and prayed for us to win, it just wouldn't matter because all the really good looking girls would still go out with the guys from Mohawk because they've got all the money!" Bill Murray to the Camp North Star crew in *Meatballs*—and Penn State being denied national championships despite perfect seasons in 1968, 1969, 1973, and 1994.

8. "Look, defenseless babies!" Chevy Chase to a very angry Doberman pinscher in *Fletch*—and the 1994 Nittany Lion offense that torched every defense it encountered.

7. "Oh we've got both kinds—country and western." The bartender describing the type of music played at Bob's Country Bunker to Dan Aykroyd and John Belushi in *The Blues Brothers*—and a tip of the PSU helmet to Nittany Lion great Mike Reid, who, after his NFL playing days, started a music career in Nashville and was inducted into the Nashville Songwriters Hall of Fame in 2005.

6. "You're not going to fall for the banana in the tailpipe?" Eddie Murphy mocking a police detective in *Beverly Hills Cop*—and Anthony Scirrotto returning an Illinois onside kick attempt for a touchdown to clinch a 2006 Homecoming win over the Fighting Illini.

5. "Somebody should clean these windows. There's gook all over 'em." Chevy Chase to the airplane mechanics in *Fletch*—and that dreadful 2004 Penn State loss to Iowa. For those who have blocked that from their memory due to the emotional scars of having watched it, the final score was 6–4.

4. "Now that is what I call high-quality H2O." Adam Sandler in *The Waterboy*—and take your pick: either the 1996 Outback Bowl against Auburn or the 2010 Capital One Bowl against Louisiana State. Both games were played in a downpour of rain.

3. "Mr. Blutarsky, 0.0." The grade point average of John Belushi's character at Faber College in *Animal House*—and the number of points Woody Hayes's Buckeyes scored in the 1978 game in Columbus. By the way, the Lions scored 19.

2. "We're going streaking!" Will Ferrell's proclamation to the people of the party in *Old School*—and Penn State's 31-game unbeaten streak from 1967 to 1970.

1. "I don't know how to put this, but I'm kind of a big deal." Will Ferrell to Christina Applegate in *Anchorman*—and the Nittany Lions' entrance into the Big Ten. Penn State showed the conference that to set your sights higher than just going to the Rose Bowl is okay and that competing for national championships trumps all.

TOP 25 BRYCE JORDAN CENTER EVENTS (NON-PSU ATHLETIC) :: BY BERNIE PUNT

Whether the Bryce Jordan Center has given Penn State's hoops teams a better home-court advantage than they had at Rec Hall could be argued. What can't be argued is that the BJC, which opened in 1996, has allowed Penn State to host some of the biggest entertainers in the world. Bernie Punt, the BJC's director of sales and marketing, ranks the top 25 non-PSU athletic BJC events that have taken place. He based his rankings on attendance and significance. He said he could have easily made this list a top 50 because acts such as Aerosmith, Tina Turner, Jonas Brothers, Britney Spears, Reba McEntire, Eric Clapton, and others also have visited the arena, but they aren't included here.

25. Jay-Z (October 9, 2009). The rehearsal and North American tour opener was groundbreaking for the building, which received international exposure.

24. Will Ferrell, Zach Galifianakis, Demetri Martin, and Nick Swardson (February 11, 2008). The sold-out *Funny or Die* Tour, featuring Will Ferrell, was the highest-attended comedy show in our history (more than 11,000).

23. Cher and Cyndi Lauper (September 7, 1999). One of the most extravagant and wild nights in our history—people who came to this concert still rave that this was our best show.

22. *Walking with Dinosaurs—The Live Experience* (March 20–23, 2008). The immense tour (literally) was the largest production to ever come to the area—27 tractor-trailers and a 125-person crew, not including 17 dinosaurs.

21. Prince (April 18, 2004). A rare concert tour, it was followed by one of the most impressive performances in our history.

20. Kenny Chesney, Keith Urban, and Dierks Bentley (April 30, 2004). The all-star lineup of country headliners was the No. 1 tour at the time.

19. Pearl Jam (May 3, 2003). This was the last date of its North American tour that turned out to be the longest concert in our history. The band continued its encore until close to 1 a.m.!

18. Bon Jovi (February 8, 2003). This was another rehearsal and North American tour opener for the building.

17. Rod Stewart (February 29, 1996). This was our first center-stage set-up and the concert that had everyone talking about the BJC. Stewart (an avid soccer fan) kicked balls into the upper deck during his long set of hits.

16. Bill Clinton, Spring Commencement (May 10, 1996). President Clinton spoke to a capacity crowd that had hundreds of Secret Service employees in position at every nook and cranny of the building.

15. Eagles (June 20, 1996). This was the concert that officially put the BJC on the map with agents and promoters.

14. Rusted Root (January 18, 1996). This was the very first concert at the Bryce Jordan Center.

13. George Strait (September 6, 1996). This concert featured an artist who rarely comes east, and it immediately sold out. The success of this show set up our booking for Garth Brooks the following year.

12. The Dead and The Allman Brothers (October 13, 2008). A reunited band tied to a presidential election brought people in from all over the United States, and it gave us national exposure.

11. Taylor Swift (August 29, 2009). This was the fastest sell-out in Jordan Center history—12 minutes—and Swift put on an impressive performance.

10. Tim McGraw and Faith Hill (September 8, 2000). The duo went on their first-ever date at the BJC (jeep ride) when Faith opened for Tim in 1996. The couple returned and purchased the jeep, which they have on their farm in Tennessee. Our building still has a special place in their hearts.

9. Philadelphia 76ers vs. Washington Wizards (October 22, 2001). This was a sold-out exhibition NBA game, as Michael Jordan returned from retirement to play in his first game for the Wizards. It also was an uplifting patriotic event because it was just after 9/11.

8. Dave Matthews Band (April 5, 2002). The band would later go on as one of the most successful touring acts for the next decade. This night was standing room only.

7. Shania Twain (December 12, 1998). No one knew at the time that this would be her only performance in the area—more than 15,000 witnessed her rare concert.

6. Elton John and Billy Joel (January 16, 2002). The Face 2 Face Tour offered one of the most highly sought-after tickets. Many locals consider this the best concert in our history.

5. Bruce Springsteen and the E Street Band (February 28, 2000). The band rehearsed and opened its North American tour, something that was becoming commonplace.

4. Neil Diamond (November 10, 1998). His first concert in our venue brought in people from all over the Northeast. We didn't have enough seats.

3. Backstreet Boys (February 11–12, 2000). This boasted two sold-out shows and another rehearsal and North American tour opener for the building. The decibel level of screaming girls made it one of the loudest concerts in our history.

2. Billy Joel (November 1, 1998). Not only was this the largest-attended event in our 14-year history (15,722), but Joel also rehearsed and opened his North America tour at the building—many other artists soon followed this route.

1. Garth Brooks (April 3–7, 1997). Five straight sold-out nights turned Penn State into Garth country. Besides entertaining more than 15,000 people each night, Brooks played basketball with the Lady Lions, learned how to body check from the Penn State Icers, and even participated in some spring drills with the football team.

TOP OFF-COURT MEMORIES :: BY KELLY MAZZANTE

During her four seasons as a Lady Lion (2000–04), Kelly Mazzante was a *must* see. And plenty of people did see her, as the team set attendance records during her career. Name a Penn State scoring record, and she likely holds it. Her 2,919 career points are not only the most in Lady Lion history; they are the most in Big Ten history, women or *men's* basketball. Mazzante certainly enjoyed plenty of on-court memories—the 49 points against Minnesota in 2001, leading her team to an Elite Eight appearance in 2004, and making two other Sweet 16 showings—but she also had some off-court experiences that stood out for her.

5. Pregame. It was the same thing for every game. We'd go to the gym six hours before the game and have our shoot-around and pregame practice. Everyone would eat together as a team. We'd hang out. It was like clockwork. I'd go to the training table and the trainer would work on me, and I'd fall asleep every time.

4. Fall semester 2004 (Mazzante returned to Penn State and took two classes that she needed to graduate. It was after her final season as a Lady Lion and following her first in the WNBA). That was the least amount of stress I've ever had. It was a good semester. I actually enjoyed just being a student. I still worked out, but it was nice enjoying college life and feeling like a normal student.

3. Family time. My parents came to every home game, and a lot of parents were there as well. That was one of the coolest parts of the whole experience. My mom would bring goodies, and the parents would talk and socialize. Looking back, it was great to have that opportunity to have my family watch me play.

2. Community involvement. We did THON every year. We did the cancer walk every year. We would go to the therapeutic horseback riding facility and be with the kids there. Even if we could make a difference in just one kid's life, it was great to get out and do those things. We had a good time doing all that during the preseason.

1. Tailgate parties. Prior to our seasons starting, when the football season was happening, Rene [Portland] would have these tailgates for the team. Former players would come. Everyone would bring a certain dish. They were always packed. Families would come. Seeing some of the former players was cool because you knew you were carrying on the tradition. This was a neat thing Rene did, bringing the former and current players together. Then you would feel excited to start a new season.

WE ALL SCREAM FOR ICE CREAM
:: BY JENNIFER PENCEK

Being a Penn State fan, or a sports fan in general, probably means that if you have a significant other, they are either a fan themselves or *very* patient with the time you spend supporting your teams. They might not understand the need to tailgate at 9 a.m. for an 8 p.m. game, but, hey, they'll go along or at least allow you to take up an *entire day* to cheer for Dear Old State. Our wives, neither of whom is a PSU grad, deserve sainthood, as they say, for putting up with all the time, money, and energy we have put into our teams. One way of saying thanks is having our wives participate in this book. David's wife, Jennifer, works at Penn State, and her office isn't too far from the famous Berkey Creamery, which *USA Today* ranked as the top ice cream parlor in Pennsylvania. Jennifer has "taken one for the team" and sacrificed some of her time to become familiar with the flavors there, so here are her top recommendations—just remember, no mixing those flavors!

10. Coconut Chip. Add the word *chip* to any ice cream flavor and I may just try it. Also a popular flavor, Coconut Chip might just have to be on my to-do list next time I get a hunkering for some heaven in a cup.

9. Butter Pecan. Although I do not usually get this flavor, it is one of the top Creamery sellers, so people seem to be drawn to the butter-almond flavored ice cream with pecans. Also, as it is my father-in-law's favorite, it has to be on the list.

8. WPSU Coffee Break. Not being a fan of drinking coffee, I'm still somewhat amazed at how much I enjoy coffee ice cream. It must be that Creamery magic. Also, this is David's favorite, so it has to be on the list.

7. Cookies 'n Cream. Vanilla ice cream with Oreo cookie crumbles makes a yummy treat. I just love biting into the chunks of cookie and enjoying the tasty vanilla ice cream.

6. Peanut Butter Swirl. Next to chocolate, my second biggest craving is peanut butter. My husband can attest to the fact that some of my evening snacks often consist of a spoon and a jar of peanut butter. By mixing the tasty swirls with vanilla ice cream, the Creamery makes my love of peanut butter oh so much better.

5. Bittersweet Mint. I've always loved anything with mint—chocolate with mint, mint candies, and more. The Creamery doesn't disappoint with its Bittersweet Mint—the perfect mint flavor that tickles my tongue—really.

4. Vanilla. With so many creative flavors available, some may wonder why the simpler Vanilla makes the list. The reason is that in the majority of tasty flavors, Vanilla plays a huge part, and it's even tastier on its own.

3. Death by Chocolate. Every now and again, I need to have a chocolate infusion and feel chocolate running through my veins. The result often is the feeling I may actually die from too much chocolate—but what a way to go. For chocolate lovers nothing beats Death by Chocolate, with all its yummy chocolate gooiness.

2. Peachy Paterno. Anyone who knows me knows I never mix fruit and my desserts, but Peachy Paterno still makes the list because it may just be the most talked-about flavor the Creamery offers. Whether it's those who want to bite into the ice cream that honors the beloved football coach or those who actually enjoy fruit and ice cream, the flavor is often seen in cones and dishes across campus.

1. Chocolate Chip Cookie Dough. Maybe it's the flashbacks to my childhood of sneaking bites of raw cookie dough from the mixing bowl into my mouth—I know, not the healthiest—but the Creamery's Chocolate Chip Cookie Dough always tops my list when I have a craving. Chocolate chips and chunks of cookie dough—you can't go wrong there!

WE ARE... PENN STATE—FROM AN OUTSIDER'S PERSPECTIVE :: BY SHANNON PENCEK

For those of us who have grown up being a part of Nittany Nation, we know what makes rooting for Penn State special. Family events being scheduled around those 11 or 12 Saturdays in the fall are the norm. For those who don't understand, the simplest response to them is "It's a Penn State thing." Matt's wife, Shannon, a University of Delaware grad, has had to cope with the fact that the Nittany Lions are now a large part of her life. Even though "The Miracle of Mt. Nittany," Gregg Garrity's catch, and Pete Giftopoulos's interception probably still don't cause much of an emotional ripple for her, what has occurred is a great appreciation, even an embrace, of some of things that make Penn State great.

7. Tailgating. One of our first dates was the 2000 Kickoff Classic against USC held at Giants Stadium. I was pretty impressed at the elaborate tailgates. I also was a little star struck: Several of his friends apparently had press passes, and others were drinking beer and hanging out of an RV. Penn State didn't win that game, but fun was still had by all. Over the years I've hit quite a few tailgates and games, some in amazing fall weather, others hotter than hell, or colder than the Arctic. I've sat in the rain and so high up in the stadium that I could practically touch the Nittany Lion weather vain. I always remember the fan atmosphere and how practically everyone is chanting, "We Are... Penn State" or wearing blue or white.

6. Road trips. I should have known that my husband was a Penn State sports nut when we stopped planning our first vacation together to somewhere warm and sunny in order to go wherever the PSU basketball team was going to be playing during March Madness (hey, vacations happen every year; Penn State playing in the NCAA Tournament is such a rare occurrence that it had to be seen firsthand). The worst-case scenario was Boise, Idaho, but, fortunately for me, the Nittany Lions' destination was New Orleans. It was my first trip to the Big Easy and so much fun! PSU won both games, and we thoroughly enjoyed the Hurricanes at Pat O'Brien's!

5. Never growing up. We were engaged the weekend of Arts Fest in 2002. I proudly showed off my ring while doing cherry bombs at the Phyrst. I realized why my husband loves to go back to State College: You get to relive college over and over—without the exams.

4. Having Penn State embedded into my life. Although I wouldn't allow a cardboard life-size image of JoePa or a big inflatable Nittany Lion at our wedding reception, we did make our entrance into the reception as husband and wife to a recording of the Blue Band's "Lion Fanfare" and "The Nittany Lion."

3. The Nittany Lion Shrine. I realized that at some point I was going to have to give in and allow our Christmas card to be a picture of the family at the Nittany Lion Shrine. Matt got lucky one year because somehow a complete stranger managed to snap a picture of us and our two boys all looking at the camera with smiles on our faces.

2. Emotion. Although I don't quite understand the craziness of it all, I can't help but get excited while watching the game. I get chills when we watch the *Penn State Football Story*, and I'll probably cry at JoePa's last game.

1. All this hype for a game that does not count?! I must be a true fan because I don't mind driving four hours to partake in the Blue-White Game festivities, and I couldn't wait to get my kids a Lion Hoodie with ears. I like to give Matt a hard time, but I enjoy the fanfare—as long as most trips end with a visit to the Creamery!

TOP TEN FAMOUS NONSPORTS FIGURES WHO ATTENDED PENN STATE

We'd like to take a brief pause to recognize some of those who came to Penn State and made names for themselves in ways other than throwing, hitting, or shooting a ball. It would be impossible, or at least take a whole book, to mention every famous or nearly famous Penn Stater. So, here are ten who we think are some of the school's notable former students—some of them are alums, whereas some were here for just a brief time. They show just how far and wide Penn State's tentacles have spread.

10. Herman Fisher (1921). In 1930 Fisher created Fisher-Price Toys with Irving Price and Helen Schelle. Creating a toy company in the middle of the Depression was a risky venture, but the three brought 16 of their wooden toys to the International Toy Fair in New York City. According to the company's website, "The whimsical nature and magical surprises of those first toys quickly caught on and became the hallmarks of Fisher-Price ever since."

9. Valerie Plame Wilson (1985). It's okay to write her name now, right? The former CIA undercover officer became the center of controversy when Richard Armitage "leaked" her name to syndicated columnist Bob Novak. Wilson has gone on to write about her life and the incident in a book titled *Fair Game: My Life as a Spy, My Betrayal by the White House*. It was made into a movie starring Naomi Watts as Wilson. It also stars . . .

8. Ty Burrell (1997 grad student). When he's not starring in the hit comedy *Modern Family* as Phil Dunphy, Burrell is appearing in movies such as *Fair Game*, *National Treasure: Book of Secrets*, and *The Incredible Hulk*.

7. Steve McCurry (1974). He may be famous for his "Afghan Girl" photo that appeared on the cover of *National Geographic* in June 1985, but McCurry has done so much more while becoming one of the more renowned photojournalists. And how's this for a way to make a living: In a 2009 interview with *Town&Gown* he said his greatest accomplishments "have been managing to stay alive, despite being in a plane crash in 1989, being almost drowned by a bunch of thugs in Bombay in 1992, being jailed twice in Pakistan, being robbed at gunpoint twice in Afghanistan, as well as being bombed and repeatedly shot at over the past 15 years."

6. Jonathan Frakes (1974). He starred as Commander Riker in *Star Trek: The Next Generation* and some of the *Star Trek* movies that followed. And a bit of *Star Trek* trivia—Frakes is one of only two Star Trek regulars to appear in four different *Star Trek* series. Besides *The Next Generation*, he also appeared in *Deep Space Nine*, *Voyager*, and *Enterprise*. Majel Barrett-Roddenberry, wife of *Star Trek* creator Gene Roddenberry, appeared in all six television series.

5. Jef Raskin (1967 grad student). Raskin taught art, photography, and computer science at the University of California, San Diego, in the early 1970s. Oh, yeah, he eventually went on to start the Macintosh project for Apple Computers. Raskin envisioned an easy-to-use computer for the masses. Though he left Apple in 1982, it's safe to say he achieved that goal.

4. Guion Bluford Jr. (1964). Astronaut Bluford made history in 1983 when he became the first African American in space. He flew and conducted experiments on four separate shuttle missions and was inducted into the International Space Hall of Fame in 1997. Prior to his space flights, Bluford had flown 144 combat missions in Vietnam and was awarded ten air medals. He is a Penn State Distinguished Alumnus.

3. Hugh Rodham (1935)/John Aniston (1955). These two gentlemen accomplished much on their own, but perhaps their greatest achievements are being fathers to two of the world's most famous women. Rodham, of course, was father of current Secretary of State and former First Lady and Senator Hillary Rodham Clinton. He had a successful career in the textile-supply industry. He died in 1993, just a few months after his daughter became First Lady of the United States. Aniston is known for his role as Victor Kiriakis on *Days of Our Lives* and for being the father of Jennifer Aniston, whom you may occasionally see on covers of tabloid magazines.

2. Richard James (1939). The inventor of the Slinky. Enough said!

1. Gene Kelly (1933). One of the most iconic performers in American history, Kelly is best known for his performance in *Singin' in the Rain*. He was the top star for Hollywood musicals until the genre declined in the late 1950s. Despite starring in classics such as *Singin' in the Rain*, *Anchors Aweigh*, and *An American in Paris*, Kelly garnered just one Academy Award nomination for Best Actor. Still, he's considered one of Hollywood's greats, and in 1999 the American Film Institute ranked him 15th on its list of Greatest Male Stars of All-Time.

WHY THE 1982 POLLS GOT IT RIGHT BY VOTING PENN STATE OVER SMU

The 1982 football season will live forever for those Penn State fans who witnessed it unfold. The Nittany Lions won their first official national championship, but it was not without controversy. Though the Sugar Bowl game against Georgia was a No. 1 vs. No. 2 matchup, after the New Year's Day bowl games ended, the SMU Mustangs were the only undefeated team in the country, with an 11–0–1 record. In a reversal of what some of Joe Paterno's earlier teams experienced, this Nittany Lion squad was on the winning side of the pollsters' whims. SMU partisans cried foul, but were they justified in their claims? Here are five reasons why the Nittany Lions were correctly crowned kings of 1982.

5. Penn State had more talent. The Nittany Lions had four All-Americans (Curt Warner, Walker Lee Ashley, Kenny Jackson, and Mark Robinson). In addition, quarterback Todd Blackledge and Warner both finished in the top ten in the Heisman voting. The number of All-Americans on SMU? One, just one—that would be running back Eric Dickerson. After seeing the Lions' defense stop Heisman-winner Marcus Allen in the Fiesta Bowl the year before and what it did to 1982 Heisman-winner Herschel Walker in the Sugar Bowl, picturing a scenario in which SMU's offense would have success against Penn State if the two teams had played is difficult.

4. Pitt was itt. The last two games the Panthers played that season were against Penn State in the regular-season finale and SMU in the Cotton Bowl. Both games were played in less-than-stellar weather conditions and both were basically Pitt road games with the Cotton Bowl played in SMU's hometown of Dallas. Pitt was the loser in each contest. So what can we glean from each game? Penn State threw for 140 yards against the Panthers compared to SMU's 101. How about the "Pony Express" of Dickerson and Craig James? The Mustangs racked up 153 yards rushing in the Cotton Bowl; the Nittany Lions rushed for 210 the day after Thanksgiving. SMU won by four points, 7–3, whereas Penn State defeated Pitt by nine, 19–10.

3. SMU cheated. SMU is the only school in NCAA history to receive the "Death Penalty," the suspension of its football program. The recruiting violations that led to this severe penalty all occurred in the 1980s. The 1981 team, which featured Dickerson and James, was on probation and thus was not eligible for the Southwest Conference championship or participation in a bowl. According to the book written by David Whitford, *A Payroll to Meet*, a number of Mustang players were paid $300 a month, and some, such as Eric Dickerson, were given cars—usually a Nissan 280Z.

2. Strength of schedule. Unlike today, when all you basically need is a pulse to be invited to play in a bowl game, there were only 16 such games in 1982. Six of Penn State's 11 regular-season opponents played in bowls, including Pitt in the Cotton and Nebraska in the Orange. SMU played just one team that went to a bowl (Arkansas in the Bluebonnet).

1. SMU did not go for the win. All this would be moot if only the Mustangs were able to defeat Arkansas in their regular-season finale played in Texas Stadium. The Mustangs trailed the Razorbacks 17-10 with six minutes remaining when quarterback Lance McIlhenny scored on a two-yard keeper. The Mustangs eschewed the chance to win the game with a two-point conversion and opted to kick the extra point. The game ended in a 17-17 tie. Contrast that to Penn State's similar situation in 1978. Owning a No. 1 ranking and a date in the Sugar Bowl with Alabama, Penn State trailed Pitt 10-7 with five minutes to play. The Nittany Lions had a fourth-and-2 from the Pitt 4. Joe Paterno went for the win, and Mike Guman's touchdown run gave the Lions the lead in an eventual 17-10 victory.

WHY THE VOTERS GOT IT WRONG IN 1994

We can spend all day speculating whether Penn State, with its juggernaut offense, would have beaten Nebraska in 1994. At the very least, that the Lions and Cornhuskers didn't split the national title is one of the biggest shames in recent history; instead, Nebraska finished No. 1 in both the AP and Coaches polls. Here are five reasons why we think those voters got it wrong.

5. Big Ten vs. Big 8. In 1994 the Big Ten had five teams finish with winning records. The Big 8 had only three. The Big 8 went 2–2 in bowl games. The Big Ten went 4–1. The Big 8 also had one team—Iowa State—finish winless. More on them later.

4. October 29. Penn State entered this day ranked No. 1 in both polls. The Lions proceeded to thump No. 21 Ohio State, 63–14, whereas Nebraska beat undefeated Colorado, 24–7, in Lincoln. Nebraska jumped over Penn State to No. 1 in the AP poll (thanks, surprisingly, to some voters from Big Ten cities changing their votes), whereas the Lions still held the edge in the Coaches poll. The victory over the Buffalos was Nebraska's hallmark win of the season. But how good were the Buffaloes? They did beat Wisconsin at home early in the season, but they needed a miracle Hail Mary to beat Michigan, barely defeated an average Texas team, and struggled to a 17–3 win over what ended up being a three-win Oklahoma State team.

3. November 5. Anyone who watched the PSU-Indiana game this day knows what happened, but obviously some coaches who voted in the Coaches poll didn't watch. Penn State led 35–14 with a little more than six minutes remaining. JoePa put in his second- and third-teamers to finish up the game. The Hoosiers scored two late TDs, including one on a Hail Mary on the last play of the game, to make the 35–29 score appear closer than the game actually was. Nebraska overtook PSU in the Coaches poll and strengthened their position in the AP poll. Mind you, Indiana did finish the season 6–5. So if the Lions were "punished" for a "close" game with a 6–5 team, surely the Cornhusker would be punished if they had a close game with, say, a winless team. In the words of Lee Corso, "Not so fast," because the very next week Nebraska played . . .

2. Iowa State. The Cyclones were one of the worst teams in Division I in 1994. They finished with a 0–10–1 record. But on November 12 Iowa State played Nebraska tough and trailed just 14–12 after the third quarter. The Cornhuskers scored two TDs in the fourth quarter to win 28–12, but the fact that they were in a tight contest with a winless team didn't harm them. They maintained their No. 1 ranking in both polls.

1. 1997. Although the 1997 season has nothing to do with what happened in 1994, it does serve as a source of frustration and, maybe, evidence into the politics that were involved in what happened that season. Just three years after Penn State went undefeated, rolled through the Big Ten, won the Rose Bowl, and yet didn't earn a share of the national title, voters somehow decided to split the 1997 national championship between Michigan and Nebraska. The AP, including its voters from Big Ten towns, gave the title to Michigan; the Coaches gave it to the Cornhuskers and head coach Tom Osborne, who, before the bowl games, announced he was retiring. Why is it that what made sense in 1997 didn't make sense in 1994? One can only speculate.

1959—THE SEASON THAT ALMOST WAS
:: BY RICHIE LUCAS

The 1959 season holds a special place in the history of Penn State football. For most of the campaign Penn State was challenging for a major bowl bid and a chance at the national championship. Leading the team was one the greatest Lions—Richie Lucas. Lucas led the offense in passing and rushing, and on defense he led the team in interceptions. He also was primed to win the top individual prize in college football—the Heisman Trophy. Lucas, who lives in State College, offers his reflections on the great ride of 1959.

5. Setting the tone. Penn State and many of the schools in the region were considered "lowly eastern" football programs. A season opening 19–8 win at Missouri (which would end up playing in the Orange Bowl) made people take notice of our team. A few weeks later we beat Illinois. [PSU would start the season 7–0 and reached a high-water mark of No. 7 in the AP poll. Then . . .]

4. Heartbreaking losses to Syracuse and Pitt. We lost by two points (20–18) to Syracuse [who was ranked No. 4]. We missed an extra point after our first touchdown [a Roger Kochman 17-yard run]. We were chasing that point the rest of the day. We missed a two-point try in the fourth quarter [following a Kochman 100-yard kickoff return]. Two weeks later we lost at Pitt (22–7). It seemed like we always played at Pitt [Lucas did] because their stadium was twice as large as ours.

3. The Heisman Trophy vote. There were not the prebanquet events for the Heisman like there are today, and there was not the TV coverage of the award that you now see. I found out that I finished second to Billy Cannon when I picked up a newspaper at an airport in Arizona. I didn't even know the Heisman was a big deal. Later on, when I met Cannon, I jokingly told him that I formed a committee of my buddies to look into the voting results and they reported back that the voters did not do a good job.

2. The Liberty Bowl. We weren't aware of the behind-the scenes politics that required Penn State to play in the Liberty Bowl [it was the first Liberty Bowl and it was played in Philadelphia] instead of playing a game in a southern city. I thought it was a good thing Bear Bryant did by agreeing to not only play a "lowly eastern" school but also play them in a northern cold environment. Back then, southern teams did not travel north to play teams in our part of the country.

1. Joe Paterno. You could tell back then that he was going to be a great head coach [Paterno was Lucas's position coach]. Rip Engle was such a good coach himself; he was a gentleman, and when he retired I was worried that the university would make the wrong choice and not name Paterno as his replacement. I was glad they did the right thing.

COULD'A... SHOULD'A... WON THE HEISMAN

The first Heisman Trophy was awarded following the 1935 season. Only one Nittany Lion—John Cappelletti in 1973—has won the coveted award. Cappelletti's acceptance speech, when he dedicated the Heisman to his younger brother, Joey, who was dying of childhood leukemia, is generally regarded as one of the greatest Heisman moments.

Given the grand tradition of Penn State football and the number of great players who have worn the Blue and White, should other Nittany Lions have won the Heisman? Three were runners-up and one finished third. Those four are on this list along with a few others who received accolades for a fine season but came up short at the awards ceremony.

10. Chuck Fusina—1978. He led Penn State to consecutive 11–1 seasons in his final two years in Happy Valley. He was the quarterback who guided the Nittany Lions to their first No. 1 ranking in the AP poll when Penn State finished the 1978 regular season at 11–0. That more than anything propelled the Pittsburgh native to a second-place finish behind Oklahoma running back Billy Sims in the Heisman Trophy voting. Actually, Fusina's junior season was more productive. He completed 58 percent of his passes, throwing 15 touchdowns and nine interceptions. There was a slight drop in his 1978 numbers—56 percent completion rate, 11 TDs, and 12 INTs. Fusina did win the Maxwell Award in 1978, presented to the best player in the country.

> **Verdict:** Could'a. Fusina actually got more first-place votes than Sims (163–151), but Sims more than made up for it with a 152–89 advantage in second-place votes. However, it's hard to argue against Sims's winning—he led the nation in rushing and scoring.

9. Curt Warner—1982. The 1982 season had a loaded field of Heisman contenders, including two on the Nittany Lion roster—running back Warner and quarterback Todd Blackledge. Warner rushed for 1,041 yards and scored eight TDs. He finished tied with Nebraska running back Mike Rozier for tenth in the Heisman voting as the award went to Georgia running back Herschel Walker.

Warner showed he was worthy of Heisman consideration as he went head-to-head with Walker in the Sugar Bowl that decided the 1982 national championship. Warner scored two touchdowns and out-rushed Walker 117 yards to 107—the second consecutive year Warner out-rushed the Heisman winner in a head-to-head bowl match-up.

Verdict: Could'a. Walker was the dominant player in college football, so he deserved the trophy.

8. Mike Reid—1969. Not many players on defense get strong Heisman consideration. Reid's stellar 1969 season, however, was good enough for a fifth-place finish in the Heisman voting, with Oklahoma running back Steve Owens winning the award. Reid was the anchor of the defense that led Penn State to a second consecutive undefeated season. He registered 89 tackles and returned an interception for a touchdown against Maryland. Reid won the Maxwell Award and the Outland Trophy, which is given to college football's best interior lineman.

Verdict: Could'a. Though upgrading Reid to Should'a is tempting, Owens had a monster season for the Sooners rushing for a then-Big 8 single-season record 1,536 yards, and he broke O.J. Simpson's NCAA record for carries with 357.

7. Michael Robinson—2005. Few PSU quarterbacks have done more for their team than what Robinson did in 2005. The senior led the Lions to the Big Ten title, passing for 2,350 yards and 17 TDs and rushing for 806 yards and 11 touchdowns. Just as impressive as the numbers was Robinson's leadership: He was the driving force in bringing the Nittany Lions back to relevance in college football. He won the Big Ten Offensive Player of the Year Award and finished fifth in the Heisman voting in one of the most talented fields in recent memory. USC running back Reggie Bush won the award over Texas quarterback Vince Young, USC quarterback Matt Leinert, Notre Dame quarterback Brady Quinn, and Robinson.

Verdict: Could'a. Any other year and Robinson probably wins this. But this was the year of Texas and USC, so either Bush, Leinert, or Young were going to win the Heisman. Although now, technically, nobody won it after Bush forfeited the trophy in 2010 because of an investigation that showed he had received improper benefits while at USC.

6. Lydell Mitchell—1971. Mitchell held the top spot as the all-time Nittany Lion career rusher until Warner broke his mark in 1982. Of Mitchell's 2,934 career yards, 1,567 came in his 1971 senior season. He was the primary weapon in Penn State's third 11-win season in four years. He finished his career with a 147-yard effort in the Nittany Lions' 30–6 rout over Texas in the Cotton Bowl, earning him Offensive Player of the Game honors. He finished fifth in the Heisman voting, as the award went to Auburn quarterback Pat Sullivan.

Verdict: Could'a. Again, moving him up to Should'a is very tempting, but it's tough to jump Mitchell over Sullivan, who passed for 20 touchdowns, or Oklahoma running back Greg Pruitt, who rushed for 1,760 yards.

5. Todd Blackledge—1982. The triggerman of Air Paterno, Blackledge put up a record-setting season. His 22 touchdown passes are still a Penn State single-season record. His efforts helped Penn State become the first team to win the national title while passing for more yards than rushing in a season. Blackledge finished sixth in the Heisman voting.

Verdict: Could'a. Although Blackledge presents a stronger case than Warner, there's still no getting past Walker with his 1,616 yards rushing and all the NCAA records he broke during his three-year college career.

4. Kerry Collins—1994. Not just Penn State, but all of college football had not seen as well-balanced and explosive of an offense than what the 1994 Nittany Lions rolled out en route to their first Big Ten title. State scored at least 31 points in each of its 12 games—all victories. Leading this attack was senior quarterback Collins. He broke Penn State's single-season records for passing yards (2,679) and completion percentage (66.7). He also finished with the fourth-highest passer rating in NCAA history at 172.8. With Collins, the Nittany Lion offense broke 14 school records, led the nation in scoring (47.8 ppg), and also was tops in the country in total offense (520.2 ypg). Despite finishing fourth in the Heisman voting, Collins took home many of the other major awards. He won the Maxwell Award, the Davey O'Brien Award (given to the nation's top quarterback), ABC-TV Player of the Year, and the Big Ten Conference Player of the Year.

Verdict: Should'a. Perhaps teammate Ki-Jana Carter's (second in the Heisman voting) presence took away votes that may have gone to Collins, but one of the greatest seasons a college quarterback has ever had deserved a better fate. Colorado running back and 1994 Heisman-winner Rashaan Salaam was only the fourth player in NCAA history to top 2,000 yards in a season. But as we will soon see on this list, 2,000 yards does not always guarantee the Heisman. Collins's numbers are truly awesome, even more so when you consider that so many of Penn State's games were over by halftime and either Collins was running a conservative offense in the second half or watching from the sidelines as the backups played out the rest of the game.

3. Richie Lucas—1959. The Riverboat Gambler, Lucas was the all-purpose king for the 1959 Nittany Lions. In the era of the two-way player, he did it all—leading Penn State in rushing (325 yards) and passing (913 yards). Lucas also was the team's punter and picked off five passes while playing safety on the defensive side of the ball. With him, Penn State went 9–2, including a 7–0 win over Bear Bryant's Alabama Crimson Tide in the Liberty Bowl. Lucas's season was good enough for a second-place finish in the Heisman voting to LSU's Billy Cannon. Lucas did, however, win the Maxwell Award for his outstanding senior year.

Verdict: Should'a. When comparing the stats between Cannon and Lucas, I have to ask: *How in the heck did Cannon win the Award!?* Cannon rushed for 598 yards—*as a running back!* Lucas had 325 playing quarterback. Cannon had 161 yards receiving, but how does that trump Lucas's production as a passer? I don't think it does (though I am sure some folks from the Bayou won't agree). Cannon also played defense and had four interceptions, which, and correct me if I am wrong, is one less than Lucas's five. Even in the pre-Paterno days, Penn State was receiving little support from the national media.

2. Ki-Jana Carter—1994. As mentioned earlier, the 1994 Penn State offense was one of the (and I argue *the*) most explosive, well-balanced offenses in the history of college football. While Collins was lighting it up in the air, Carter was equally impressive in his final season as Penn State's running back. His three touchdowns and 210 yards rushing at Minnesota was the opening salvo of one of the greatest single seasons for a Penn State running back. He topped the century mark in seven of the next nine games and ended the regular season with another 200-yard performance, rushing for 227 against Michigan State. Oh, by the way, Carter found the end zone five times that day! He also had something left for the Oregon Ducks in the Rose Bowl, rushing for 156 yards—83 coming on a touchdown run on Penn State's first offensive play. He would add two more touchdowns and win the MVP of the game.

Verdict: Should'a. I know, we already have a Should'a from 1994, but if you take Carter's season just as an individual mark, he also should have won the Heisman that year. At worst, he and Collins should have shared the award. The most compelling argument for Carter: 7.7 to 6.9. Carter averaged 7.7 yards per carry compared to Salaam's 6.9. Sure, Salaam topped 2,000 yards, but he needed 98 more carries to get there. Also, just as in Collins's case, Carter was sitting out large portions of the second half due to many of the lopsided wins Penn State had that season.

1. Larry Johnson—2002. Some of the greatest single seasons by a Penn State running back are represented on this list. The *greatest* season by a Nittany Lion rusher was, as the team's play-by-play announcer Steve Jones described it, "2K for L.J." In his only season as State's primary ball carrier, Johnson averaged 7.7 yards per carry for 2,087 yards. How about these numbers in his final four regular-season games: 279 yards vs. Illinois, 118 against Virginia, 325 at Indiana, and 279 yards *in the first half* against Michigan State. Johnson didn't play in the second half against the Spartans, as the game was well out of hand, and Penn State cruised to a 61–7 win. Maybe JoePa should have left Johnson in to crack 400 yards and boost his Heisman chances. His work for the season earned L.J. the Maxwell Award, Walter Camp Award (best player in college football), the Doak Walker Award (best running back), and a third-place finish in the Heisman voting.

Verdict: Should'a. USC quarterback Carson Palmer and Iowa quarterback Brad Banks finished ahead of Johnson. Banks threw for 2,573 yards and 26 touchdowns. Palmer threw for 3,942 yards and 33 touchdowns. Okay, maybe it is not as clear-cut for Johnson as initially believed (especially compared to Palmer's stats), but ponder this: If Johnson played at Tailback U and Palmer for Penn State and they both had the same stats, who wins the Heisman in 2002? Regardless, for those who watched Johnson in 2002, it was an awesome show!

GREATEST QUARTERBACK CONTROVERSIES

Penn State has never been confused as being a quarterback factory like their linebacking counterparts. However, the position does invite a large amount of scrutiny and debate among fans, reporters, and even coaches on the staff—not every year, but it sure seems as if two or three seasons can't go by without a good old-fashioned quarterback controversy sparking the typical questions of "Who should start" and "Who should be benched?" In the 120-plus years of Penn State football, more than 60 seasons involved one Joseph Vincent Paterno having a major say in who would be the Nittany Lions' signal caller. Rip Engle gave him a great deal of authority in the decision during Paterno's 16 years as the quarterbacks' coach. Obviously, JoePa has had some input (putting it mildly) during his time as head coach. What were the biggest QB battles and how did they play out?

10. Michael Robinson vs. Anthony Morelli—2005. In hindsight, it is hard to believe there was a strong debate on this one. Penn State was coming off their fourth losing season in five years. Robinson had limited experience as quarterback, mostly playing when predecessor Zack Mills was injured. Morelli was the prized recruit whom the Nittany Lions pilfered from Pitt, and he was the more traditional pocket passer, whereas Robinson could utilize his mobility to create plays on his own. What many underestimated was Robinson's leadership. Being the upperclassman usually is positive in these decisions for Paterno, and Robinson earned the starting job. A thrill-packed season followed, including a come-from-behind win at Northwestern, the birth of the "Greatest Show in College Football" with the victory over Ohio State, a Big Ten championship, and a victory over Florida State in the Orange Bowl. Robinson passed for 2,350 yards, 17 touchdowns, and was named the Big Ten's Offensive Player of the Year.

9. Mike Cooper/Bob Parsons/John Hufnagel—1970. As the start of the 1970 season loomed, Paterno was left with the challenge of replacing Chuck Burkhart, who had led the Nittany Lions to back-to-back Orange Bowl victories and two perfect seasons. His backup, then-senior Mike Cooper, started the season under center. The first African American quarterback in Penn State history led the Lions to a 55–7 victory over Navy. The offense regressed as the team went deeper into the season, and Cooper and Parsons began to share time as QB. After the Lions suffered a 24–7 loss to Syracuse, sophomore Hufnagel earned the start at Army, and Penn State would close out the season with five consecutive wins. The following season, with Hufnagel now established as the starter, Penn State went 11–1, including a rout over Texas in the Cotton Bowl. In his senior year Hufnagel became the first Nittany Lion quarterback to pass for more than 2,000 yards, as he was named an All-American.

8. Matt Senneca/Zack Mills/Zac Wasserman—2001. Paterno's options prior to the 2001 season were all short on experience. Senneca had 46 pass attempts as Rashard Casey's backup in 2000. Mills and Wasserman were true freshmen. Wasserman dropped out of the competition early when he left the team for personal reasons. With Senneca starting, the Nittany Lions dropped their first four games primarily due to an offense that generated a measly average of 7.75 points a game. Senneca's finest moment occurred in the fifth game at Northwestern. He passed for 234 yards, throwing for one touchdown and rushing for two others. With the Wildcats leading 35–31 late in the game, Senneca was injured, and Mills directed the Lions to a winning touchdown drive. The following week at home against Ohio State, Senneca could not prevent his team from falling 18 points behind. Again, Mills came off the bench and rallied the team to the victory that allowed Paterno to break Bear Bryant's record for most wins by a Division 1-A coach. Mills would go on to set school records for total offense in a career with 7,796 yards and career touchdown passes (41).

7. Don Bailey vs. Milt Plum—1954. Here is a rare moment when Paterno's choice was overruled and it turned out to be the correct decision. Paterno favored Plum, so it was the New Jersey native who started in the season opener at Illinois. However, Plum could not move the team, and head coach Rip Engle replaced him with Bailey. Bailey led the Lions to a 14–12 win and was the starter for the rest of the season. Penn State would go 7–2 and Bailey would go on to win the Most Valuable Player award of the East/West all-star game at the conclusion of the season. Plum would still have a great career at PSU, starting in 1955 and 1956, and became one of the team's best QBs in clutch moments.

6. Tony Sacca vs. Tom Bill—1988–90. This was an odd battle. Bill began 1988 as the starter and led Penn State to a 2–0 start. In the third game against Rutgers, Bill was injured, and with backup Lance Lonergan nursing a thumb injury and third-stringer Doug Sieg out with a bad back, true freshman Sacca was called in to attempt to salvage what would eventually be a 21–16 loss to the Scarlet Knights. Bill was out for the season, so Sacca would start five games that year. At the start of 1989 Bill and Sacca alternated series in an opening loss to Virginia. Weeks later Bill was off the team when he was cited for public drunkenness. Sacca would start the rest of the way and lead the team to a win in the Holiday Bowl over BYU. At the start of 1990 Sacca had the starting job, with Bill now in the role as backup. However, Paterno did not appear to be comfortable with the junior leading the team. Sensing the Lions needed a spark at Alabama in the seventh game of the season, Paterno had Bill take over for Sacca in the third quarter in what would be a 9–0 win. Sacca got the hook in the second quarter the following week at West Virginia as Bill rallied the Lions to a 31–19 win. Bill concluded his senior season in another relief role, leading Penn State to a win at Pitt. When Sacca's Penn State career concluded the following season, he held school records for career and single-season passing yardage.

5. Kevin Thompson vs. Rashard Casey—1998–99. This was another pocket passer "game manager" in Thompson versus the quarterback with dual-threat potential in Casey. Thompson emerged from the 1998 competition as the starter. Casey, like most backups, was more of the people's choice, especially after the Nittany Lions finished 5–3 in the Big Ten and were downright ugly in those losses, being outscored 79–12. Thompson threw only six touchdowns to eight interceptions. In not one of Nittany Nations' finest moments, Thompson was booed at a PSU basketball game when the football team was honored for the past season. He was able to turn those boos into cheers, however, in 1999 when his 79-yard touchdown pass to Chafie Fields gave the Nittany Lions a come-from-behind 27–23 win at Miami. He led the Lions to a 9–0 record, and as the calendar turned to November, Penn State was undefeated and poised to play for the national championship. Then the last-second loss to Minnesota, the blowing a fourth-quarter lead to Michigan, and, sadly, a seven-point loss at Michigan State had fans, who only weeks earlier were planning on a New Year's Eve party in New Orleans (site of the BCS title game), asking for their bowl-trip deposits back when Penn State accepted the invitation to play in San Antonio's Alamo Bowl—the first non-January 1 bowl for the Lions in nine years. Thompson was injured in the lead-up to the bowl game, so Casey started, and Penn State shut out Texas A&M, 24–0. However, the big tease that was Rashard Casey failed to fulfill the expectations. With the starting job his in 2000, the Lions' season was a loser, as they finished 5–7.

4. Gary Wydman vs. Jack White—1964. When assistant coach Joe Paterno and head coach Rip Engle's wife, Sunny, have a terse exchange of words about the quarterback situation, you know you have a controversy. As recounted in *Joe Paterno: Football My Way*, written by Mervin D. Hyman and Gordon S. White Jr., Paterno was out on an island as he seemed to be the only man supporting Wydman. Fortunately for Wydman, Engle gave Paterno the authority in the quarterback department. Wydman was not impressive in the 1964 spring practice sessions, but as the regular season approached, he was Paterno's choice as the starter, a decision that led to disagreements with the other members of the coaching staff. When the Nittany Lions started the season 1–4, the other coaches began to turn up the heat to make a change, and the fans were becoming vocal in their displeasure with the play of the quarterback. Things became tense at a cocktail party when Sunny Engle suggested to Paterno to change quarterbacks. Paterno responded, "Don't put in your two cents Sunny. If Rip wants to change quarterbacks, you tell Rip to come and see me himself." Though tested to the limits, Paterno's faith in Wydman paid off when the Lions closed out the season with five consecutive wins, including a 27–0 upset rout over second-ranked Ohio State in Columbus.

3. Daryll Clark vs. Pat Devlin—2008. Entering the 2008 season, Clark and Devlin appeared to be even in the race for the starting position. Clark's claim to fame to that point was a brief but successful appearance in the 2007 Alamo Bowl win over Texas A&M. Devlin was a prized recruit who backed out of his commitment to Miami when the Hurricanes made a head coaching change. Once again, seniority won out and Clark received the nod in the season opener against Coastal Carolina. Maybe as an indication that the decision to start Clark was not a consensus, Devlin would see meaningful action in the early part of the season. When conference play started, it was apparent that this was Clark's team, as the offense was tailored to his skills. As the triggerman for the newly dubbed "Spread HD Offense," Clark led the Nittany Lions to an 11–1 regular-season record and a third Big Ten title for the program. Following the conference clincher over Michigan State, Devlin left the team and eventually transferred to Delaware. For his 2009 encore Clark became the first Nittany Lion to pass for more than 3,000 yards in a season (3,003), and he threw for 24 touchdowns. He was the co-MVP of the Big Ten and left Penn State holding school records for career-touchdown passes (43), season-touchdown passes (24), and season-passing yardage (3,003).

2. Todd Blackledge vs. Jeff Hostetler—1980. Two talented quarterbacks, both would have great college careers, but there was room for only one at Penn State. Let us take you back to 1980, when redshirt freshman Blackledge and sophomore Hostetler were the two candidates for the top job. Hostetler was named the starter in the opener against Colgate, but Blackledge saw significant playing time in the 54–10 win. Hostetler also was No. 1 on the depth chart in the 21–7 home loss to seventh-ranked Nebraska. The following week at Missouri, Blackledge was named the starter for good. Hostetler would transfer to West Virginia, where, in two seasons, he passed for 4,261 yards and 26 touchdowns. Blackledge would go down as one of the greatest quarterbacks in Penn State history. Individually, he set school records for career- and season-touchdown passes. He directed the Nittany Lions to 29 wins in his 33 starts, which, of course, included the Sugar Bowl win over Georgia that won the 1982 national championship.

1. John Shaffer vs. Matt Knizner—1986. Thanks to two starts in 1984 as a sophomore, Shaffer began 1985 as the top signal caller. It was a job he kept the entire season, thanks in large part to the fact that the Lions kept winning. Penn State finished the regular season 11-0 and ranked No. 1 in the nation, heading to an Orange Bowl matchup with Oklahoma to determine the national champion. Shaffer's regular-season stats, however, were lacking. He completed only 45.1 percent of his passes, with eight touchdowns and 10 interceptions. The door to a quarterback controversy blew wide open following the 25–10 loss to the Sooners. Paterno cited an ineffective passing attack playing a large role in the defeat, as Shaffer could only muster a 10-of-23, 74-yard, three-interception performance. During the off-season the *Harrisburg Patriot News* ran a poll asking fans whom they wanted to start the 1986 season—Shaffer or Knizner. Knizner won in a landslide, but when the season started, it was Shaffer under center against Temple in the opener. The senior was solid, as Penn State scored more than 30 points five times in the regular season. He threw for nine touchdowns and cut the interceptions down to four. Another undefeated regular season also helped quell the naysayers. Penn State had another opportunity to win a national title when it faced top-ranked Miami in the Fiesta Bowl. Shaffer's Fiesta Bowl stats were not much better than his Orange Bowl's, as he went 5-of-13 for 53 yards and one interception. Give Shaffer this: He directed the only legitimate touchdown drive of the game. The Hurricanes had taken a 7–0 lead in the second quarter after a Shaffer pick in PSU territory. He atoned for the mistake by driving the Lions 74 yards, highlighted by a 23-yard completion to Eric Hamilton on a third-and-12. Shaffer capped the drive with a four-yard rollout keeper. The Nittany Lions won, 14–10, and with Shaffer graduating, Knizner was now in charge of a defending national champion in 1987. He could not meet the expectations Nittany Nation placed on him the summer before, as he was 113-of-223 for 1,478 yards with seven touchdowns and 12 interceptions. Penn State would go 8–4 and lose, 35–10, to Clemson in the Florida Citrus Bowl.

LINEBACKER U

You must be doing something right to earn the nickname "Linebacker U." Penn State's ability to turn out top-notch linebackers has become legendary. Two of the linebackers on this list are in the College Football Hall of Fame. Two others hold the distinction of being two-time All-Americans. The Nittany Lions are recognized for being the best at producing linebackers, so here are our best of the best.

10. Charlie Zapiec. He played only one season at linebacker, after being a starting guard on the offensive line of the 1968 and 1969 undefeated teams, and became an All-American. In his senior 1971 season Zapiec set the single-game record for solo tackles by a linebacker with 18 at Iowa.

9. Sean Lee. He was a 2007 All-American and a first-team member of the 2009 All-Big Ten team. He finished his career with 325 tackles, good for fourth on PSU's list.

8. Andre Collins. He had 130 tackles in 1989 in becoming an All-American and a top-five finalist for the Butkus Award. Also, Collins was a Lion coleader in punts blocked in a single season (3) and career (4).

7. Dan Connor. The Lions' leading career tackler with 419, Connor was a 2006 and 2007 All-American. In 2007 he was first-team All-Big Ten and won the Bednarik Award given to the top defensive player in the nation.

6. Greg Buttle. He was a 1975 All-American and was named a winner of the Butkus Silver Anniversary Award in 2000. With 343 career tackles, he held PSU's career-tackling record for more than 30 years.

5. LaVar Arrington. A 1998 and 1999 All-American and 1999 winner of the Butkus, Bednarik, and Lambert awards, Arrington also was first-team All-Big Ten in 1998 and 1999. He was known for his "leaping" abilities—especially with his signature "LaVar Leap" play against Illinois.

4. Dennis Onkotz. A 1968 and 1969 All-American, he shares the team record for interceptions returned for a touchdown (3) and is a member of the College Football Hall of Fame. Many credit him for starting the Linebacker U tradition.

3. Jack Ham. He was a 1970 All-American and the only Nittany Lion to be in both the College and Pro Football halls of fame. He made 90 tackles and had four interceptions during his senior season in 1970.

2. Shane Conlan. Conlan was a 1985 and 1986 All-American and a 1986 Butkus Award finalist. With eight tackles and two interceptions, he was the defensive MVP of the 1987 Fiesta Bowl win over Miami that gave Penn State its second national title. When he graduated, he had more solo tackles (186) than any Penn Stater.

1. Paul Posluszny. He was a 2005 and 2006 All-American and the 2005 winner of the Butkus and Bednarik awards. He also was a two-time first-team All-Big Ten team member and ranks second in career tackles with 372. Posluszny was one of the best leaders in PSU history and helped the program's resurgence after four losing seasons in five years.

THE START OF SOMETHING SPECIAL :: BY JACK HAM

In Penn State's great Linebacker U tradition, Jack Ham is arguably the best of the bunch. He certainly had one of the more storied football careers that you can find. In college he starred on one of the great defensive units in college football (Penn State's 1968 and 1969 teams) that led to two undefeated seasons, and he became an All-American his senior year in 1970. In the NFL he was an All-Pro on the Steel Curtain defense that led the Pittsburgh Steelers to four Super Bowl titles. He is a member of the College Football Hall of Fame (Class of 1990) and the Pro Football Hall of Fame (Class of 1988), and he now teams with play-by-play man Steve Jones, providing commentary on the radio broadcast of Penn State games.

But everything seemed to begin with those 1968 and 1969 teams—Ham's great career, the tradition of Linebacker U, the Nittany Lions' becoming a national power, and the legend of the young head coach at the time, Joe Paterno.

5. Fighting for respect. We were in a situation in which people got us confused and thought we were in Philadelphia—they thought we were the University of Pennsylvania. Going undefeated and beating the likes of UCLA and Kansas State as well as in the bowl games beating Missouri and Kansas—it's an overused cliché trying to get respect, but it played out right. We were not only gaining respect for ourselves but also for eastern college football.

4. It begins up front. Our great defense—it started with our front four. You had Mike Reid and Steve Smear at tackles; you had Gary Hull and John Ebersole on the ends. Three of those guys played professionally—Mike Reid was drafted No. 1. That front four could really get after it and put so much pressure on the other team. Every great defense has to have a great front four. I go to the Pittsburgh Steelers and play with the likes of L.C. Greenwood and Joe Greene, so during my whole career I never knew what bad linemen were.

3. Linebacker U. It started with Denny Onkotz, and I was after him, and it continued. Great defenses—that was Joe's philosophy then and it still is. You saw it with Sean Lee and Navorro Bowman. You build a reputation from winning, and we were winning a lot of football games. If you're a linebacker and want to be the best, you'd look to go to a university like Penn State.

2. No ordinary Joe. I went down to watch practice in the spring [of 2010] and [Paterno] was yelling to the linemen about blocking. He sounded like that 40 years ago when he was yelling at Smear and Mike Reid. It's amazing. I guess if you're around young people it helps if you remain young. When I played, he had the offer from the Pittsburgh Steelers to coach before they went with Chuck Noll. He stayed at Penn State. Joe was meant for college football. Of course, I was just trying to make the football team back then. I wasn't thinking about the legacy of Joe Paterno. One thing: Joe was against athletic dorms in college, so a lot of guys were in fraternities. Football is just part of your college experience. If you're always around the same people, that's not a good experience. He believed you needed to be diversified, and I totally agree with that. It added to my college experience.

1. Team, team, team. We had different guys who made big plays. That's how we were able to go 11–0 for two years. You had Mike Reid sacking Bobby Douglas twice in the Orange Bowl against Kansas. You had big interceptions from George Landis against Missouri. Denny Onkotz made big plays. Different people put that streak together; it wasn't just one guy. That's what was so special about that time.

DYNAMIC DUO :: BY LYDELL MITCHELL

Few backfields in college football history can match what the Lions had with Lydell Mitchell and Franco Harris. The two played three seasons together from 1969 through 1971. Three times they each rushed for at least 100 yards in the same game, and once, against Boston College in 1969, the two were joined by Charlie Pittman, as all three broke 100 against the Eagles. As Penn State's featured back in 1971, Mitchell became an All-American and finished fifth in the Heisman Trophy race, rushing for a then-team record of 1,567 yards (Larry Johnson broke that mark in 2002). He also scored a NCAA record 29 touchdowns that season (Oklahoma State's Barry Sanders broke the record in 1988). As a result of his outstanding career at Penn State, Mitchell was inducted into the College Football Hall of Fame. Both Mitchell and Harris went on to have great success in the NFL—Mitchell with an All-Pro career for the Baltimore Colts, where he established franchise rushing and receiving records for a back, and Harris as a Pro Football Hall of Fame running back for the Pittsburgh Steelers. Through it all the two have remained close friends and also are business partners. Mitchell reflects on the top moments for the Dynamic Duo.

8. How it began. Both Franco and I came from South Jersey. (Harris was from Mt. Holly, and Mitchell was from Salem.) Ernie Accorsi (who was then Penn State's assistant sports publicity director) and Joe Paterno were flying over South Jersey. Joe pointed down there and said, "There's two guys down there that if we get those two guys we can be a pretty good football team." They arranged for us to visit Penn State the same weekend. We hung out, shot pool, went out to dinner. Franco committed to Penn State before me because I was being heavily recruited by Woody Hayes at Ohio State and had given him a tentative verbal commitment. I had to tell Coach Hayes I wasn't coming. Talk about a tough call for a kid to make! I can still hear his shrill voice in my ear more than 40 years later. Then I made the commitment to Penn State.

7. 1969. Charlie Pittman was a senior on that team and we were sophomores. Charlie was our mentor. He was the man. He taught us a lot. Franco and I weren't starters at the beginning of the season. Charlie got hurt and I started my first game against Kansas State. We beat them and I rushed for over 100 yards. I was known to be a little cocky back then because I had a lot of confidence in myself, but that game was like a proving ground and elevated me to the next level. The three of us eventually all started. I was more the wingback and would play flanker. Charlie would occasionally play wingback and I'd be the running back. Franco was always in the backfield playing fullback.

6. 1970 Orange Bowl. I remember getting ready for the Orange Bowl and the coaches put the game plan in. They put *one* running play for me. Franco and Charlie had all of the running plays. I had the pass plays. I was upset, and when we were running one of the pass plays in practice and I wasn't going 100 percent, I turned around and Joe was there. He said, "What's wrong with you?" I said, "You gave me one running play!" I was mad about that. He said, "I put this pass play in for you and you're going to score a touchdown." And wouldn't you know that ended up being the play that scored the winning touchdown (and the game's only touchdown in Penn State's 10–3 win over Missouri). So once again, Joe Paterno was right. Even today Joe never misses an opportunity to remind me about it. You know, over the years, a lot of us who played for him have said that the older we become, the smarter Joe gets.

5. Rousing speech leads to—a loss. I remember our junior year. We went out to Colorado, but it didn't go very well and we ended up getting beat, which ended our three-year winning streak. So we finally made a *Sports Illustrated* cover, but it has a Colorado guy killing Franco on a play. The next week we went to Wisconsin, and Joe was furious before the game. He was mad, and he took the *Sports Illustrated* and he flings it. He said, "I wish I could play!" Franco and I both weren't big on pep talks, but this time we were all fired up—the team was ready to tear the hinges off the door. We ran out on the field—and Wisconsin promptly beat the heck out of us. Looking back, it's a funny story, but the reality was that we were struggling at the time. The coaches were starting to make some changes to offense. They were getting me and Franco to run the veer offense, and that wasn't our style. It just didn't work for us.

4. Sharing the wealth. Joe always made Franco and I think we were a package deal. During the first game of our senior year, we opened against Navy and I scored five touchdowns. Joe came up to us after the game and asked me how many touchdowns I had. Then he asked Franco how many he had, and he hadn't had any. Joe said, "Don't worry. You'll get yours next week." The next week against Iowa, Franco had over 100 yards and four touchdowns. Joe figured out how to make us both happy. I don't ever remember competing against Franco. We just went out and did what we had to do to win the football game. But there's a reason Joe Paterno is a college football legend.

3. 1971 season. I didn't see it coming. It just happened. Franco was hurt for a few games, so I got to carry the ball more. Because I got more touches, I had a great year. Joe never promoted anyone for the Heisman because it was always about the team. Basically, Ed Marinaro (from Cornell) and I split the eastern vote, and I finished fifth in the voting. But I think Joe learned from that because, two years later, Cappelletti wins it and Joe pushed the issue there. Joe and I are great friends, and to this day I believe that if he would have pushed for me to win the Heisman, I would have won it. But he didn't do it because it was team, team, team, and I have no problem with that.

2. 1972 Cotton Bowl. That was a very important game. I remember that, as a team, we were reluctant to play the Cotton Bowl because of all the tension in the country with the civil rights movement and having to go Texas to play. We didn't think it was a good place, but we decided to go. It was pretty much what we expected: People there didn't think much of eastern football. They seemed to think, "This is our birthright down here." All week long we heard how we were going to get killed. But you give Joe Paterno an opportunity to prepare for a bowl game, and we're going to beat you unless the talent is so much different. We went there and we spanked Texas, 30–6. It was so gratifying. It was the first time Texas hadn't scored a touchdown with their wishbone. It was a great feeling. I was Offensive Player of the Game (Mitchell rushed for 146 yards and one touchdown), so we could stick our chests out after that. That win put us on the national map: Penn State beat Texas. It proved we could play football with anybody. That game solidified our existence as a major power in college football. (Note: Mitchell was later elected into the Cotton Bowl Hall of Fame.)

1. A lasting friendship. Going to Penn State together worked out perfectly for Franco and me. Some relationships just happen. We still do things together all the time. He's a wonderful person; in fact, I can't think of a better person I know. We stay in constant contact with each other. I remember when I was with the Chargers and was sick in the hospital in San Diego. I had a Staph infection and was gravely ill. I was in the hospital for two or three weeks, and who comes in to see me? He flies in from Pittsburgh and takes time to visit me in the hospital. That's what it's all about. And to think—it all started at Penn State: a lifelong friendship more valuable than any trophy or treasure.

TOP PENN STATE NON-BCS BOWL GAMES

In addition to winning national championships and winning major bowl games, the Nittany Lions also have had some big moments in the "other" bowls. For the purpose of this list, the Rose, Orange, and Sugar Bowls (three of the current BCS bowls) obviously aren't included. The Fiesta Bowl started playing on New Year's Day in 1982, so any games after that point also aren't included. The Cotton Bowl was a major bowl until the 1994 season. The Lions played in three Cotton Bowls during the period of time when the game was considered a major bowl, so those contests weren't considered either. Yes, it's a bit confusing, so to summarize, any bowl game that was not considered a major bowl at the time of the contest was considered for this list. Got it?

10. Fiesta Bowl—December 25, 1977: No. 8 Penn State 42, No. 15 Arizona State 30. Play of the game: Leading 14–7 in the second quarter, the Nits' Jimmy Cefalo returned a punt 67 yards that set up a Matt Bahr field goal. Cefalo would finish the season as the second-best punt returner in the nation.

9. Gator Bowl—December 30, 1961: No. 17 Penn State 30, No. 13 Georgia Tech 15. Play of the game: Trailing 9–7 with under a minute left in the first half, Nittany Lion quarterback Galen Hall's lofted pass found Roger Kochman in the corner of the end zone for a touchdown. It was the only time all season that Tech had allowed more than one touchdown in a game.

8. Liberty Bowl—December 22, 1979: Penn State 9, No. 15 Tulane 6. Play of the game: Following a Green Wave field goal that tied the game, 6–6, with 2:40 to play, the Nittany Lions had one more chance for victory. Fourth-string tailback Joel Coles on the option-pass play connected with Tom Donovan for 40 yards with 35 seconds remaining. It set up kicker Herb Menhardt's game-winning 20-yard field goal.

7. Florida Citrus Bowl—January 1, 1994: No. 13 Penn State 31, No. 6 Tennessee 13. Play of the game: Ki-Jana Carter's 13-yard touchdown sprint with three seconds remaining in the first half ended up being the winning score, as it gave the Lions a 17–13 halftime lead.

6. Gator Bowl—December 30, 1967: Penn State 17, Florida State 17. Play of the game: Facing fourth-and-inches at its own 15-yard line, PSU was pitching a 17–0 shutout. Joe Paterno, in an uncharacteristic move, decided to go for it. Tom Sherman's QB sneak was stuffed short by the Seminoles. The stop changed the momentum of the game and led to 17 unanswered Florida State points.

5. Fiesta Bowl—December 26, 1980: No. 10 Penn State 31, No. 11 Ohio State 19. Play of the game: The first offensive play for the Nittany Lions gave them their first points of the day, as Curt Warner burned the Buckeye defense on a 64-yard touchdown run.

4. Outback Bowl—January 1, 2007: Penn State 20, No. 17 Tennessee 10. Play of the game: Early in the fourth quarter the Lions and Volunteers were tied, 10–10, with Tennessee approaching the "red zone" looking to take the lead. UT running back Arian Foster fumbled prior to being tackled. Penn State's Tony Davis scooped up the ball and raced 88 yards for the touchdown and eventual winning score.

3. Liberty Bowl—December 19, 1959: No. 12 Penn State 7, No. 10 Alabama 0. Play of the game: The only score of the game. With just five seconds remaining in the first half, Penn State lined up for a field goal at the Alabama 18-yard line. Quarterback Galen Hall served as the holder. When he received the snap, Hall executed a fake and completed a pass to halfback Roger Kochman, who eluded tacklers and eventually dove into the end zone for the touchdown.

2. Capital One Bowl—January 1, 2010: No. 13 Penn State 19, No. 12 Louisiana State 17. Play of the game: Playing on one of the worst field conditions in Nittany Lion bowl history, Penn State's Collin Wagner kicked from an angle at the right hash mark, connecting on a 21-yard try with 57 seconds left in the game to give the Lions the lead and eventual victory.

1. Holiday Bowl—December 29, 1989: No. 18 Penn State 50, No. 19 BYU 39. Play of the game: There are so many to choose from, but for this list the top play goes to the one that clinched the Lions' win. It was a crazy end to an offensive shootout. Penn State led, 43–39, with just 63 seconds remaining. However, BYU, led by future Heisman Trophy–winner Ty Detmer, had the ball, and its offense had been nearly unstoppable in the second half. Facing third-and-3 from the Penn State 38, Detmer went back to pass. Converted running back and now strong safety Gary Brown attacked on a blitz, got his hands on Detmer, and then pulled the football away from the BYU quarterback—all in the same motion. Brown raced untouched for a 53-yard touchdown.

TOP MAJOR BOWL VICTORIES

Some have resulted in national championships, whereas others were statement games. Penn State has made success in the "major" bowls part of its status as an elite football program. Although the Nittany Lions had winning seasons and bowl victories prior to when Joe Paterno became head coach, he is the only Penn State coach to win a major bowl. Of Paterno's college-football best 24 bowl victories, 12 have occurred in the majors, BCS, or whatever these games are being called today. To clarify, we are counting the Cotton Bowl victories because those games were considered a major bowl at those times, and we are not counting Penn State's first two Fiesta Bowl victories because the game had not achieved major New Year's Day status until the 1982 contest. So here are the rankings of all 12 of the Lions' major bowl wins.

12. Fiesta Bowl—January 1, 1997: No. 7 Penn State 38, No. 20 Texas 15. Play of the game: In the third quarter, after regaining the lead, the Nittany Lions had the ball deep in their own territory. On a double reverse, Chafie Fields rushed 84 yards to the Longhorn 5. The play set up Anthony Cleary's one-yard touchdown run.

11. Cotton Bowl—January 1, 1975: No. 7 Penn State 41, No. 12 Baylor 20. Play of the game: Tom Shuman's 49-yard touchdown pass to freshman Jimmy Cefalo in the third quarter gave Penn State a 17–14 lead—and the Nits never trailed again.

10. Fiesta Bowl—January 1, 1992: No. 6 Penn State 42, No. 10 Tennessee 17. Play of the game: Trailing 17–7 in the third quarter, the Nittany Lions would score 35 straight points, including 28 in a less than four-minute span that covered the end of the third quarter and start of the fourth quarter. The last of those points came when defensive back Derek Bochna hit Volunteer quarterback Andy Kelly, knocking the football out of Kelly's hands and into the hands of linebacker Reggie Givens, who took it in for a 23-yard touchdown.

9. Fiesta Bowl—January 1, 1982: No. 7 Penn State 26, No. 8 USC 10. Play of the game: In the second quarter the Lions took the lead for good when quarterback Todd Blackledge hit Gregg Garrity on a 52-yard touchdown pass that made the score 14–7, Penn State.

8. Orange Bowl—January 3, 2006: No. 3 Penn State 26, No. 22 Florida State 23 (3 OTs). Play of the game: After missing a game-winning attempt near the end of regulation and a 38-yard attempt in the first overtime, freshman kicker Kevin Kelly finally ended this marathon with a game-winning 29-yard field goal in the third overtime.

7. Cotton Bowl—January 1, 1972: No. 10 Penn State 30, No. 12 Texas 6: Play of the game: John Hufnagel found a *wide* open Scott Skarzynski for a 65-yard touchdown pass, giving the Nittany Lions a 17–6 third-quarter lead. According to *The Penn State Football Encyclopedia,* Skarzynski said after the game that he was so open that "my grandmother could have made the play."

6. Orange Bowl—January 1, 1974: No. 6 Penn State 16, No. 13 Louisiana State 9. Play of the game: Trailing 7–3 in the second quarter, Chuck Herd's one-hand in-stride grab of a Tom Shuman pass went for 72 yards and the go-ahead touchdown.

5. Orange Bowl—January 1, 1970: No. 2 Penn State 10, No. 6 Missouri 3. Play of the game: The only touchdown of the game occurred in the first quarter, when running back Lydell Mitchell caught a 28-yard pass from Chuck Burkhart for the score.

4. Rose Bowl—January 1, 1995: No. 2 Penn State 38, No. 12 Oregon 20. Play of the game: Could there be any doubt? On the Nits' first play from scrimmage, Ki-Jana Carter blows past the Duck defense and is off to the races for an 83-yard touchdown.

3. Orange Bowl—January 1, 1969: No. 3 Penn State 15, No. 6 Kansas 14. Play of the game: With 15 seconds left, Penn State had pulled to within one point when quarterback Chuck Burkhart scored on a keeper from three yards out. The Nittany Lions went for two points and the win. Burkhart's pass sailed over tight end Ted Kwalick, falling incomplete and all but giving the Jayhawks the win—until a penalty flag was thrown and the official's call on the field signaled that Kansas had too many men on the field for that play. Given second life, running back Bob Campbell punched into the end zone for the winning points.

2. Sugar Bowl—January 1, 1983: No. 2 Penn State 27, No. 1 Georgia 23. Play of the game: This is arguably the signature play in the history of Penn State football. Wide receiver Gregg Garrity's diving 47-yard touchdown catch in the fourth quarter clinched the national championship for the Lions.

**1. Fiesta Bowl—January 2, 1987: No. 2 Penn State 14, No. 1 Miami 10.
Play of the game:** There are so many great plays to choose from—Shane Conlan's fourth-quarter interception, D.J. Dozier's winning touchdown—but for *the* play of the game, it has be Pete Giftopoulos's interception of Vinny Testaverde at the goal line, denying the Hurricanes' their last chance and starting the celebration of Penn State's second national championship in five seasons.

MOST MEMORABLE CALLS :: BY STEVE JONES

When it comes to some of the great moments in Penn State athletics over the past few decades, Steve Jones has seen most of them firsthand. Jones is *the* voice of Penn State sports. He'll be entering his 30th season of doing radio play-by-play for the men's basketball team. The 2011 football season will be Jones's 12th as the play-by-play man and 20th overall of helping with the broadcasts. He also is the main voice for the State College Spikes of the New York-Penn League. With all the teams and all the seasons he's seen, Jones has obviously had some great games and moments to call. Here are his top ten.

10. August 3, 2006—State College Spikes vs. Williamsport Crosscutters. Nathan Southard hit a tenth-inning walk-off inside-the-park home run, and I described him belly-flopping into home plate.

9. March 23, 1995—Penn State at Iowa, NIT Quarterfinal. Pete Lisicky hit a shot at the buzzer in the NIT quarterfinal. When the ball was in the air, I said, "Lisicky for three and Madison Square Garden—goooood!"

8. November 23, 2002—Michigan State at Penn State. Larry Johnson got to the end zone on a 38-yard run, and I said, "2 K for L.J."

7. October 8, 2005—Ohio State at Penn State. The emotion in Beaver Stadium was never higher. The nation knew Penn State was back.

6. March 15, 1991—Penn State vs. UCLA, First Round NCAA Tournament. Penn State had won the Atlantic 10 Tournament in its last season in the conference. No one gave them a chance in the Carrier Dome. The Lions beat the fourth-seeded Bruins, 74–69.

5. October 25, 2008—Penn State at Ohio State. Penn State had not won in Columbus since 1978. The winner was in the driver's seat for the Rose Bowl. Penn State played a perfect defensive game, and ending on a Lydell Sargeant interception was appropriate.

4. March 18, 2001—Penn State vs. North Carolina, Second Round NCAA Tournament. Penn State had not been to the Sweet 16 since 1955. In the Superdome the setup was perfect. North Carolina was a big name with a big reputation but started two football players. Penn State had seniors who had beaten Kentucky, Michigan State, Pitt, Ohio State, Temple, and Indiana that year. The Lions upset the second-seeded Tar Heels, 82–74, to advance to the Sweet 16.

3. October 27, 2001—Ohio State at Penn State. 324 for Joe Paterno, and I had a front-row seat to announce history for a great moment and a great man.

2. April 2, 2009—Penn State vs. Baylor, NIT Championship. It was my 27th season of announcing Penn State basketball. I had seen so many up and downs, so to see them cut down the nets with 36 busloads of fans on hand was incredible.

1. January 3, 2006—Penn State vs. Florida State, Orange Bowl. Penn State kicker Kevin Kelly finally wins it in a game with incredible twists and turns.

THE GREATEST GAMES AGAINST THE BIG TEN

Starting in 2011 there will be 12 teams in the Big Ten. We guess brand trumps logic in this conference. Some games were important to winning a conference title, whereas others were just thrilling contests. Since playing their first conference football game in 1993, the Nittany Lions have some memorable battles against their fellow Big Ten members.

Illinois—November 12, 1994, Memorial Stadium. Penn State dug itself into a 21–0 hole in its attempt to clinch the Big Ten title. The Nittany Lions then capped off a long drive in the second quarter with a Brian Milne touchdown to get on the board. Trailing 31–28 midway in the fourth quarter, they had the ball at their own 4-yard line. Several minutes and 14 plays later, Milne plunged into the end zone for his third touchdown of the day and a 35–28 win. At a rally in Rec Hall when the team returned from Champaign, radio play-by-play announcer Fran Fisher belted into a microphone, "Rose Bowl!" letting all know Penn State's New Year's Day destination.

Indiana—November 13, 2004, Memorial Stadium. Heading into the 2004 season, the Hoosiers were the only team to never have defeated the Nittany Lions in conference play. On this sunny afternoon in Bloomington, they had to think that they had their best chance to end that losing streak. It wasn't that the Hoosiers had a strong team in 2004—sporting a 3–6 record, they didn't. Penn State, at the time, was having one of its worst seasons ever. The Nittany Lions were 2–7 overall and an unthinkable 0–6 in Big Ten play. Trailing 22–18, the Hoosiers found themselves with first-and-goal at the Lions' 1-yard line in the closing minutes. They had four chances to win the game—each was denied. On the last attempt running back Chris Taylor was kept out of the end zone by a pack of Lions. The win is credited to being the springboard to Penn State's 2005 Big Ten championship season.

Iowa—September 15, 1984, Kinnick Stadium. We're taking a little liberty with this one. Unfortunately, most of the memorable Penn State/Iowa games since 1993 have ended up being Hawkeye victories. Prior to joining the Big Ten, Penn State would occasionally play Iowa, as was the case in 1984, when the No. 12 Lions visited the fifth-ranked Hawkeyes. Early in the fourth quarter PSU quarterback Doug Strang scored on a one-yard keeper that gave Penn State a ten-point lead at 20–10. Iowa came right back, and with just over ten minutes to play, Hawkeye quarterback Chuck Long countered with his own one-yard touchdown, making the score 20–17. The Hawkeyes would have only one more possession the rest of the game, and it ended when Ray Isom, Duffy Cobbs, and Michael Zordich stuffed running back Ronnie Harmon on fourth-and-1 from the Penn State 29.

Michigan—October 15, 1994, Michigan Stadium. This was one of the great Penn State regular-season wins in history. The Nittany Lions built a 16–0 first-half lead, only to see the Wolverines go in front 17–16 in the third quarter. With just under three minutes to play in a game tied 24–24, Penn State's Kerry Collins hit Bobby Engram for a 16-yard touchdown. Penn State would hold on for a 31–24 win and take the No. 1 ranking in both the AP and Coaches polls.

Michigan State—November 25, 1995, Spartan Stadium. This game had all the ingredients for a classic two-minute drill leading to victory. Time: 1:47 remaining. Score: Michigan State 21, Penn State 17. Starting position: Penn State 27. Nittany Lion timeouts remaining: 0. No problem for quarterback Wally Richardson. The junior hit 9 of 12 passes, bringing the ball to the Spartan 4-yard line with 13 seconds remaining. On his 13th pass attempt of the drive, Richardson dumped the ball off to Bobby Engram, who ducked under two defenders and dove into the end zone, giving the Lions a 24–20 win.

Minnesota—October 7, 2006, Metrodome. Minnesota tied the game 21–21 late in the fourth quarter to send the contest into overtime. After the Golden Gophers scored a touchdown in the extra session, a missed extra point made the score 27–21. The Lions survived a replay challenge on a fourth-and-9 Anthony Morelli-to-Derrick Williams pass near the sidelines. Penn State kept the ball with the first down ruling. Later, Tony Hunt's 11-yard touchdown run and Kevin Kelly's extra point made the final score 28–27 in favor of Penn State.

Nebraska—September 25, 1982, Beaver Stadium. Any doubts it would be the Miracle of Mount Nittany? Widely considered the greatest regular-season game in Penn State history, the Nittany Lions led 14–0 in the second quarter. The Cornhuskers would eventually come all the way back to take a 24–21 lead with 1:18 left in the game. Starting at its own 35-yard line and led by quarterback Todd Blackledge, Penn State made the most of its limited time, driving to the Husker 2. Then Kirk Bowman, the man nicknamed "Stonehands," scooped up Blackledge's pass inches from the turf for his second touchdown of the day, giving Penn State a 27–24 win.

Northwestern—September 24, 2005, Ryan Field. After four losing seasons in five years, Penn State was not exactly dominant in its three nonconference games (South Florida, Cincinnati, and Central Michigan) to start 2005. That style of play continued in its Big Ten opener at Northwestern. At one point the Nittany Lions trailed 23–7 and were down 29–27 when they began their final drive late in the fourth quarter. The drive almost did not get beyond their first series of downs. Facing fourth-and-15 deep in Penn State territory, senior quarterback Michael Robinson connected with tight end Isaac Smolko for 20 yards and the first down. The drive ended with Robinson hitting wide receiver Derrick Williams for a 36-yard touchdown and a 34–29 win.

Ohio State—October 8, 2005, Beaver Stadium. There were so many great images and positive results from this game. It was the birth of "Paternoville" and the atmosphere that Penn State markets as "The Greatest Show in College Football." After trailing 3–0, the Nittany Lions scored 17 unanswered points and then, in classic Paterno style, turned the game over to the defense. Ohio State narrowed the margin to 17–10 and was driving to tie the game late in the fourth quarter when Tamba Hali belted Buckeye quarterback Troy Smith. The hit jarred the ball loose, and Scott Paxson recovered for Penn State. The win pushed Penn State's record to 6–0, signaling that the Lions were back as a national power.

Purdue—October 23, 1999, Ross-Ade Stadium. With Penn State leading 31–25 late in the fourth quarter, Purdue QB Drew Brees drove the Boilermakers to the Lions' 12-yard line. With 31 seconds remaining, he had four pass attempts to give Purdue the lead and end second-ranked Penn State's undefeated season right there. However, all four attempts fell incomplete, and the Lions survived. Two of Penn State's defensive stars scored TDs in this game. Linebacker LaVar Arrington scored in the second quarter when he sacked Brees, forced a fumble, and went two yards into the end zone. Defensive end Courtney Brown then scored in the third quarter on a 25-yard interception return that gave PSU a 28–14 lead.

Wisconsin—October 5, 2002, Camp Randall Stadium. After a heartbreaking overtime loss to Iowa the week before, the Nittany Lions bounced back very nicely at one of the more challenging venues in the conference. They jumped out to a 10–0 lead, but B.J. Tucker's 65-yard pick-six off of Zack Mills in the second quarter gave the Badgers a 14–13 lead. No matter, star running back Larry Johnson put Penn State in the lead for good, scoring on a nifty run on the following possession. He added a two-point conversion to give the Lions a seven-point lead. Penn State held on for a 34–31 win.

ROAD TRIP EATS :: BY FRANK BODANI

One of the things many Penn State fans enjoy is traveling with the Nittany Lions. They usually come to the visiting towns on Friday, watch the games on Saturday, and return home on Sunday. That leaves limited time to see and really experience what these other college towns have to offer.

Frank Bodani has covered the Penn State football team for the *York Daily Record* since 1994. He has become the unofficial restaurant guru on the beat, as he looks for different spots for himself and some of the other reporters to try. Bodani gives his top restaurants to hit in each Big Ten town, including the newest member, Nebraska. This will hopefully help you in your travels with the Lions.

11. Nebraska—Misty's Restaurant and Lounge (6235 Havelock Avenue, Lincoln, Nebraska). They have great steaks, chops, and chicken, including a buffalo ribeye. Plus, you get treated to the Big Red pep band parading through the place on Friday nights before games!

10. Michigan State—Traveler's Club International Restaurant and Tuba Museum (2138 Hamilton, Okemos, Michigan). There's no other place like it, not with more than 200 beers to choose from and tubas of all shapes and sizes adorning the walls. Plus, the menu "travels" from Asian to Latin to Middle Eastern influences, with simple dishes each month.

9. Northwestern—Davis Street and Fish Market (501 Davis Street, Evanston, Illinois). This is another late-night option close to the stadium that's perfect for after the game. They have a satisfying selection of fresh fish, featuring some interesting fusion and side-dish options, including a grilled skate wing special.

8. Illinois—Radio Maria (119 North Walnut Street, Champaign, Illinois). They boast a varied menu that features tapas (small plates) for sharing and a knockout wine, beer, and cocktail list. Late-night Latin dancing around the bar accentuates everything from the fried goat cheese to the stellar steaks.

7. Indiana—Casablanca Café (402 East 4th Street, Bloomington, Indiana). This is a Moroccan restaurant in a renovated house where the waitress pours hot tea perfectly into cups from about two feet off the table—a nice start. There are dishes with Mediterranean and even Italian touches throughout.

6. Purdue—Triple XXX Family Restaurant (S.R. 26 West and Salisbury, West Lafayette, Indiana). It's been there forever, is almost always open, and serves just about the most legendary hamburgers and sides and root beer in the state.

5. Wisconsin—Chautara (334 State Street, Madison, Wisconsin). This is an interesting find that serves Nepalese—the food of Tibet. There are plenty of vegetarian options and lots of influences from India and even the Mediterranean.

4. Minnesota—Chino Latinos (2916 Hennepin Avenue, Minneapolis, Minnesota). It's sleek and hip and where beautiful people hang out to get huge plates of food from the "hot zones." We're talking Jamaica to Asia to the Americas, and it's best to go with a group in order to share offerings such as the Cuban Roast Pork Crisis.

3. Iowa—Graze (115 East College Street, Iowa City, Iowa). This has a dark, modern martini bar-feel, with impressive martinis, of course. But the draw is the gourmet, meal-sized appetizers served on "grazing towers" for the table to share. Big hits are the "chicken lips" (chicken tenders), pizzas, and sliders.

2. Michigan—Pacific Rim by Kana (114 West Liberty Street, Ann Arbor, Michigan). A nice selection of seafood stands out on the Pan-Asian menu, and the well-designed, unique dessert offerings add a nice ending to an intimate meal. It serves late, so it's perfect after a 3:30 p.m. game!

1. Ohio State—Kihachi Japanese Restaurant (2667 Federated Boulevard, Columbus, Ohio). This is authentic—meaning no elaborate sushi bar or knife-wielding chefs making onion volcanoes; rather, the daily specials are written in Japanese (and are translated by your bilingual waitress) and feature small-plate selections such as baby octopus, sea urchin, and a braised eel omelet-like dish—to go with plenty of tempura (fried) vegetables, and noodle and rice dishes.

BEST PIZZA IN THE KEYSTONE STATE
:: BY MIKE MUNCHAK

Although major cities such as New York and Chicago claim that they make the greatest pizza, there are those (including the two authors of this book) who have tasted the pizza made in Northeastern Pennsylvania and would rate that the best. Somebody who also agrees with that sentiment is NFL Hall of Famer and Nittany Lion great Mike Munchak. Munchak is from Scranton, Pennsylvania. Nearby is Old Forge, home to the famous Old Forge Pizza. Playing his entire career for the Houston Oilers, Munchak says great pizza places were not as abundant in Houston as they are back home. Named head coach of the Tennessee Titans in February 2011, he says he forgoes eating pizza the month prior to his returning to his hometown for a visit so he can enjoy feasting on the many options available in Old Forge and Scranton; he says he feels like he gains five to ten pounds after each trip. Here, he offers his favorite pizza places in the Scranton area as well as those he enjoyed in State College when he was a member of one of the greatest offensive lines in Penn State history.

8. Buona Pizza—Scranton. They offer round-style pizza and are a great place to walk in and grab a slice or two for a snack.

7. Hi-Way Pizza—State College. This is another great place to walk in and have a few slices. A bonus when I was in school was that they regularly had live music.

6. Brothers Pizza—State College. I loved the Friday special—two cuts and a soda. Brothers is a round pizza similar to Buona. If I was walking along College Avenue, I would have to stop in and have some pizza, even if I was not hungry.

5. Alfredo's—Scranton. They have gotten a lot of national attention lately because of the many references on the TV show *The Office*. Square-style pizza, the difference between Alfredo's and other places in the Old Forge/Scranton area is the blend of a variety of cheeses.

4. Revello's—Old Forge. This is typical Old Forge, square-style pizza. The best thing about this type of pizza is that you can eat seven to eight slices and not feel bloated.

3. Pizza by Pappas—Scranton. Located near what was Scranton Central High School, Pizza by Pappas is round, greasy—in a good way—and with a crispy crust.

2. Bell's Greek Pizza—State College. This was the best pizza to eat when hanging out in the dorms or apartments when I was going to school at Penn State. I roomed with linebacker Chet Parlavecchio, and he would order Bell's three times a week. That was his routine: eating Bell's pizza and watching his hockey games on TV.

1. Arcaro and Genell—Old Forge. They have a square pizza dough with a light crust that sets it apart from the other places. What also makes it great is their blend of different cheeses. They have this backroom where about 30 of my family members get together when I am back in town and we eat pizza all night. When I was playing, I kept talking about Arcaro and Genell to my Oiler teammate Bruce Matthews. I finally got him to Old Forge and he loved their pizza.

Gone but Not Forgotten: Biff's Pizza—Scranton. Biff's also was that square-tray pizza that had a good crispy crust.

ALL-TIME BARS IN STATE COLLEGE :: BY JEFF BYERS

In a college town you know you're going to have a wide selection of places to enjoy some adult beverages, food that probably isn't good for you, and some quality entertainment—good times to be had by all. Having grown up in State College, Jeff Byers, Penn State's longtime play-by-play man for wrestling, has become quite familiar with Happy Valley's nightlife. Here are his top all-time State College bars.

13. Lion's Den. The Den has a different feel to it at different times. There is an outside deck, an inside bar and dance area, and a downstairs that has a more elegant vibe.

12. Mad Mex. With its outside seating in the spring and summertime, it has flourished as a hot spot. It is famous for its margaritas and Mexican bar food.

11. The Shandygaff. Good times and great oldies, the Gaff is fun for students and alumni alike. Prepare for your shoes to stick to the dance floor and for the wide range of personalities you'll come across. The dance floor is usually hopping, with the DJ playing a mix of current and old stuff.

10. Mr. C's/Players/Indigo. If you are looking for the modern dance scene and the creative side of the area, this is your place. Flashier dress and fancier moves have long been the hallmark of this popular hot spot.

9. The Scorpion. This now-defunct bar was a staple for students and alumni alike in the 1970s. It was a fun bar with a diverse clientele.

8. The Saloon. There is fun in State College, and then there is Monkey Boy fun. The Saloon's signature pitchers, available in many flavors, help the crowd get warmed up for Friday nights with Velveeta.

7. The Brewery. This is just a good, old-fashioned bar with plenty of live music and good specials. It is similar to the Skellar in terms of its feel and its place in Penn State lore. Local musicians have long made their names here.

6. Champs. Known for good food, hot waitresses, and great coverage of sports events on the omnipresent TVs, Champs has long been a staple for sports fans in the area. Stanley's Wonder Wings, Ultimate Nachos, and Bloody Marys are among the many popular offerings here.

5. The Brickhouse. One of the best live-music venues of its time, in its heyday it was the gathering place for local musicians and those who appreciated them.

4. The Crowbar. The site and name of this bar has changed many times over the years, but when it was the Crowbar, Saturday nights with Sideshow Bob were a must for the college crowd and alumni alike. Its size and diversity of musical acts gave it an edge over other venues.

3. Café 210. Always a popular lunch spot, it has become a force on the music scene and also has good, reasonably priced food. It also has a large dance area and plenty of outdoor seating available in the front and the back.

2. The Phyrst. A downstairs venue that features Saturday night sing-alongs with the Phyrst Phamly that are legendary. Cherry bombs and table wars are the hallmarks of this feel-good venue. It is impossible to stay here long and be in a bad mood.

1. The Rathskellar. This bar holds a unique place in Penn State lore. Famous for its now-defunct Rolling Rock case races on St. Patrick's Day, it is the ultimate hole-in-the-wall college bar. You can't really say you've been to Penn State until you've been to the Skellar.

WHAT'S IN A NAME?

Penn State has produced some of the greatest players in college football history. Those names populate the all-time letterman roster. Other big-time *names* also are on the list. In those cases, the person who actually played for the Nittany Lions may not be well known, but they happen to share the same moniker as some rather famous (or infamous) people.

14. Don James (1914). Not the College Football Hall of Famer and former head coach of the University of Washington.

13. Charles Wilson (1950–51) and Charlie Wilson (1968–70). Neither was the famed Texas Congressman portrayed by Tom Hanks in the movie *Charlie Wilson's War*.

12. Dave Clark (1985–86). Not the front man for the 1960s band the Dave Clark Five.

11. Joe Jackson (1973–74). Not "Shoeless" Joe Jackson who was banned for life from baseball after the 1919 "Black Sox" scandal, nor the musician who had the hit "Is She Really Going Out with Him?"

10. Mike Garrett (1982, 1984). Not the 1965 Heisman Trophy winner from USC.

9. Tom Jackson (1967–69). Not the former Denver Bronco and current NFL analyst for ESPN.

8. John Booth (1971). Not the infamous assassin of Abraham Lincoln.

7. George Allen (1968). Not the former Los Angeles Rams and Washington Redskins head coach.

6. Gary Carter (1968–70). Not the Baseball Hall of Fame catcher.

5. Patrick Duffy (1990). Not the actor who played Bobby Ewing on the hit TV show *Dallas*.

4. Phil Collins (1993–94). Not the Grammy Award–winning singer.

3. Jim Brown (1978–81). Not the Pro Football Hall of Fame running back.

2. Tony Stewart (1997–00). Not the NASCAR champion driver.

1. Douglas McArthur (1968, 70). Not Douglas *MacArthur*, the US Army general.

BASKETBALL NAME

Mike Lang (1980–83). Not Mike Lange, the longtime voice of the Pittsburgh Penguins.

JOEPA COMMERCIALS

If you have watched a Joe Paterno press conference in the past 20 years, you might get the impression that Penn State's football coach does not like the spotlight. On the rare occasion, however, Paterno has joined an industry that many other sports celebrities thrive in—that of a product pitchman in a commercial. Though few in number, Paterno's commercials have been memorable.

5. R Super Foods' Super Donuts and Super Buns. The company owned by former PSU great Franco Harris had Paterno on its boxes of donuts and sticky buns. It was a promotion to honor sports figures who have "immersed themselves in their local communities, providing initiatives and community service that helps others." At a promotional event, Harris was with Sue Paterno, who said about the donuts, "I couldn't stop at just one. Joe has more discipline."

4. Wheaties. Though there was no corresponding television ad, we would be remiss if we did not include Paterno's side profile gracing the cover of Wheaties' boxes. As it has many times in its existence, the cereal company used a high-profile sports figure to bring attention to its product. Paterno was chosen as the "cover boy" for this campaign in the early 2000s. However, the football teams back then looked as if they needed to eat more Wheaties.

3. Bell of Pennsylvania Yellow Pages. During the mid-1980s Paterno was the front man for the Yellow Pages. The highlight of the ad was Paterno tapping into his quarterback skills from his playing days as he executes a play-action fake with the phone book in place of a football.

2. Milano Bread. This ad campaign used just about every thinkable media outlet available. There were TV ads, radio ads, print ads, and billboards featuring Paterno and Milano Bread. During an interview on the Big Ten Network, former Nittany Lion Anthony Adams said that escaping the shadow of Paterno while playing at Penn State was impossible: "His face is everywhere. It seemed like the more you were mad at him, the more you saw him . . . you can't even get bread without seeing his face!"

1. Big Ten Network. This is the one that will probably have the longest staying power. The 2008 commercial utilized all the conference's football coaches in pretending to "recruit" viewers to watch the BTN. The final pitch was made by Paterno, who basically yelled into the camera with what appears to be an angry look, "Come to Penn State!!!"

JOEPA PRODUCTS

3. 1970s Paterno and Penn State Coca-Cola tray.

2. Joe Paterno mask.

1. Cardboard stand-up Joe Paterno.

JOE PATERNO FASHION STATEMENTS

Penn State's head football coach has earned iconic status mainly due to his success on the field. At various points in his career, however, Joe Paterno has been criticized for not keeping up with the times. Although most of that is probably directed to his game plans, it also could be applied to his attire. When he started his tenure as head coach in 1966, Paterno's style was in line with his contemporaries. However, as the disco seventies begat the preppy eighties, which led to the grunge nineties, other coaches began to dress down. Paterno kept to his own classy style, which he still sports today.

5. Parka. Over the years Paterno has sported several winter coats to fend off the early central Pennsylvania winters. Our favorite is the navy blue parka with fur-lined hood. Bonus points to any photographer who has a picture of JoePa covering his head with that hood.

4. Sportcoat vs. sweater vs. windbreaker. For most of the 1960s, seventies, and early eighties, if the weather permitted, Paterno would don a sports coat to go with his button-down shirt and tie. Somewhere in the mid 1980s the sports coat gave way to the sweater over the tie—think 1987 Fiesta Bowl. As the Nittany Lions started their Big Ten play, the windbreaker came into play. Now it seems as if the windbreaker is the go-to cover no matter what the weather.

3. Tie and button shirt. As referenced earlier, no matter what he has on top, Paterno has stayed true to going with a button-down shirt and tie. Where most coaches today dress as if they are playing in a weekend foursome at the local golf course and looking for the beer cart, Paterno remains classy with the tie.

2. Rolled-up khaki pants. Whether they are plain or briefly flashy with whale prints, the bottom of Paterno's pants legs are rolled up, drawing snarky flood pants comments. The story of the pants legs is nearly as legendary as the coach himself. In his early years Paterno's wife, Sue, grew tired of having to deal with grass and dirt stains collecting on the pants from Paterno's pacing the sidelines. To counter the effect of the football fields, Paterno began rolling up his pants to keep them clean.

1. Glasses. These are probably the first thing people think of when describing Paterno's look. Thanks to laser surgery, however, he no longer needs the glasses. But what would Joe Paterno be without them? Like Bear Bryant's hat, Paterno's glasses—big, thick, and tinted—are his calling card.

WHAT PATERNO DOES NOT WEAR THAT MOST OF HIS PEERS DO:

2. Baseball hats. This is probably why he still has a full head of hair.

1. Headsets. This is definitely why he and assistant coach Mike McQueary are constantly talking on the sidelines.

FAVORITE JOEPA PRESS CONFERENCE MOMENTS :: BY NEIL RUDEL

Joe Paterno has obviously had many, many memorable moments on the field. But he's also had some memorable moments off the field during his meetings with the media. Neil Rudel of *The Altoona Mirror* has covered Penn State football since his junior year at *The Daily Collegian* in 1977, so he has seen Paterno in just about every situation and mood imaginable. Here are five of his favorite press conference moments with JoePa.

5. Surpassing the Bear (Beaver Stadium Media Room, 2001). Penn State had just beaten Ohio State, 29–27, which allowed Paterno to win his 324th game, passing Bear Bryant's all-time record for most victories as a Division I-A coach. JoePa was carried on the shoulders of his players to an awaiting flatbed truck, where a tribute took place. Afterward he came to the Media Room and was joined by his family. Still touched, he kept his remarks short, but he did thank the media and said, "No one has had the run with the press that I've had."

4. A win is a win, right? (Beaver Stadium Media Room, 1986). Penn State was in the midst of building a pair of teams that would play for the national title, the 1985 entry that lost to Oklahoma in the Orange Bowl and the 1986 team that beat Miami to capture the Lions' second title. After a closer-than-expected struggle with Cincinnati in which the Nittany Lions ultimately prevailed, 23–17, Mike DeCourcy, then of the *Pittsburgh Press* and now of *The Sporting News*, asked JoePa if Cincinnati posed a greater threat than Paterno and the Lions anticipated. JoePa lost his cool. He yelled, "You guys drive me absolutely up a wall!" and he slammed his fist on the podium, shaking the microphone. These were days before every press conference was beamed by satellite, so the outburst didn't become a Mike Gundy–like video clip. But it certainly reflected Paterno's intensity and lack of patience for when he got a question, fair or not, that he didn't like.

3. It's like looking in a mirror (The Capital One Bowl, 2002). It was a couple of days before the game against Auburn, and a number of the southern writers from Auburn and Orlando were trying to dig deeper into the Paterno legacy. One asked him about the stand-up Joe, a cardboard cutout that Mike Poorman of the Barash Group conceptualized and marketed for many years. Somebody wondered if JoePa had one in his house. He smiled and told a story in which his wife, Sue, had one in a downstairs sewing room. One day, when he was in the basement looking for something, he flipped the light on in the room and, he said, "It scared the hell out of me." The room broke up, and so did Joe when one of the Penn State writers interjected, "Now you know how we feel!"

2. Banter with Bernstein (Beaver Stadium Media Room, 1991). Over the years no writer had a better rapport with JoePa than the late Ralph Bernstein of the Associated Press, who covered Paterno since he was hired. They were roughly the same age—Bernstein died in 2007 at the age of 85—and JoePa liked the veteran Philadelphia writer, as the two would frequently exchange playful jabs. Bernstein was the "leadoff man" on each Tuesday teleconference until his retirement in 1994 (Penn State hosted a dinner in his honor, in Philadelphia, that JoePa attended, offering a toast to Bernstein). On this day Penn State was coming off an unimpressive 21–10 loss at Southern Cal a few days earlier when the press-conference moderator called on Bernstein. "Joe, I sat home and watched TV Saturday night, and saw two things that were ugly—Miss New York and your offense." Even JoePa couldn't resist a laugh.

1. Finally, national champs (January 2, 1983, at the New Orleans Hilton). After stalking the national title and having three unbeaten teams that finished shy of No. 1, the Nittany Lions—who had one loss, to Alabama at midseason—delivered in the Sugar Bowl, beating Georgia, 27–23, to claim the coveted prize. The next morning saw a relieved and grateful Joe Paterno posing with the national championship trophy. First, classy Georgia head coach Vince Dooley spoke and offered congratulations to Paterno. When the traditional question-and-answer was over, many of the writers converged on JoePa, who on this morning was in no rush. He diagrammed the Lions' defensive strategy of taking the right angles so that Herschel Walker "could never get his shoulders squared," and he talked about finally reaching the top of the mountain. When a southern writer asked about his relationship with Bear Bryant, JoePa looked up and asked, "Is Paul here?"

GREATEST PENN STATERS FOR EACH NFL TEAM

With the exception of the league's newest team, the Houston Texans, every current NFL franchise has had at least one Nittany Lion on its roster at some point in its history. However, the wealth is not evenly spread across the NFL landscape. Whereas some teams, such as the Pittsburgh Steelers, can boast multiple Pro Football Hall of Famers who once played for Penn State, other teams have only a few former Penn Staters to ever start a game for their franchise. By scouring each NFL team's all-time roster, we compiled the greatest Nittany Lions to play for each team. It might be nice if the Texans decided to join the party.

Atlanta Falcons—Chuck Sieminski (1966–67). Sieminski gets the nod here because the defensive tackle started all 14 games for Atlanta in 1966. Other than that, there's not too much else to tell.

Arizona/Phoenix/St. Louis/Card-Pitt/Chicago Cardinals—Levi Brown (2007-present). Quantifying the play of offensive linemen is difficult, so let's go with these tidbits: Brown has started 43 of 45 games since being drafted by the Cardinals. Prior to his arrival in the desert, the Cardinals had one playoff appearance in Arizona. Since Brown became a fixture on the line, they have had two playoff appearances, four playoff wins, and one NFC championship with a subsequent Super Bowl appearance.

Baltimore Ravens—Kim Herring (1997–2000). He was a key member of one the greatest defensive units in league history. The strong safety had three interceptions in the Ravens' 2000 Super Bowl winning season. He added another pick in the Super Bowl when he intercepted New York Giant QB—and former Penn State teammate—Kerry Collins early in the third quarter.

Buffalo Bills—Shane Conlan (1987–92). Three-time Pro-Bowler and three times named second-team All-Pro linebacker, Conlan helped lead the Bills to three Super Bowls.

Carolina Panthers—Kerry Collins (1995–98). What a way to start a career! Collins was the first-ever selection of the Carolina Panthers (fifth overall in the 1995 draft). The quarterback led the Panthers to a 7–6 record in his 13 starts that year. The encore of 1996 was a trip to the Pro Bowl following an NFC West title and helping the Panthers advance to the NFC championship game.

Chicago Bears/Staleys/Decatur Staleys—Matt Suhey (1980–89). Paving the way for Walter Payton's record-breaking career was fullback Matt Suhey. Suhey also could tote the ball, racking up a career high 681 yards in 1983, and he scored a touchdown in the Bears' demolition of the New England Patriots in Super Bowl XX.

Cincinnati Bengals—Mike Reid (1970–74). Reid was a dominant defensive tackle in each of the five seasons he played for the Bengals. Every season he was at least a member of the first-team All-AFC team. In 1972 he was named second-team All-Pro in the first of two straight Pro Bowl seasons.

Cleveland Browns—Matt Bahr (1981–89). Accuracy and longevity defined Bahr's career with the Browns. The kicker played nine seasons in Cleveland, and during that time he connected on 74.1 percent of his field goal attempts, including an NFL best 87.5 percent in 1983.

Dallas Cowboys—Tom Rafferty (1976–89). He was the first and, for most of the franchise's existence, only Nittany Lion to play for the Cowboys. Rafferty was a consistent starter on the offensive line, missing only three games from 1977 through 1988. He had an All-Pro career and was named to the Cowboys' all-time team in 2003. He also is the only Cowboy lineman to block for both Roger Staubach and Troy Aikman.

Denver Broncos—Pete Liske (1969–70). Liske started nine games as quarterback in 1970, leading the Broncos to a 5–4 record.

Detroit Lions/Portsmouth Spartans—Eddie Drummond (2002–07). Drummond was one of the NFL's elite returners, highlighted by the 2004 season, when he was named first-team All-Pro. That season he returned two punts and two kickoffs for touchdowns.

Green Bay Packers—Dave Robinson (1963–72). Robinson was a star linebacker for the Packers dynasty in the 1960s. He was a first-team All-Pro in 1967, winning Pro Bowl MVP honors that year. He also is a member of the 1960s NFL All-Decade team, as selected by voters of the Pro Football Hall of Fame.

Houston Texans—None.

Indianapolis/Baltimore Colts—Lenny Moore (1956–67). Playing his entire career for Baltimore, Moore was a star on a team of stars. A dual threat in the backfield, he finished his career with 6,039 yards receiving, 48 touchdown catches, 5,174 yards rushing, and 63 touchdowns on the ground. He led the NFL in yards-per-carry in 1956–58 and 1961. A member of the 1950s All-

Decade team, he was inducted into the Pro Football Hall of Fame in 1975.

Jacksonville Jaguars—Kyle Brady (1999–2006). A big receiving target at tight end for the Jags during their run of success near the turn of the current century, Brady caught 343 passes for Jacksonville, including a career high 64 in 2000.

Kansas City Chiefs/Dallas Texans—Larry Johnson (2003–09). For a two-year stretch (2005–06), L.J. was one of the NFL's elite running backs. He put together consecutive seasons of more than 1,700 yards rushing. He also scored 37 touchdowns in that period of time.

Miami Dolphins—O.J. McDuffie (1993–2000). An impact player at receiver and returning kicks, McDuffie led the NFL in receptions with 92 in 1998. That season he also achieved career highs in yards receiving (1,050) and touchdowns (7).

Minnesota Vikings—D.J. Dozier (1987–90). Dozier scored seven touchdowns in his four seasons with Minnesota.

New England/Boston Patriots—Todd Rucci (1993–99). A standout offensive lineman for the Patriots during the 1990s, Rucci started for the Pats during their 1996 AFC championship season. He was named to the Patriots' 1990s All-Decade Team.

New York Giants—Rosey Grier (1955–62). One of the top players on the NFL's marquee defenses during the 1950s. Grier was named first-team All-Pro defensive tackle in 1956 and was a second-team All-Pro in 1958 and 1959.

New York Jets/Titans—Mickey Shuler (1978–89). A consistently productive tight end for the Jets, Shuler averaged 65.2 catches, 715 yards, and five touchdowns per season from 1984 through 1988.

New Orleans Saints—Bruce Clark (1982–88). The defensive end recorded 39.5 sacks during his eight seasons with New Orleans, including a monster year in 1984 with 10.5.

Philadelphia Eagles/Steagles—Kenny Jackson (1984–88, 1990–91). The wide receiver's most productive seasons were his first four. During that period he averaged 29.3 receptions, 516.8 yards, and 2.8 touchdowns per season.

Pittsburgh Steelers/Pirates/Steagles/Card-Pitt—Jack Ham (1971–82). This was the most difficult selection of all the teams, as Ham edged out fellow Pro

Football Hall of Famer Franco Harris. Ham was named first-team All-Pro linebacker each season from 1974 through 1979. He was part of the Steel Curtain defense that helped lead Pittsburgh to four Super Bowls in a six-year span. Ham was elected to the Hall of Fame in 1988. His presenter that day in Canton, Ohio, was his college coach, Joe Paterno.

Oakland/Los Angeles Raiders—Steve Wisniewski (1989–2001). Wisniewski missed only two games in 13 seasons with the Raiders. He was named first-team All-Pro twice and was an eight-time Pro Bowler.

St. Louis/Los Angeles/Cleveland Rams—Rosey Grier (1963–66). Grier makes his second appearance on this list. He was a member of LA's Fearsome Foursome defense during his four seasons with the Rams.

San Diego/Los Angeles Chargers—John Cappelletti (1980–83). Cappelletti was a role player for the "Air Coryell" Chargers in the early 1980s. In his first two seasons with San Diego he averaged 309 yards rushing and 4.5 touchdowns.

San Francisco 49ers—Ted Kwalick (1969–74). Kwalick was a first-team All-Pro in 1972, when he achieved career highs with 751 yards receiving and nine touchdown receptions. He also made the Pro Bowl three times (1971–73).

Seattle Seahawks—Curt Warner (1983–89). When the Seattle portion of his career ended, Warner held nearly every significant franchise rushing record. In his seven seasons with the Seahawks, he averaged 957.8 yards rushing, 7.8 touchdowns, and 27.5 receptions. He led the AFC in rushing his rookie season and helped Seattle to the AFC title game, where it lost to the Los Angeles Raiders. He was inducted into the Seahawks' Ring of Honor in 1994.

Tampa Bay Buccaneers—Mark Robinson (1988–90). The strong safety snagged 12 of his 15 career interceptions in his three seasons with the Bucs.

Tennessee Titans/Houston Oilers—Mike Munchak (1982–93). A member of the NFL's 1980s All-Decade team at offensive guard, Munchak was a four-time first-team All-Pro. He was inducted into the Pro Football Hall of Fame in 2001.

Washington/Boston Redskins/Boston Braves—Chuck Drazenovich (1950–59). Drazenovich was the top linebacker for the Redskins during the 1950s, appearing in four Pro Bowls and twice being named second-team All-Pro. In 2002 Drazenovich was on the list of the 70 greatest Redskins ever. Washington came out with the list to celebrate its 70th season.

PRO CHAMPIONSHIP GAME PERFORMANCES BY PENN STATERS

Penn State has long been respected as a top producer of pro football talent. In fact, the NFL Network rated the Nittany Lions as the seventh-best school of all time for cranking out pro players. As you might expect, some of these players have been key contributors for championship teams, including the first four Pittsburgh Steelers' Super Bowl titles. The timeline for this list spans more than 60 years of pro-football history.

10. Chuck Fusina—1984 USFL Championship: Philadelphia Stars 23, Arizona Wranglers 3. Pipe down—we were big USFL fans in the mid-1980s, so deal with it. The Philadelphia Stars reunited the Penn State passing duo from the late 1970s in quarterback Chuck Fusina and wide receiver Scott Fitzkee. Add to that Pete Kugler, Tom Donovan, Dave Opfar, Roger Jackson, and Ron Coder, and the Stars roster was loaded with former Penn Staters. Fusina was name the game's MVP as he completed his first ten passes and finished 12-of-17 with 158 yards.

9. Matt Bahr—Super Bowl XXV: New York Giants 20, Buffalo Bills 19. The game is more remembered for the Bills' kick at the end of the game that missed rather than Bahr's efforts. Playing in his second Super Bowl, Bahr's 28-yard field goal midway through the first quarter opened the scoring in the contest played in Tampa Stadium. Midway in the fourth quarter, with Giants trailing 19–17, New York's time-consuming drive stalled at the Buffalo 14-yard line. The G-Men called on the former Nittany Lion star, and Bahr delivered with the 21-yard field goal that proved to be the winning score.

8. Matt Millen—Super Bowl XXIV: San Francisco 49ers 55, Denver Broncos 10. It was Millen's third Super Bowl appearance, and it ended up being his third Super Bowl win. He registered four and a half tackles, including one for a loss in the 49ers' rout over the Broncos.

7. Lenny Moore—1958 NFL Championship: Baltimore Colts 23, New York Giants 17 (OT). One of the iconic games in NFL history saw former Nittany Lion Moore play a vital role. Although he gained only 24 yards on the ground, his 99 receiving yards on five catches helped put the Colts into the first overtime game in league history. Moore also was the one who threw the key block that cleared the way on Alan Ameche's game-winning touchdown.

6. Matt Millen—Super Bowl XVIII: Los Angeles Raiders 38, Washington Redskins 9. This was another fine Millen effort on a Super Bowl winning team. He had five solo tackles, and his sack of quarterback Joe Theismann in the second quarter helped end a Redskins' drive and set up the Raiders' second touchdown of the game.

5. Jack Ham—Super Bowl XIII: Pittsburgh Steelers 35, Dallas Cowboys 31. This was the most productive of the three Super Bowls Ham started for the Steelers at linebacker. He had seven solo tackles, including dropping Dallas's Tony Dorsett for a three-yard loss at the Cowboy 24-yard line in the second quarter.

4. Matt Suhey—Super Bowl XX: Chicago Bears 46, New England Patriots 10. The longtime blocking back for Hall of Famer Walter Payton, State College native Suhey earned some individual glory in this Super Bowl rout. He scored the first touchdown of the game on an 11-yard run in the closing seconds of the first quarter. He would rush for 52 yards on 11 carries and had one reception for 24 yards.

3. Franco Harris—Super Bowl XIV: Pittsburgh Steelers 31, Los Angeles Rams 19. Harris's one-yard run in the second quarter was the Steelers' first touchdown of the day, and his one-yard run with just under three minutes remaining in the game clinched Pittsburgh's fourth title in six years. In addition, Harris's 32-yard pass reception from Terry Bradshaw on the Steelers' first drive of the game helped set up fellow Penn Stater Matt Bahr's 41-yard field goal.

2. Lenny Moore—1959 NFL Championship: Baltimore Colts 31, New York Giants 16. Moore was on the receiving end of Johnny Unitas's 60-yard touchdown pass that opened the scoring as the Colts defended their title in a rematch of the previous year's classic game.

1. Franco Harris—Super Bowl IX: Pittsburgh Steelers 16, Minnesota Vikings 6. Franco's Italian Army rolled to the MVP award as the Steelers won their first championship. Harris set a then–Super Bowl record with 158 yards rushing, and his nine-yard TD run in the third quarter gave Pittsburgh a 9–0 lead and ended up being the winning score.

OTHER NOTABLE EFFORTS:

4. Dave Robinson—Super Bowl II: Green Bay Packers 33, Oakland Raiders 14. Robinson was a starting linebacker for Vince Lombardi's dynasty of the 1960s. In Super Bowl I he recorded three tackles in the victory over the Chiefs. In Super Bowl II he had two tackles, and on the first play of the fourth quarter, he recovered a fumble by Raider halfback Pete Banaszak at the Packer 47-yard line.

3. Scott Fitzkee—1985 USFL Championship: Baltimore Stars 28, Oakland Invaders 24. Fitzkee caught a 16-yard touchdown pass from Fusina to open the scoring, which was punctuated by one of Fitzkee's TD-celebration ball spins.

2. Joe Jurevicius—Super Bowl XXXVII: Tampa Bay Buccaneers 48, Oakland Raiders 21. Jurevicius caught four passes for a team-high 78 yards in helping the Buccaneers to their first title.

1. Kim Herring—Super Bowl XXXV Baltimore Ravens 34, New York Giants 7. Herring intercepted former Nittany Lion teammate Kerry Collins on the Giants' first possession of the second half.

LION KILLERS

Penn State has ruined many a Saturday afternoon for players and fans of other programs. Though the reverse has not happened as often, there have been players who have had great success against Penn State. For the most part we tried to avoid those "one-hit wonders"—those players who had a singularly huge day against the Nittany Lions. There are two players on this list, however, who do fit that description and merit inclusion. For the most part, what we wanted was sustained greatness against Penn State, with individual and team success coinciding for at least a two-to-three-year stretch. Whether they were tearing up Rip Engle's teams or carving up Nittany Lion defenses that would win national or conference championships, here are ten who slew the Lions.

10. Doug Flutie. Yes, he was only 1–2 against Penn State as a starter and 1–3 during his four-year Boston College career, but, to paraphrase Dennis Green, Flutie was who we thought he was—which was a great quarterback. Flutie made a relief appearance in his 1981 freshman season, passing for 135 yards in the fourth quarter of what was a 38–7 Penn State rout. That served as a preview for the next three seasons. In 1982 Flutie racked up 520 yards, but turnovers keyed another Nittany Lion romp, 52–17. His lone win came in 1983 in Foxboro, Massachusetts. Flutie threw for 380 yards and two touchdowns as the Eagles triumphed, 27–17. For his final Beaver Stadium playing appearance, the eventual 1984 Heisman Trophy winner passed for 447 yards, but somehow it was not enough, as Penn State won their sixth and final victory of the season by a 37–30 score.

9. Curtis Dickey. Our first "one-hit wonder" was dominant on September 22, 1979. It was a game that gave proof that Penn State was going to suffer a "hangover" season from losing the national championship game against Alabama in the Sugar Bowl nearly ten months earlier. The Texas A&M senior running back rushed 31 times for 184 yards. Dickey had touchdown runs of 69, 21, and 11 yards in the Aggies' 27–14 win at Beaver Stadium.

8. Brad Banks. The second "one-hit wonder" was part of one of the most entertaining games of the 2002 season. The Iowa Hawkeye quarterback had his team poised to leave Beaver Stadium with a victory, leading 35–13 midway through the fourth quarter. Banks had thrown three touchdowns and would finish the day with 261 yards in air. Incredibly, the Lions would rally for 22 unanswered points to tie the game and send it into overtime. Like he had in regulation, Banks tormented Penn State's secondary, connecting with C.J. Jones for a six-yard touchdown pass that would become the winning score of a 42–35 Iowa victory.

7. Walter Lewis. The stats that Lewis accrued in his three starts against the Nittany Lion belie his overall impact on those games. Make no mistake: The quarterback for Bear Bryant's wishbone and later Ray Perkins's offense was the main reason the Crimson Tide won two games against Penn State and nearly a third in Lewis's senior season. In the 1981 Beaver Stadium contest Lewis attempted only ten passes, but two of his six completions went for touchdowns. Those six completions netted 167 yards in the air in Alabama's 31–16 win, which allowed legendary head coach Bear Bryant to tie Amos Alonzo Stagg for most career wins (314). The following year, in Birmingham's Legion Field, the Tide handed the Lions their only loss in their national championship season, winning 42–21. Lewis was 'Bama's leading rusher, with 86 yards. His most productive passing day occurred in 1983. The portable lights at Beaver Stadium added to the high drama of the late-afternoon start. The Lions took a 34–7 lead into the fourth quarter, when Lewis put on a show and nearly stole a victory. He led Alabama on three scoring drives, including two capped by touchdown passes to Jesse Bendross, to pull his team within six points at 34–28. With less than three minutes remaining, Lewis took the field for his final drive, needing 51 yards to reach the end zone. He made up 30 of those yards with four completions. He would move the Tide to the Penn State 4-yard line. On fourth down his final pass of the day appeared, at first, to be his fourth touchdown pass of the day. Preston Gothard juggled the ball in the back of the end zone and landed on the ground in possession of what many thought was the winning score. However, the back judge ruled the pass incomplete, and in an era without video replay, that call stood and the Nittany Lions escaped with the victory.

6. Adrian Clayborn. The man knows how to ruin a Penn State party. Early in the fourth quarter of the 2009 contest, the Nittany Lions were clinging to a 10–5 lead over Iowa in an attempt to avenge their only loss of the 2008 season. Like that game, the Hawkeyes would rally for a win. Clayborn provided the spark when the defensive end blocked a punt and returned it 53 yards for a touchdown and an 11–10 lead (the two-point conversion attempt failed). Iowa went on to a 21–10 victory. In the 2010 Big Ten opener Clayborn harassed the Lions' offense all night, registering ten tackles, including three for losses, totaling 19 yards in the 24–3 Hawkeye win.

5. Pete Dawkins. He played on Army teams that defeated Penn State in three consecutive seasons. Dawkins's two rushing touchdowns led the Black Knights to a 27–13 win in 1957. The following season he was recognized as the best player in the nation, winning the Heisman Trophy and Maxwell Award. The October 4 game against the Nittany Lions at West Point played a role in his receiving those honors. Dawkins rushed for 73 yards and one touchdown and had a 72-yard touchdown reception in a 26–0 shutout over Penn State.

4. Tony Rice. The Notre Dame quarterback came within a failed two-point conversion attempt to sweep all three games he started against the Lions. That attempt occurred in Penn State's 1987 regular-season finale. Rice had 67 yards rushing, scoring two of the Fighting Irish's three touchdowns in the 21–20 loss. The following season, when he led Notre Dame to the national championship, Rice passed for 191 yards and one touchdown. He also rushed for 84 yards and a touchdown in the Irish's 21–3 win. In his senior season (1989), Rice rushed for a career-high 141 yards and scored two touchdowns in a 34–23 Notre Dame win at Beaver Stadium.

3. Gary Beban. Beban was a dual threat in all three of his starts against Penn State, which were all victories for the UCLA quarterback. He rushed for 74 yards, scoring two touchdowns on the ground, and passed for 76 yards in a 24–22 win at Beaver Stadium in 1965. The following year at the L.A. Coliseum, 132 was the number. Beban rushed for 132 yards and passed for 132 yards. Add in another two rushing touchdowns, and the Bruins were on their way to a 49–11 rout. Beban's Heisman Trophy–winning season of 1967 saw him have his least productive day against Penn State. Still, his 108 passing yards and 46 yards rushing were good enough to lead UCLA to a 17–15 win.

2. Mike Hart. The Michigan Wolverine running back seemed always to be at his best against Penn State. The Nittany Lions won the 2005 Big Ten title, but their only loss of the season was the controversial 27–25 game in Ann Arbor. Hart rushed for 108 yards and one touchdown. The following season, in front of a Beaver Stadium "white out," he would go four yards better on the ground and add a touchdown in a 17–10 Wolverine win. In 2007 he racked up 153 yards and scored a touchdown in a 14–9 victory in Ann Arbor.

1. Bear Bryant. When it comes to head coaches, one could make the case that Lloyd Carr and/or Kirk Ferentz belong on this list. Carr, the former Michigan coach, won his last nine meetings against the Lions, including three times when Penn State was undefeated. Ferentz, the head man at Iowa, has gone 8–2 against Penn State, including victories in eight of the last nine meetings, many in memorable fashion—two overtime games, the 2008 victory that derailed Penn State's undefeated season, and does the score 6–4 sound familiar? But Bear Bryant receives the spot on this list because, well, he's the Bear—and the fact that Joe Paterno *never* defeated him. Paterno, at least, beat Carr in their first two meetings and has bested Ferentz twice. Bryant did lose his initial matchup against Penn State, 7–0, in the 1959 Liberty Bowl. Paterno, of course, was an assistant under Rip Engle during that time. But in his head-to-head contests against Paterno, Bryant was 4–0. The Tide defeated the Lions, 13–6, in the 1975

Sugar Bowl, which was played on New Year's Eve. Three years later—same Superdome, same result, as the Tide won the national championship, 14–7, thanks to the infamous (from the Penn State perspective) goal-line stand. The Bear was instrumental in establishing the regular-season series between the two powers during the 1980s. As mentioned earlier, 'Bama won the 1981 contest, 31–16, as Bryant tied Amos Alonzo Stagg's record for most victories. The following year, his last as Crimson Tide head coach, Bryant handed Paterno's team its only loss (42–21) of Penn State's national championship season.

SURPRISING FOOTBALL HEROES

Whether they were "one-hit wonders" or an unexpected outstanding effort that signaled a bright future for a player, here are some of the surprising one-game standout football performances.

6. Chris Eberly. In 1996 Eberly was buried behind workhorse running back Curtis Enis on the depth chart. In the ninth game of the season at Indiana, Enis injured his shoulder and could not continue. However, the Nittany Lions did not miss a beat, as sophomore Eberly rushed for 110 of his 281 total yards for the season against the Hoosiers. He also scored a touchdown in the 48–26 win. Eberly would rush for only 146 yards for all of 1997 and 153 in 1998. But on that late October 1996 day in Bloomington, he had his "one shining moment."

5. Joe Nastasi. As a redshirt freshman, Nastasi rarely saw meaningful game action in 1995. Some may remember his name from the "Snow Bowl" game against Michigan at Beaver Stadium. Many more remember his play—and the fact that a major snowstorm hit the Centre Region a few days prior to the game, so the stands were filled with snow, which, obviously, led to plenty of snowballs being tossed about among the students and onto the field. Penn State led Michigan, 20–17, with just over two minutes to play. The Nittany Lions lined up for a 16-yard field goal. Nastasi was the holder and, upon receiving the snap, bolted into the end zone for the touchdown and the all-important two-score margin that ultimately resulted in a 27–17 win.

4. Shelly Hammonds. Another redshirt freshman who made a surprising impact was Shelly Hammonds. The Nittany Lions dropped their first two games of the 1990 season, and after righting the ship, they were 2–2 heading into the Boston College game at Chestnut Hill, Massachusetts. Injuries to Gary Brown and Leroy Thompson meant they would have to play the game without their two main running backs. Joe Paterno had to dig deep into the depth to find a gem in Hammonds. Hammonds obliterated the Eagles defense by rushing for 208 yards and ripping off touchdown runs of 65 and 48 yards. He had a third TD (59 yards) that was called back because of a clipping penalty.

3. Larry Cooney. In 1947 the junior from Pittsburgh was a backup running back to Wally Triplett as the Lions had a perfect 9–0 record in the regular season. The reward: a trip to the Cotton Bowl to face 9–0–1 SMU. After Penn State spotted the Mustangs a 13–0 first-half lead, Cooney caught an Elwood Petchel pass and scored a 38-yard touchdown just before halftime. Earlier in the second quarter, Cooney ended a Mustang drive by knocking down a pass on fourth down from the Penn State 30. The game would eventually end in a 13–13 tie.

2. Chuck Penzenik. It was quite a stage to make the first start of his career. A month earlier Penzenik was listed fourth on the depth chart at cornerback, but with injuries to Cliff Dingle and Kim Herring, he was moved to free safety for the Rose Bowl game against Oregon. In the first quarter he intercepted a pass from Duck quarterback Danny O'Neil. That alone would have been a great end to the story, but Penzenik wasn't finished. As the sun began to set over the San Gabriel Mountains in the third quarter, Penn State had gone in front 21–14, but Oregon was mounting a drive in an attempt to tie the game. Penzenik picked off O'Neil for a second time at the Nittany Lion 43 and weaved his way to the Ducks' 13-yard line. Three plays later, Ki-Jana Carter scored and the Rose Bowl rout was on.

1. Kirk Bowman. He was the ultimate "one-hit Penn State wonder." In 1982 tight end Kirk Bowman had two receptions: Both occurred in the same game, and both were touchdowns—the second immortalized forever in the images of Penn State fans who witnessed it in person or on TV. The classic 27–24 Nittany Lion victory over Nebraska is referenced several times in this book, due mostly to the thrilling nature of the game and the importance of the contest. Bowman did not even start the game. In fact, his only career starts—both of them—occurred in his senior season of 1983. His first touchdown reception came from a 14-yard pass from Todd Blackledge that capped an 83-yard drive and opened the scoring at 7–0. The second occurred with four seconds remaining and led to one of the biggest on-field celebrations by Penn State fans in Beaver Stadium history.

TOP WALK-ONS UNDER JOE PATERNO

Walk-ons have always had a special place in Joe Paterno's heart. It may be because these players probably had the talent to play somewhere else (albeit at a program that wasn't as prominent as Penn State) and even receive a scholarship. But for whatever reason, they took a chance to join the Nittany Lions with no guarantees of anything. Most walk-ons spend their careers on practice squads and have the first-stringers beat up on them. Some may actually see playing time and earn a varsity letter or two. Then there are the *really* special ones who not only play and earn a scholarship but also have an impact and become important contributors. Here are ten such players. Although we could put quarterback Matt McGloin on this list right now, we preferred to wait to see how his career plays out.

10. Tom Bradley (1977–78). He is now known for his coaching abilities as the team's current defensive coordinator, but more than 30 years ago Bradley was basically Penn State's version of Rudy. At 5-9, 167 pounds, he made the most of his physical abilities and became captain of the special teams unit in 1978. He earned the nickname "Scrap Iron" because of his scrappy play and fearlessness in taking on all blockers on kick coverages.

9. Jeremy Boone (2007–09). Two years after Boone came to Penn State, the Lions brought in a punter on scholarship, Ryan Breen. Boone, however, had bided his time backing up Jeremy Kapinos for two seasons. He won the starting job in 2007 and never let it go. He became the Lions' career leader in punting average and earned second-team All-Big Ten honors his senior season. Breen, by the way, left the program following the 2009 season.

8. Joe Iorio (1999–2002). He's still the only true freshman walk-on to start for Joe Paterno. Injuries along the offensive line in 1999 gave Iorio the opportunity to start at guard. He ended up starting 31 games in his career, most at center. During his senior season he anchored the offensive line that helped Larry Johnson Jr. rush for more than 2,000 yards.

7. John Bruno (1984–86). Bruno walked on in 1982, and no one will forget what he did in the 1987 Fiesta Bowl. He, as much as anyone, played a huge role in helping the Lions upset Miami to win the national title. His punts consistently kept Miami deep in its own territory, thus allowing the Lion defense to dominate the way it did. Sadly, Bruno died in 1992 from skin cancer.

6. Josh Hull (2006–09). He never seemed to receive the credit he deserved. While the star linebackers such as Sean Lee and Navorro Bowman dealt with injuries, Hull was a reliable force for the linebacker unit during the 2008 and 2009 seasons. He started at middle linebacker in 2008 for Lee, who had a torn ACL, and was second on the team in tackles. The next season, he led the Lions in tackles with 116.

5. Gregg Garrity (1980–82). Obviously known for his diving TD catch in the 1983 Sugar Bowl, Garrity was more than just that play. He was a great clutch receiver during his PSU career. He led the team in receptions in 1981 and had a 52-yard TD reception against USC in the 1982 Fiesta Bowl. In the win against Nebraska during the 1982 regular season, he had several key receptions that kept drives alive.

4. Robbie Gould (2001–04). From walk-on to the Super Bowl, Gould could have gone on to play professional soccer but chose to try out for the Lions. He became the starting kicker and led the team in scoring in 2003 and 2004, and he is sixth on the team's career-scoring list. In the NFL he's become a Pro Bowl kicker and helped the Chicago Bears win the NFC title and advance to the Super Bowl in 2007.

3. Troy Drayton (1991–92). He started out as a fourth-string wide receiver but became a solid tight end, even earning third-team All-American honors his senior year. During the 1992 season he set a team record for receptions by a tight end in one season with 36.

2. Deon Butler (2005–08). Of all the great receivers Penn State has had—Bobby Engram, O.J. McDuffie, Kenny Jackson, and so forth—former walk-on Butler is the one who is No. 1 on the career-receptions list with 179. Butler was part of the great receiving corps that included Derrick Williams and Jordan Norwood. The three helped the Lions win two Big Ten titles in four seasons. His 22 career TD receptions also ranks third on the Penn State list.

1. Neal Smith (1967–69). A first-team All-American his senior season, Smith still holds the Penn State record for interceptions in a career, with 19. After walking on in 1966, he became a key member of the outstanding 1968 and 1969 defenses that helped Penn State go a combined 22–0 those years. He came up with huge performances in the Lions' bowl wins those seasons. In the 1969 Orange Bowl he partially blocked a Kansas punt with 1:16 remaining. That gave the Lions the ball at their own 49 and led to a TD drive and eventual 15–14 win. In the Orange Bowl the next season he had two interceptions in the 10–3 win over Missouri. His ten INTs in 1969 are tied for most in one season by a Penn State player.

MISSED BASKETBALL OPPORTUNITIES

The Penn State basketball program has been around nearly as long as the football program. Yet, unlike football, Nittany Lion basketball success has been few and far between. They have appeared in only nine NCAA Tournaments. They do have one Final Four on the résumé, and schools with a richer basketball tradition such as Missouri can't even claim that. However, for more than 40 years one big question continues to surface about PSU hoops—why can't they field a consistent winner? Along the way the university has missed some great opportunities to have a strong program.

5. Not hiring Bobby Knight. This was a great crossroads moment in the history of the program. After three seasons at Army (in which he compiled a 51–21 record, including two NIT appearances with one trip to the Final Four), Knight made it known that he wanted the Penn State job following the resignation of John Egli. However, Penn State didn't want what Knight was offering and instead hired John Bach. What Bach offered in his ten seasons was the definition of mediocrity, posting a record of 122–121. His last four seasons were far from mediocre, as the Lions limped to a 40–61 mark. Bach failed to take Penn State to an NCAA Tournament or even an NIT. One of two things would most likely have occurred if Knight had coached Penn State: He would have generated success that a few years later would have propelled him to a bigger gig, or he would have stayed at Penn State, the Nittany Lions would have been regular participants in March Madness, and Rec Hall would have become the northeast version of Duke's Cameron Indoor Stadium. Either way, Penn State basketball would have been in a much better situation than it is today.

4. Not joining the Big East. In a 2009 interview with the *New York Times*, former Big East commissioner Mike Tranghese said his predecessor Dave Gavitt wanted Penn State to join the emerging basketball powerhouse conference. In 1982 the proposal to invite Penn State was voted on by the Big East schools. Despite Gavitt's efforts, Penn State missed joining the conference by one vote. Tranghese was an assistant to Gavitt at that time and told his boss, "We will rue the day over this decision." He added in the 2009 interview about that quote, "It has been pretty prophetic." That was likely in reference to the conference's football standing, because the Big East has obviously enjoyed great basketball success, including programs rising from nowhere to become winners. In 1983 Connecticut was 12–16 and Seton Hall occupied the Big East cellar, with an overall record of 6–23. Six years later Seton Hall played for the national title, losing in overtime against Michigan. The following season Connecticut started its current run of success as an elite program. No doubt being in the Big East would have made appearing in the NCAA Tournament on a regular basis a realistic expectation for Penn State.

3. Failure to take advantage of the 1996 season. 1996 was supposed to be a "We've turned the corner" season. The Nittany Lions were ranked in the top 25 most of the year, finishing 11th in the final poll, the Bryce Jordan Center opened, and the team made a rare trip to the NCAA Tournament. Surely, that would have led to an upgrade in talented recruits, which in turn would help sustain that success. That didn't happen—and please don't call me Shirley. The Lions went 10–17 in 1997. They did make the NIT championship game in 1998, and in 2000 they needed a mini-miracle run in the Big Ten Tournament just to have the winning record that they needed in order to be eligible for the NIT. Like they often do when making the "little dance," they parlayed the invite into a trip to the NIT Final Four. However, going to the NIT is the basketball equivalent of a football team going to the Meineke Car Care Bowl: It's nice, but it is a far cry from playing in a BCS bowl. Certainly there should have been more success in selling to recruits a program that was ranked in the top 20, made the NCAA Tournament, and was playing in a new arena than what actually occurred. Similarly . . .

2. Failure to take advantage of the 2001 season. Penn State won at Kentucky, beat Temple, and beat Pitt in the nonconference part of the schedule. It defeated Big Ten regular-season champ Illinois in conference play. It upset Michigan State in the Big Ten Tournament. It won NCAA Tournament games against Providence and North Carolina, and it advanced to the Sweet 16 for the first time since 1955. All that success led to . . . consecutive 7–21 seasons and the departure of head coach Jerry Dunn.

1. The "national search" for Dunn's replacement. Athletic director Tim Curley used that phrase in the 2003 search for a new basketball coach. Some eight years later it is a phrase that draws snickers from many of the remaining few dozen avid followers of Penn State basketball. Curley did have talks with former UCLA coach Steve Lavin and Iowa State and Chicago Bulls coach Tim Floyd (thank goodness he was not offered the job). Former University of Pennsylvania and current Temple head coach Fran Dunphy, with his Philadelphia-area high school pipeline, expressed interest in the position. Dunphy was eschewed, as the "national search" all along seemed to be limited in its geography to Johnson City, Tennessee, where a PSU graduate and former assistant coach had just taken East Tennessee State to the NCAA Tournament. Though the fan base received the announcement of Ed DeChellis as head coach with mixed reactions, there were some merits to the hire at the outset. DeChellis was one of those guys who is probably on the "bleeds blue and white" list. This was his dream job, meaning he was not going to use Penn State to enhance his resumé and jump to something bigger and better. He built a bad ETSU program into a consistent winner. However, in 2011–12, entering his ninth season at Penn State, DeChellis has produced only two winning seasons and has one NCAA Tournament appearance.

FAMILY TIES

Penn State alumni and fans have always thought of themselves as one big, happy family—"We Are . . . Penn State" and all that. Some *actual* families, however, have shown that the blue and white really runs in their veins. You've seen their names appear on the roster during different eras and generations. Here are our top ten families that have played football for Dear Old State.

10. Hamilton. Harry and Lance were two of the best scholar-athletes to play for Penn State. The two brothers from Wilkes-Barre were Academic All-Americans their junior and senior years, and both played for teams that played for a national title. Harry came first (1980–83). He started at "Hero" during the 1982 national championship season and was the leading tackler his senior year, when he earned third-team All-American honors. Lance played from 1983 through 1985 and came up with some big moments during the Lions' undefeated regular season in his senior year. He forced a fumble in the season-opening win at Maryland and had a team-high nine tackles in the win versus Alabama.

9. Shuler. Same name, same position, same number for this father-son combination. Mickey Sr. was an outstanding tight end for the Lions from 1975 through 1977. He was a second-team All-American his senior year, when he caught 33 passes for 600 yards. He also turned out to be a fine tight end for the New York Jets. Thirty years later his son, Mickey Jr., was wearing No. 82 and playing tight end for JoePa. Although he didn't put up the numbers that his old man did, Mickey Jr. was a solid tight end for the Lions and helped them win a Big Ten title in 2008. He had his best season during his senior year in 2009, when he caught 11 passes and had two touchdowns.

8. Garrity. Father, Jim, and son, Gregg, were excellent pass catchers for the Nits. Jim played from 1952 through 1954 and was one of the top receivers in the nation during those years. He was a cocaptain on the 1954 team that went 7–2. He also was an outstanding defensive lineman. Jim also did Penn State a great service when he talked Gregg into walking onto the team in 1979. Gregg had planned to go to Clarion, but because of his father's encouragement, he chose to take a chance and become a walk-on. Of course, the rest is history. Gregg made one of the most memorable catches in Penn State history, with his diving touchdown reception in the 1983 Sugar Bowl that all but sealed the win over Georgia for the national title. He had a team-high 116 receiving yards that game. He also led the Lions in receptions his junior year with 23 catches.

7. Smith/King. Both Terry Smith and his stepson, Justin King, helped Penn State come back from losing seasons. At 5-foot-8, Smith may have been a small receiver, but he had big-play talent and abilities. His freshman year in 1988 saw Penn State suffer its first losing season under Paterno. He then helped the Lions return to their winning ways, as they went 28–8–1 between 1989 and 1991. He ranks ninth on the team's all-time receptions list with 108. A cocaptain his senior year, he led the Lions with 55 catches for 846 yards. In 2005 King, along with Derrick Williams, helped bring the Penn State program back after four losing seasons in five years. They were two of the most highly recruited seniors in high school, and both chose to come to Penn State. King played both offense and defense during the 2005 Big Ten title season that resurrected the program. He eventually became a full-time cornerback, where he was second-team all-conference his sophomore year. He left for the NFL after his junior season, but he and Williams will always be remembered for putting the program back on the winning track.

6. Johnson. Most people know about Larry Jr. and his 2,000-yard season in 2002. His brother, Tony, wasn't a bad receiver during those years. In fact, he ranks tenth on the team's all-time receptions list with 107. During Larry's remarkable 2002 season, Tony was third on the team in receptions behind Bryant Johnson (no relation) and his brother. He led the team in catches in 2003. Oh, their father, Larry Sr., yeah, he hasn't done too bad at Penn State either as the team's defensive-line coach and one of its top recruiters.

5. Pittman. Unbelievably, in games in which either dad, Charlie, or son, Tony, started at Penn State, the Lions went 45–0–1. Maybe even more remarkable is the fact that despite the two playing for a combined three undefeated teams, neither won a national title—thanks, pollsters. Charlie played 1967 through 1969 and is considered the first superstar running back in the Paterno era. He led the Lions in all-purpose yards all three seasons, including 1,262 yards in 1968. He also led the team in scoring his last two seasons, as the Lions went undefeated in 1968 and 1969. Tony was a solid cornerback for the Lions in the early 1990s. He led the team with five picks in 1993 and was a key member of the 1994 team that went undefeated and won the Big Ten championship.

4. Bahr. The kicking game was in good hands, uh, feet for most of the 1970s, as brothers Chris and Matt Bahr became first-team All-Americans for the Lions. Chris kicked from 1973 through 1975 and is the Lions' best-ever kicker from long range. He kicked six field goals of 50 or more yards during his career, including four in 1975. Matt (1976–78) picked things up right where his brother left off. He's tied for team record for most field goals in a season, with the 22 he kicked in 1978 to help the Lions go 11–0 in the regular season and be ranked No. 1 for the first time. The Bahrs weren't too bad at soccer either—both were All-Americans in that sport as well.

3. Collins. Frances Collins and husband, Charles, of Cinnaminson, New Jersey, had 19 children. Five of them played for the Lions from 1986 through 1997. The first, Andre, was the best of the bunch. He was a first-team All-American linebacker his senior year in 1989, when he had 130 tackles and blocked three kicks. In the 1989 Holiday Bowl he intercepted Ty Detmer on a two-point attempt and returned it 102 yards to give Penn State two points in its 50–39 win over the Cougars. Brothers Gerry (1989–91), Phillip (1993–94), and Jason (1994–95) followed and were mostly backups during their careers. Aaron was the last, as he played from 1994 through 1997. He started 36 consecutive games at linebacker and was a cocaptain on the 1997 team that was ranked No. 1 during part of the year.

2. Wisniewski. This family did the dirty work in the trenches. Leo (1979–81) was a defensive tackle and one of the inspirational leaders on the 1981 team that was ranked No. 1 during the season and ended the year 10–2. He was the Defensive Player of the Game in the Lions' win over USC in the 1982 Fiesta Bowl. During that game Leo tackled Heisman-winner Marcus Allen three times for big losses, and he recovered a fumble. His younger brother, Steve, played at Penn State from 1985 through 1988 and is one of the program's best-ever offensive linemen. He was a starter his sophomore season in 1986 and helped the Lions win the national title. He then became a two-time first-team All-American (1987 and 1988). His nephew—Leo's son—Stefen also became a dominant offensive lineman. Stefen became a starter his freshman year in 2007, and even though he was moved from guard to center and then back to guard during his time at Penn State, he was one of the rocks on the Lions' lines during his four years.

1. Suhey. The Suheys are definitely the First Family of Penn State football. The line goes back to Bob Higgins, who was an All-American in 1915 and 1919 and was Penn State's head coach from 1930 to 1948. He became the father-in-law to Steve Suhey, who played for Higgins and the Lions in 1942 and 1946–47 and also married Higgins's daughter. After serving in World War II, Suhey became a first-team All-American offensive lineman in 1947. He helped the Lions go 9–0–1 that year. Three of his sons went on to play for Penn State during the mid-1970s. Larry, the oldest, was a backup fullback in 1975 and 1976. He suffered a serious knee injury his freshman year and never fully recovered. Paul played from 1975 through 1978 and was a captain on the 1978 team. He was a starting outside linebacker and was second on the team in tackles his senior season with 63. Matt followed both and played from 1976 through 1979. Although he's most remembered for his failed touchdown plunge in the 1979 Sugar Bowl, Matt became one of the best fullbacks to play at Penn State. He finished his career with 2,818 yards and 26 touchdowns. He still holds the team record for punt-return yards in a game with 145 against North Carolina State in 1978. Matt's son, Joe, will be a senior fullback for the Lions in 2011. Although the Lions have gone to more of a spread offense, which has minimized the role of the fullback position to an extent, Joe has been a steady player—and doing the Suhey name proud.

WHY I LOVE HAPPY VALLEY :: BY MIKE MCQUEARY

Twenty years ago Mike McQueary would have been one of the last people you'd expect to talk about how much he loves Penn State and Happy Valley. Known for his trademark red hair, he moved to State College with his family in the 1980s when he was six years old. For all of his youth, including when he attended State College Area High School, he was a Notre Dame fan. He even wore No. 9 during his high school playing days in honor of former Notre Dame quarterback Tony Rice. In fact, he'll tell you that he "hated" Penn State. All that changed, however, when Joe Paterno took a chance on giving McQueary a scholarship. In 1997 McQueary finally became the starting quarterback for the Lions. He threw for 2,211 yards and 17 TDs that year, helping Penn State, who was ranked No. 1 for part of the year, to a 9–3 record. He's been on the coaching staff for more than ten years; he's now the wide receivers' coach and recruiting coordinator. Since taking over the latter position in 2004, the Lions have had some of their best recruiting classes since joining the Big Ten, which helped them win two conference titles in four seasons. And if McQueary has his way, he'll never leave Happy Valley. Here are some of his top reasons why he's grown to love the place.

7. My barber. I've been going to same barber at Fetterolf's since I was six years old. He's the best.

6. Meyer Dairy. I love Meyer Dairy milk. I don't buy my milk from anywhere else. I wouldn't drink milk from a grocery store.

5. State High's Memorial Field. I think to have a high school stadium right downtown is unique. I think it's a great thing to have for the community.

4. Town-Campus connection. It's great how the town comes right up on campus, and Beaver Stadium is right on campus. It's a great game-day atmosphere, in which you have downtown State College and all the people flow onto campus. It's not a metropolitan area at all, which I love.

3. But. . . . Thanks to Penn State, there's a metropolitan-type feel and we have a lot of world-class opportunities here. We have access to a lot of things.

2. The people. It's an educated community and very diverse. When I was in high school, we had people from every walk of life. It's a loyal community and very supportive.

1. It's the perfect place. One of our receivers, Shawney Kersey, who is from Woodbury, New Jersey, said, "This is utopia." You look at the green mountains and the blue skies. We have high school coaches come here for camps, and this is like a vacation for them. It's very peaceful and a good change of pace for them. Penn State has been the best thing that has ever happened to me. I'm just an average guy who's been unbelievably lucky. I never want to leave here if I don't have to. I'm totally in love with Happy Valley.

ALL-TIME TOP ATHLETES FROM CENTRE COUNTY :: BY RON BRACKEN

Although great athletes have obviously come from Penn State, the high schools around Dear Old State haven't been too shabby in producing some talent of their own. During his 41 years as sports editor and columnist for the *Centre Daily Times*, Ron Bracken saw many of those prep stars go on to play for the Nittany Lions or take their talents elsewhere. Bracken, who covered Penn State football from 1968 through 2007 and is now retired, gives his top ten all-time athletes from Centre County.

10. Josh Hull. A graduate of Penns Valley High, Hull walked on at Penn State and became a two-year starter at linebacker for the Nittany Lions. He was a seventh-round draft choice of the St. Louis Rams and had made the final roster for the 2010 season before suffering a season-ending knee injury in the second week of the regular season.

9. Eric Milton. An outstanding pitcher for Bellefonte High School, Milton played baseball at the University of Maryland and became the No. 1 draft choice of the New York Yankees. He later played for the Minnesota Twins, Philadelphia Phillies, Cincinnati Reds, and Los Angeles Dodgers. He retired in 2010.

8. Mike Condo. Bald Eagle Area's first Big 33 and all-state football player, Condo was also a district champion in the 100-yard dash at a time (1964) when BEA did not have a track team. He went on to become a starter in the secondary for the University of Minnesota.

7. Jon Condo. A three-sport standout at Philipsburg-Osceola, Condo was an all-state and Big 33 selection in football, a PIAA wrestling champion, and an all-state selection in baseball. He was a four-year letterman in football at the University of Maryland and is currently the long snapper for the Oakland Raiders.

6. Quentin Wright. Wright was a two-time PIAA wrestling champion at Bald Eagle Area and also placed second in the PIAA tournament as a sophomore. He became an All-American wrestler at Penn State his freshman season and won a national title in 2011 as a redshirt sophomore.

5. Cal Emery. Emery graduated from Centre Hall High School and went to Penn State. He was instrumental in leading the Nittany Lions to the 1957 College World Series, where he was named the Outstanding Player. He was drafted by the Philadelphia Phillies and played one year in the Major Leagues. He later served as a coach with the Chicago White Sox.

4. Larry Suhey. An all-state and Big 33 tailback at State College in 1972, Suhey also was a two-time PIAA wrestling champion. He went on to participate in both of these sports at Penn State, but a knee injury shortened his career.

3. Dave Joyner. He was an all-state football player and PIAA wrestling champion at State College. He went to Penn State, where he became an All-American in both football, as an offensive tackle, and wrestling, placing second in the NCAA Wrestling Championships. He was a cocaptain of the 1971 Penn State football team that went 11–1.

2. Ron Pifer. A two-time PIAA wrestling champion at Bellefonte (1957, 1958), he went on to become an NCAA runner-up at Penn State. He later coached at Army and then served as the head wrestling coach at State College Area High School two different times.

1. Matt Suhey. Suhey was a three-time all-state tailback and a Big 33 selection at State College Area High School from 1973 through 1975. He went to Penn State and became a four-year starter at fullback. The Chicago Bears drafted him in the second round in the 1980 draft, and he played ten years with the Bears, where he helped open up running holes for Walter Payton. He scored the first touchdown in the Bears' 1986 Super Bowl win over the New England Patriots.

A HAPPY VALLEY BUCKET LIST

To truly appreciate the region where Penn State is based—aptly called Happy Valley—you have to have some experiences beyond what happens inside Beaver Stadium (although that's important too). Here are some places to visit, events to check out, and more that everyone should attempt at least once before they kick the you-know-what.

10. Happy Birthday, America. At the Central PA 4th Fest, not only do you have a chance to see one of the largest fireworks displays in the country, but there also are concerts, activities for the whole family, and more. Wish America a Happy B-day in style.

9. Visit Boalsburg and Bellefonte. It's fairly easy to become too focused on State College and Penn State and just take in things that are right there. But do yourself a favor and travel just a few miles outside and hit Boalsburg and Bellefonte. Boalsburg stakes its claim as the birthplace of Memorial Day and has great little shops and restaurants. Bellefonte is known for its Victorian homes and has one of the best parks in the region in Talleyrand Park. Take some time to feed the ducks and enjoy concerts at the Gazebo in the summer.

8. Get lost, and find your way out of the Stacks. Walking into the Pattee/Paterno Library can be pretty intimidating if you don't know your way around. Still, it's worth venturing into the Stacks of Pattee Library, or, at least, it feels like a rite of passage for any true Penn Stater.

7. Arts Festival. Whether you're there for the art or more for the festival, this is the highlight of every summer in Happy Valley. Be sure to try the Chicken on the Stick.

6. Have a beer at Otto's. The local brewery moved into its new location in 2010, so now parking is even easier. Some of their great beer selections include Apricot Wheat, Red Mo Ale, Mt. Nittany Pale Ale, and Double D IPA. If you haven't had their beers before, try a sampler selection.

5. Grilled Stickies. Sure, you've had cinnamon rolls before, but you haven't tasted anything if you haven't had one of The Diner's Grilled Stickies. They're truly a treat, especially if you heat one up and add a scoop of ice cream. Oh, and speaking of ice cream . . .

4. The Creamery. You obviously have to have some ice cream from the Creamery if you're a Penn Stater or just visiting the university. Heck, Ben and Jerry learned some of their tricks from the Creamery's correspondence course in ice cream making.

3. Climb Mount Nittany. Okay, it's not Everest or Kilimanjaro, but it does offer great views of Beaver Stadium and the Happy Valley region.

2. Have your photo taken at the Nittany Lion Shrine/JoePa statue. It used to just be the Lion Shrine, but you now have to include JoePa's likeness. Of course, if you get a photo next to the real JoePa, then don't worry about the statue.

1. Attend a White Out. A White Out means a night game, which means tailgating all day and a big-game opponent—they don't just have White Outs for anybody. It also means you're part of one of the coolest spectacles and atmospheres in all of sports.

TOP TEN THINGS WE'D LOVE TO SEE AT PENN STATE

As great as Penn State is, there are a few areas where it can improve. We don't believe these are unreasonable requests we're making, so we hope to see some or all of these things happen within the next few years.

10. The return of the Chicken Cosmo Sandwich. These chicken patties were the best things the dining halls offered during our college days. Unfortunately, Penn State was the only institution buying them from Pierce Chicken Products, the chicken cosmo vendor, so the company stopped making them in 2008. "Treating yourself to several chicken cosmos" was featured on a list of Top Ten Things to Do Before You Graduate Penn State. Whatever has replaced the chicken cosmo on that list certainly can't taste as good.

9. Concerts at Beaver Stadium. If hallowed grounds such as Fenway Park and Wrigley Field can host major musical acts, why not the Beav? We'd like to suggest Jimmy Buffett or Kenny Chesney. More than 100,000 Parrotheads—that's got to be some kind of record.

8. Making ice hockey a Division I sport again (and we're getting our wish starting in 2012–13). With a great mix of Flyers and Penguin fans, Happy Valley has a solid hockey fan base, and the Icers have a loyal following as a club sport. Some students make it a tradition to go to their games on Friday and Saturday nights before hitting the town. It's time to see Penn State, which had a varsity team from 1939 through 1940 and 1945 through 1946, take on the likes of Michigan and Boston College on the ice—and maybe even make a run to the Frozen Four.

7. Bring back the whale pants. For our money, JoePa never looked so good as when he wore his infamous khaki pants with images of little blue whales on them back in 1982. It would be great to see them make a comeback just one more time before Paterno's final game. And hey, the team did win a national title in 1982, so they did bring him a little luck.

6. Rename it Paterno Field at Beaver Stadium. Something like this will likely happen when and if JoePa retires. Some think it should be done before then, especially when you see Duke having Coach K Court at Cameron Indoor Stadium. But honestly, that just doesn't seem to be Paterno's style, and we applaud him for that. So wait until his amazing career is done and then make the change.

5. Basketball returns to Rec Hall. Sure, the BJC has comfortable seats and is state of the art, but give me the cramped bleachers and poor ventilation of

Rec Hall any day when it comes to creating a hostile atmosphere for opponents. No matter how packed the BJC has been, it has never created the home-court advantage that Rec Hall had. The students were right on top of opposing players—it was great seeing Chris Webber, then of Michigan's Fab Five, trash-talking with students! Here's a request to play all the nonconference games (unless Duke or Kentucky suddenly start making trips to Happy Valley) and one or two Big Ten games at Rec Hall. Seeing basketball played in the old gym once again would be great for students and fans.

4. Combining flavors at the Creamery. This is like Penn State's version of the Soup Nazi. Come on, we live in America! There is no reason that people can't have a scoop of chocolate and a scoop of vanilla, or a scoop of Peachy Paterno and a scoop of butter pecan. Former President Bill Clinton apparently is the only one who has been able to figure out the secret to having two flavors put together.

3. Penguins-Flyers at Beaver Stadium. We already host what's been called the Greatest Show in College Football, so how about the Greatest Show in the NHL? You'd have half of the 100,000-plus in Beaver Stadium decked in yellow and black and half in orange and black. Now, that's a Winter Classic!

2. Pitt back on the schedule. There is now a generation of Penn State fans who don't know what Penn State vs. Pitt meant to Pennsylvania and to college football, especially from 1976 through 1986. That's a shame. It's amazing how every season we see USC play Notre Dame and Florida play Florida State, yet Pitt and Penn State remain in their own corners and won't figure out a way to renew the series. On the one hand, Pitt still plays West Virginia, so it has its Backyard Brawl and rivalry. Penn State, on the other hand, had the Land Grant Trophy battle with Michigan State. Not the same, and even that's gone because Nebraska joined the Big Ten.

1. JoePa to go out on top. There is no argument: Joe Paterno should go down as the greatest college football coach ever. This is not only because of his longevity and that he'll forever hold the career-wins record; it's also because of how he made college football, especially eastern college football, better. It's how he showed that you could field a winning program and have players graduate. Heck, the library here is named after him. With all that he's done, it's a little surprising that he's won only two national titles (yes, he's had four undefeated teams that weren't considered national champions but easily could have been). There is no better way for Paterno to leave the game than by winning another national title. Although he doesn't need it to validate his standing as the greatest ever, it still would be an amazing moment and the perfect "storybook ending."

ALL-TIME FOOTBALL TEAM

When your football program is one of the most successful in college history, with multiple national championships, you are sure to have plenty of star power to fill five or six rosters of all-time greats. Even a Nittany Lion all-decade team would best most other program's teams representing their entire history. In some cases the players on this list are not the all-time Penn State statistical leaders at their positions, but statistics don't tell the entire story. Here is our all-time Penn State football team.

OFFENSE

Tackle: Keith Dorney (1975–78). He was a unanimous All-American in 1978. The Nittany Lions were 22–2 in his final two seasons. In 1978 he was instrumental in assisting Matt Suhey and Booker Moore rush for a combined 1,322 yards and 13 touchdowns, and his pass protection made a Heisman runner-up out of quarterback Chuck Fusina.

Guard: Steve Wisniewski (1985–88). In his sophomore season, his first as a starter, Wisniewski helped lead a solid one-two punch of D.J. Dozier and Blair Thomas's combining for 1,315 yards rushing and 15 touchdowns. Oh, by the way, Penn State also won the national championship in 1986. The following two seasons, when the Lions had less-than-stellar seasons, including their first losing one under Paterno, Wisniewski was still dominant enough that he earned All-American honors both years.

Center: Glen Ressler (1962–64). Ressler was a great two-way player, but on our list he is the greatest center in Penn State history. He won the 1964 Maxwell Award. At the time, he was only the fifth lineman in history to be honored with the award by the Philadelphia Sports Writers Association.

Guard: Sean Farrell (1978–81). Helping to open the holes for Curt Warner and protect quarterback Todd Blackledge, Farrell was a two-time All-American. He also was a finalist for the Lombardi and Outland awards. He scored his first and only touchdown when he recovered a Warner fumble in the end zone in Penn State's 48–14 win over No. 1 Pitt in 1981. According to *The Penn State Football Encyclopedia*, head coach Joe Paterno said toward the end of Farrell's Penn State career that "if there's a better guard in the country, he's Superman."

Tackle: Dave Joyner (1968–71). In his senior season Joyner was a cocaptain and named an All-American, as he helped Lydell Mitchell rush for 1,567 yards and 26 touchdowns.

Tight End: Ted Kwalick (1966–68). "What God had in mind when he made a football player"—that was Joe Paterno's description of two-time All-American Kwalick. He set Penn State records for yards receiving by a tight end (1,343) and touchdowns (10). Finished fourth in the Heisman voting in 1968.

Wide Receiver: Bobby Engram (1991, 1993–95). Here is a time when the stats do tell the story. When Engram finished his Penn State career, he held the record for most receptions (167), most yards (3,026), and most touchdowns (31), and he was the prime target for the record-setting 1994 offense that led the Lions to the Big Ten, Rose Bowl, and—clearing throat—what also should have been a national championship.

Wide Receiver: Kenny Jackson (1980–1983). Though he has been passed a few times on the career-receiving list since playing his final game in the blue and white, Jackson earns the nod for this spot. His 25 career touchdowns set a school record, and when the Penn State offense was referred to as "Air Paterno," Jackson was receiving most of that air in the national championship season of 1982 with 41 receptions. He was Penn State's first wide receiver to be named a first-team All-American. He earned consecutive first-team honors in 1982 and 1983.

Fullback: Matt Suhey (1976–1979). Part of one of the great families in Penn State history, Suhey finished his Penn State career with 2,818 yards (second-highest total at the time) and 26 touchdowns.

Running Back: Curt Warner (1979–82). With so many great Penn State running backs, having to pick just one does not seem fair, but pick we must, and we choose Warner. We did not have to look far on the career-rushing leader chart: Warner held the record with 3,398 yards until the 2010 season, when Evan Royster broke it. Warner had back-to-back 1,000-yard seasons in 1981 and 1982. He capped his career with a two-touchdown performance in the 1983 Sugar Bowl win over Georgia that gave the Lions their first national title. In the process he out-performed Heisman Trophy winner Herschel Walker. The year before, he outshined another Heisman winner, Marcus Allen, in the Lions' win over USC in the 1982 Fiesta Bowl.

Quarterback: Chuck Fusina (1975–78). He held the triple crown for Penn State passers at the conclusion of his career, setting records for yards (5,382), completions (371), and touchdowns (32). Fusina led the Nittany Lions to a 22–2 mark over his final two seasons, including a date in the 1979 Sugar Bowl against Alabama for the national championship. In that 1978 season Fusina would finish second in the Heisman voting and win the Maxwell Award for outstanding player in college football.

Kicker: Matt Bahr (1976–78). Bahr led the team in scoring in 1977 (81 points) and 1978 (97 points). He set the NCAA record for field goals in a season with 22 in 1978, and his performance helped propel the Nittany Lions to a No. 1 ranking.

DEFENSE

End: Dave Robinson (1960–62). He was an All-American and is a member of the College Football Hall of Fame. Robinson was a dominating end on defense who also played tight end on offense. Although tackling records weren't fully kept when he played, according to Penn State historian Lou Prato in *The Penn State Football Encyclopedia*, Robinson would have been among the team's all-time leaders.

Tackle: Bruce Clark (1976–79). He's still the only Penn Stater and the first junior to win the Lombardi Award for the nation's outstanding lineman/linebacker. A first-team All-American in 1978 and 1979, Clark had 19 career sacks.

Tackle: Mike Reid (1966, 1968–69). One of the greatest Lions ever, he won the Maxwell Award in 1969 as the nation's most outstanding player. He also finished fifth in the Heisman voting that year. Reid set the tone for his career in his very first game when he recorded a record three safeties against Maryland in 1966.

End: Courtney Brown (1996–99). An All-American in 1999, Brown holds the records for career sacks with 33 and career tackles of losses with 70.

Linebacker: Jack Ham (1968–70). An All-American in 1970 when he had 92 tackles and four interceptions, Ham was a key defensive member of the undefeated 1968 and 1969 teams. He also set a record with three punt blocks in a season in 1968.

Linebacker: Shane Conlan (1983–86). Conlan was a two-time All-American in 1985 and 1986. He was the Most Valuable Defensive Player in the 1987 Fiesta Bowl win over Miami that gave the Lions their second national title. In that game he had eight tackles and two INTs, including one that he returned 38 yards and set up the game-winning touchdown. He left Penn State having more solo tackles (186) than any other Lion. He held that record for 20 years.

Linebacker: Paul Posluszny (2003–06). He was a two-time All-American in 2005 and 2006 and also was a two-time winner of the Bednarik Award (2005, 2006), given to the nation's top defensive player. Posluszny won the Butkus Award in 2005 and broke the team's all-time career-tackles record in 2006. Currently, he ranks second on that list, with 372 tackles.

Cornerback: Eddie Johnson (1985–88). A ferocious tackler in the secondary—just ask Michael Irvin and the Miami Hurricane receivers—he had a game-high 13 tackles in the Fiesta Bowl win over Miami.

Safety: Darren Perry (1989–91). He was an All-American in 1991 and is tied for second on the team's career-interceptions list with 15. Perry holds the team's all-time record with 299 interception-return yardage and also scored three touchdowns.

Safety: Neal Smith (1967–69). A walk-on in 1966, Smith became an All-American by his senior year in 1969. He holds the team record with 15 career interceptions. The ten he had his senior season is tied for the team record for interceptions in a season.

Cornerback: Mark Robinson (1980–83). Robinson was an All-American on the 1982 national championship team and had four INTs that season. He is probably remembered most for his 91-yard interception return for a touchdown that iced a 48–14 win over No. 1 Pitt in 1981.

Punter: John Bruno (1984–86). The Lions have had many outstanding punters, but Bruno earns the vote here. Besides being ranked as one of the team's career leaders in punting, he'll always be remembered for his outstanding performance in the 1987 Fiesta Bowl. He had nine punts, for an average of 43.4 yards, and kept giving Miami poor field position.